Henry E. Allison is Professor of
Philosophy at the University of
California, San Diego and associate
editor of the *Journal of the History
of Philosophy*. He is the author of
Lessing and the Enlightenment, a
book on G. E. Lessing's philosophy
of religion, and of numerous journal
articles on Kant and other topics in
the history of modern philosophy
and the philosophy of religion.

THE KANT-EBERHARD CONTROVERSY

THE
KANT-EBERHARD CONTROVERSY

An English translation
together with supplementary materials
and a historical-analytic introduction

of

IMMANUEL KANT'S
On a Discovery
According to which Any New Critique of Pure Reason
Has Been Made Superfluous by an Earlier One

Über eine Entdeckung
nach der alle neue Kritik der reinen Vernunft
durch eine ältere entbehrlich gemacht werden soll

Henry E. Allison

THE JOHNS HOPKINS UNIVERSITY PRESS
Baltimore and London

Copyright © 1973 by The Johns Hopkins University Press
All rights reserved. No part of this book may be reproduced or transmitted in any form or by
any means, electronic or mechanical, including photocopying, recording, xerography, or any
information storage and retrieval system, without permission in writing from the publisher.

Manufactured in the United States of America

The Johns Hopkins University Press, Baltimore, Maryland 21218
The Johns Hopkins University Press Ltd., London

Library of Congress Catalog Card Number 73-8113
ISBN 0-8018-1456-1

Library of Congress Cataloging in Publication data will be found on the last printed page of this
book.

To Norma

CONTENTS

PREFACE

When one thinks of Kant's "critical philosophy," he thinks primarily of the three great Critiques, secondly of some of the well known ethical writings of the "critical period" such as the *Fundamental Principles of the Metaphysics of Morals*, and finally, of works such as the *Metaphysical First Principles of Natural Science* and *Religion within the Limits of Reason Alone* which apply and develop critical principles. There are, however, numerous other writings from this period, many of them still not available in English translation, which shed a good deal of light on various aspects of Kant's philosophy. One of the most interesting and neglected of these "minor writings" is the polemical essay, *On a Discovery According to which Any New Critique of Pure Reason Has Been Made Superfluous by an Earlier One*, which was published in 1790 together with the *Critique of Judgment*.

This essay was written in response to a full-scale attack on the critical philosophy by the Wolffian philosopher and professor at Halle, Johann August Eberhard. Eberhard's main contention was quite simply that whatever is true in the *Critique of Pure Reason* was already said by Leibniz, and that wherever the Critique differs from Leibniz, e.g., in its limitation of knowledge to appearances, it falls into error. Leibnizian rationalism is thus viewed as having already overcome Humean scepticism, and the claims of rationalistic metaphysics are justified in the face of Kantian criticism. Kant, for his part, was so incensed by this attack that he abandoned his long-standing vow not to engage in any direct controversy with his critics. The result is a work which is highly polemical and often extremely bitter in tone, and in many ways an "occasional piece." It also contains, however, an important reformulation of the distinction between analytic and synthetic judgments, as well as an attempt by Kant to carefully define his philosophy vis-à-vis Leibnizian rationalism. Now Kant's conception of the distinction between analytic and synthetic judgments is generally interpreted almost exclusively in terms of the initial—and rather misleading—formulations in the Introductions to the *Critique* and the *Prolegomena*. Moreover, Anglo-American Kant interpreters and critics seem to read the *Critique* almost exclusively as an attempted answer—good, bad, or indifferent— to Humean scepticism, with the result that the equally important relation to Leibnizian rationalism is hardly considered. This has, I think, led not only to a certain one-sidedness of approach, but also to some basic misinterpretations. It thus seems vital, given the present state of Kant scholarship and discussion, to begin to seriously consider once again this whole other dimension of Kant's thought; and since this dimension is nowhere more clearly articulated than in *On a Discovery*, I have attempted an English translation of this work together with a historical-critical introduction.

Unfortunately, *On a Discovery* is written in an extremely ponderous style, even by Kantian standards, and Kant's attempts at irony often fall rather flat. Nevertheless, apart from breaking up some of the endless German sentences into slightly more manageable English ones, I have tried in my translation to render Kant's thought as accurately as possible, rather than to reformulate it in a more elegant English. Two points in the translation, however, are worthy of note. First of all, after considerable deliberation, I decided to render the German *'bildlich'* and *'unbildlich'* by the archaic English expressions, 'imageable' and 'unimageable' respectively. Despite their awkward sound, these words come much nearer to the meaning of the German expressions as used by Eberhard and Kant than the more normal English renderings: 'imaginable' and 'unimaginable' which have quite different connotations, or other possible alternatives such as 'pictorial' or 'figurative'. Secondly, I have translated the German term *'Grund'* sometimes by 'ground', and sometimes by 'reason', depending on the context and normal English usage. Thus, the text refers to the "principle of sufficient reason" and to "real" or "logical grounds."

The translation itself is based on the Prussian Academy edition of *Kant's Gesammelte Schriften*, Walter de Gruyter, Berlin and Leipzig, 1923, Vol. 8. The pagination of this standard edition is given in the margin for those who wish to compare the text with the original. In preparing the translation I have also consulted the text of the Cassirer edition, *Immanuel Kant's Werke*, edited by A. Buchanau, E. Cassirer, B. Kellermann, Bruno Cassirer (Berlin, 1914), vol. 6, and a French translation by Roger Kempf, *Reponse à Eberhard* (Paris: Librarie Philosophique, 1959. This French version is the only previous translation of the essay of which I am aware. Finally, various other materials from Kant, Johann Schulze, and Eberhard, which have a direct bearing on *On a Discovery* as well as the whole Kant-Eberhard controversy, are translated in appendices.

The historical-critical introduction, which constitutes part one of this book, is divided into three chapters. The first gives a general sketch of the background of the controversy, including the reasons that led Kant to engage in it, and provides some biographical information about Eberhard. The second attempts to give the reader a taste of the style as well as the substance of Eberhard's manner of argumentation. Accordingly, I have tried to let Eberhard speak for himself as much as possible. This unfortunately involves the introduction of some rather archaic philosophical terminology and argumentation, but I feel very strongly that at least this brief foray into philosophical archaeology is necessary if one is to fully understand the Kantian response. The third, and by far the longest chapter, deals with Kant's argument itself. This is intended to be both something less and something more than a commentary. Something less in that, although it does attempt to provide an overall view of the work and to place it within the context of Kant's thought, it is highly selective in the themes on which it concentrates, and it pays relatively little consideration to philological questions. It attempts to be something more in that it endeavors not only to analyze the argument of this particular essay, but to make a general contribution to Kant interpretation, especially in regard to the analytic-synthetic distinction and the notions of "pure intuition" and "schema." Apart from references to the *Critique of Pure Reason*, which are given in the Kemp Smith translation and cited with the standard A and B pagination, references to Kant's work are to the Academy edition, abbreviated AK, with the appropriate volume and page, and, where possible, to available English translations.

Given the vastness of the general Kant literature, the amount of material on the Kant-Eberhard controversy is remarkably small. In German, there is a summary and analysis of the controversy by W. L. G. von Eberstein, *Versuch einer Geschichte der Logik und Metaphysik bey den Deutschen von Leibniz bis auf gegenwärtige Zeit* (Halle, 1799), II: 165–291. Eberstein was himself a Leibnizian and a friend of Eberhard, but he nevertheless tried very hard to present a balanced picture. Aside from this contemporary account, however, and brief discussions in standard commentaries such as Vaihinger's or histories such as Zeller's, I have only been able to find a not particularly helpful dissertation by O. Ferber, *Der philosophische Streit zwischen I. Kant und Johann Aug. Eberhard* (Berlin, 1894). In French there is an excellent analysis on which I have relied a great deal by H. J. de Vleeschauwer in the third volume of his *La Déduction Transcendentale dans l'Oeuvre de Kant* (Paris, 1937), pp. 370–443, and an interesting, although brief discussion of some aspects of the controversy by Roger Daval in *La Métaphysique de Kant* (Paris, 1951). About the only English-speaking Kant scholar and philosopher to pay very much attention to this controversy is Lewis White Beck who has emphasized its importance in several of his articles.

Finally, I should like to express my gratitude first to Professor Beck for initially encouraging me to engage in this project; secondly to the National Endowment for the Humanities, for providing me with a fellowship for the academic year 1969–70 when I first got the idea for this study; and to the Humanities Council of the College of Arts and Sciences of the University of Florida, for providing me with financial assistance for the summers of 1970 and 1971 when I completed most of the work on it. A general expression of gratitude is also due, not only from me, but from all Kant scholars, to the publishers of *Culture et Civilisation*, for the reprinting of the works of Eberhard, Eberstein, Schulze, and many others in their excellent *Aetas Kantiana* series. Given the scarcity of the original editions, I doubt very much if I would have been able to complete this project without these reprints.

Especial thanks, however, are due to three people. First to Professors Gerd Wartenberg and George Tunstall, each of whom engaged in the laborious task of reading through my entire translation at various stages, giving me the benefit of their expertise in the German language, and correcting numerous errors. Those errors that remain, are, of course, my own. Finally, to my wife, Norma, to whom this book is dedicated. Not only did she provide the home atmosphere in which I could pursue my studies, but she typed three complete drafts of the manuscript, patiently and lovingly deciphering my illegible handwriting, and retyped the numerous changes that I made in my "final" version.

My thanks also to MacMillan & Co., Ltd., St. Martin's Press, Inc., for permission to quote from the Norman Kemp Smith translation of the *Critique of Pure Reason*; to the University of Chicago Press for permission to quote from Arnulf Zweig's *Kant's Philosophical Correspondence, 1759–99*; and to Bobbs-Merrill Company, Inc., for permission to quote from the Lewis White Beck translation of Kant's *Prolegomena to any Future Metaphysics*.

Part One

A HISTORICAL-CRITICAL
INTRODUCTION

I
HISTORICAL BACKGROUND

When it first appeared in 1781, the *Critique of Pure Reason* suffered the fate common to most philosophical classics. First it was either ignored or completely misunderstood, then it became the object of violent attacks. The misunderstandings and the attacks, of course, continued, one of the most interesting examples of both being the subject matter of the present study. At the same time, however, the *Critique* was not without its defenders. Amongst the earliest and most influential of these was Karl Leonard Reinhold, who, as we shall see, played a significant role in the controversy between Kant and Eberhard. Although he later developed a position at considerable variance with the *Critique*, his *Briefe über die Kantische Philosophie* [Letters on the Kantian Philosophy] (1786) served more than any other work, including Kant's own effort in that direction, the *Prolegomena to any Future Metaphysics* (1783), to popularize the critical philosophy and make it part of the general culture of the *Aufklärung*. Reinhold did this largely through his emphasis on the ethical force of Kant's teaching, but this also served to stimulate renewed attention to its theoretical basis. As a result of this and other efforts at popularization, the Copernican revolution in philosophy succeeded before the end of the decade in inaugurating a revolution in the intellectual life of Germany. Thus Wilhelm L. G. von Eberstein, the main historian of the Kant-Eberhard controversy, reflected that the many valid objections raised against the critical philosophy by Eberhard and his colleagues had relatively little effect, because at that time "it has become fashionable to be a critical philosopher."[1]

The revolutionary importance of the *Critique*, at least in relation to Kant's contemporaries, can be seen in terms of the question which it

[1] Wilhelm L. G. von Eberstein, *Versuch einer Geschichte der Logik und Metaphysik bey der Deutschen von Leibniz bis auf gegenwärtige Zeit*, 2 vols. (Halle, 1794 and 1799; reprinted by Culture et Civilisation, Brussels, 1970), II: 232–33.

emphasized, the answer which it provided to that question, and the implications which it derived from that answer. The question on which Kant insisted was a novel one: how are synthetic judgments possible a priori? That is to say: how is it possible for the human mind to go beyond a given concept in a judgment, and to connect it with another concept which is not logically contained in the former, and to do so a priori, i.e., necessarily and independently of experience? Kant tells us in the *Prolegomena* that he was led to a consideration of this question by his "recollection of David Hume."[2] This recollection first interrupted his famous "dogmatic slumbers," and it did so precisely by suggesting the problem of the synthetic a priori. This whole line of thought was inspired by Hume's analysis of the relation between cause and effect. The latter had seen that the decisive feature in this relation is its alleged necessity. To claim that A is the cause of B is not merely to claim that B follows A, but that it does so invariably and necessarily. But this gives rise to the question as to how any such claim of necessary connection can be justified. Upon what basis can we ever legitimately claim that "in consequence of the existence of one thing, another must necessarily exist" or, correlatively, explain how "the concept of such a combination can arise a priori"?[3] As is well known, Hume arrived at the sceptical conclusion that such a claim could be justified neither by reason nor experience. He thereby came to view it merely as a belief grounded in custom, or in Kant's uncharacteristically picturesque terms, "nothing but a bastard of imagination, impregnated by experience."[4] Now the problem of the synthetic a priori arises from a generalization of Hume's problem. Moreover, this generalization, as Kant tells us, is inspired by the realization "that the concept of the connection of cause and effect was by no means the only concept by which the understanding thinks the connection of things a priori, but rather that metaphysics consists altogether of such concepts."[5] From this, however, it was only a short step to the realization that the very possibility of metaphysics depends on a resolution of this problem, and consequently that the correct philosophical procedure is to first resolve this general problem, and only then proceed to metaphysics. This, in its barest outlines, is the critical way, and from this perspective any philosophy which engages in metaphysical speculation without first resolving this preliminary question is a species of dogmatism.

---

[2] Kant, *Prolegomena*, AK, IV: 260. English translation by Lewis White Beck (Indianapolis, Ind.: The Liberal Arts Press, 1950), p. 8. Subsequent references will be to the Academy edition and the Beck translation.

[3] *Ibid.*, p. 258.

[4] *Ibid.*

[5] *Ibid.*, p. 260.

In the Preface to the second edition of the *Critique* (1787) Kant describes his general solution to this problem as the "Copernican revolution" in philosophy. This revolution essentially involves a radical reinterpretation of the relation between knowing and being. The traditional view was that "all our knowledge must conform to objects." On that assumption, however, it proved impossible to explain how we could ever arrive at a priori knowledge of the objects. This is obvious; for if our knowledge must conform to objects, then it cannot be acquired independently of the experience of these objects, i.e., a priori. This suggested an experiment, namely, to see "whether we may not have more success in the task of metaphysics, if we suppose the objects must conform to our knowledge."[6] Despite its paradoxicality, such an assumption has the obvious advantage of being able to explain the possibility of a priori knowledge of objects; for if objects must indeed conform to our knowledge, or better, our ways of knowing, then we can determine certain necessary features of these objects independently of an experience of them, simply by means of an analysis of our cognitive faculties. These features would include the conditions under which objects can alone be given to the mind in intuition, the "forms of sensibility," which in the *Transcendental Aesthetic* Kant shows to be space and time, and the conditions under which an object can be thought corresponding to this intuition, which in the *Transcendental Analytic* Kant shows to be the pure concepts of the understanding, the "concepts of an object in general." But as Kant claims, what is presented merely as hypothesis in the Preface is definitively established in the *Critique* as a whole. The result is an epistemological subjectivism, wherein the understanding is regarded not as a passive receptor of given data but as an active ordering faculty, indeed, as the "lawgiver to nature." Such an understanding is fully capable of obtaining a priori knowledge of nature because the nature which it knows is determined by its own activity.

This triumph, however, was only achieved at what, at first at least, seemed to be a heavy price, viz., the limitation of knowledge to appearances or objects of possible experience. For if objects must conform to our subjective conditions of knowing, more specifically, to our forms of sensibility, then we can only know them in so far as they conform; that is, we can only know them in so far as they appear, and not as they are in themselves. We can, indeed, posit the existence of this mysterious thing in itself, and even think about it through our pure concepts of the understanding. But since these concepts only acquire a content in so far

---

[6]Kant, *Critique of Pure Reason*, B, xvi. All references to the *Critique* shall be the pagination of the first and second editions, A and B respectively.

as an object is given to the mind in intuition, and since for the human mind at least all intuition is sensible, such thinking by means of pure concepts remains an empty playing with the forms of thought. Legitimately used, this concept of the thing in itself, the object as it is apart from the subjective conditions of sensibility, through which alone it can be given to the mind in experience, the "noumenon in the negative sense," serves merely to remind us of the limits of our knowledge, but it does not yield any genuine knowledge of an object. Metaphysics, however, has been haunted by the illegitimate use of this concept and the categories through which it is conceived, and in this vain attempt to gain knowledge, by pure reason, of a transcendent, non-sensible reality, it thus falls victim to "transcendental illusion." This illusion arises whenever the mind ventures beyond the realm of possible experience; for then, not having any content provided for its thought, it tends to take the merely subjective logical rules or maxims in terms of which it organizes its thought, for objective, material principles which describe the nature of things. In the language of the *Critique*, it takes "the subjective necessity of a connection of our concepts, which is to the advantage of the understanding, for an objective necessity in the determination of things in themselves."[7] Moreover, this illusion, which Kant regards as both natural and inevitable, not only fails to lead to genuine knowledge, but actually leads reason into conflicts with itself or antinomies, which in turn leads to scepticism.

Nevertheless, the outcome of this analysis, which is developed in great detail in the *Transcendental Dialectic*, is far from sceptical. The denial of the illegitimate pretensions of theoretical reason serves merely to underline the rights of practical reason. Thus, God, freedom, and immortality, the basic principles of the moral life, are not only protected from any illicit encroachment from the theoretical sphere, i.e., from the "naturalist of pure reason," but are vindicated as fundamental postulates of an autonomous practical reason. This, of course, is the meaning of Kant's famous claim that he "found it necessary to deny knowledge in order to make room for faith."[8] There is a loss in the limitation of knowledge to objects of possible experience, but as Kant is quick to point out: "The loss effects only the *monopoly of the schools*, and in no respect the *interest of humanity*."[9]

The attacks on this position came from every segment of intellectual life in Germany. The romantic camp issued critiques of what they took to be Kant's excessive rationalism and his lack of attention to feeling

[7]*Ibid.*, A297/B353.
[8]*Ibid.*, B, xxx.
[9]*Ibid.*, B, xxxii.

and language. This was argued by Kant's friend J. G. Hamann in his review of the *Critique* 1781 and, in more detail, in his *Metakritik über den Purism der Vernunft* [Metacritique of the Purism of Reason] (1784), which he did not publish in deference to his friend; by Kant's former pupil, J. G. Herder, in his *Verstand und Vernunft, eine Metakritik zur Kritik der reinen Vernunft* [Understanding and Reason, a Metacritique of the Critique of Pure Reason] (1799) and *Kalligone* (1800); and by F. H. Jacobi in his *David Hume über den Glauben, oder Idealismus und Realismus* [David Hume on Belief, or Idealism and Realism] (1787). In addition to holding that feeling rather than thought is the organ through which the actual is encountered, Jacobi first raised the fundamental objection against Kant's doctrine of the thing in itself, an objection which has been repeated constantly in subsequent discussions of the critical philosophy. This objection points to the contradiction between the necessity of appealing to the thing in itself in order to explain experience and the impossibility of justifying such an appeal within the framework of the *Critique*. The essence of this objection is clearly expressed in the following passage:

I have to admit that this objection has held me up not a little in my study of the Kantian philosophy, so that for several years on end I had to keep on beginning the *Critique of Pure Reason* from the beginning again, because I was continually confused by being unable to find my way into the system without this presupposition, and of being unable to remain in it with this presupposition.[10]

Jacobi's criticism was more or less adopted by the sceptical opponents of the *Critique*, especially G. E. Schulze in his *Aenesidemus* (1792) and to some extent Salomon Maimon, although the latter was led to reinterpret rather than to simply reject the notion. From this sceptical approach the objection not only focuses on Kant's allegedly illicit use of the categories of causality and reality in regard to the thing in itself, but in light of this on the failure of the *Transcendental Deduction* to really answer Hume. The basic argument, which as we shall see was also adopted by Eberhard as one of his weapons against Kant, is that since the categories apply only to appearances, and since appearances are mere representations, Kant has failed to show that they possess any genuine objective validity. Such validity is only obtained if our concepts refer to things in themselves, and unless this possibility can be explained, one cannot explain the possibility of synthetic a priori knowledge.

The difficulties inherent in the notion of the thing in itself was also one of the guiding themes behind the development of German idealism. The basic difference, however, is that instead of coming to sceptical

---

[10] F. H. Jacobi, *Werke* (Leipzig, 1815), II: 304.

conclusions as a result of its unknowability, the idealists either completely denied or reinterpreted the concept of the thing in itself. We
cannot, of course, here trace the long and intricate history of this
movement which culminated in Hegel, but suffice it to note that,
unlike the other movements, this idealism, inaugurated by Kant's one-
time ally Reinhold and in a more definitive form by Fichte, viewed
itself, at least in its incipient phase, as a genuine development of
Kantian principles rather than as a criticism thereof. This development,
however, was in the direction of a metaphysical idealism which was
totally at variance with the Kantian limitation of knowledge to appearances. Kant made public his displeasure with the speculations of his
erstwhile disciples in his famous open letter on Fichte's *Doctrine of
Knowledge* of August 7, 1799, wherein he officially disavows any
connections with this doctrine.

Now the movements described so far can all be viewed together as
criticisms from the left; that is, from points of view which themselves
involve a radical break with the values and doctrines of the *Aufklärung*
and of its more or less official philosophy, the Leibniz-Wolffian. By far
the most extensive and vigorous criticism of the Kantian philosophy,
however, came from the right, i.e., from the defenders of the official
philosophy. Unlike the idealists, these men saw no virtue in Kant's
break with dogmatism and in his turn to the subject or Copernican
revolution, which allegedly was the only possible way to overcome the
Humean scepticism. Rather they regarded these doubts as having been
already convincingly albeit implicitly answered by Leibniz, and they
viewed the *Critique* essentially as nothing more than Berkeleian-style
subjective idealism combined with an unjustified denial of metaphysics,
that, Kant's protestations to the contrary, constituted a positive danger
to morality and religion. The leader of this group of long-forgotten
professors was Johann August Eberhard.[11]

Eberhard is one of those interesting figures whose place, however
modest, in the history of thought is due almost entirely to the people
whom he happened to attack and by whom he was attacked in return.
Moreover, his case is especially interesting in this regard because during
his long career he managed to lock horns with the two greatest minds of
his time, Gotthold Ephraim Lessing and Immanuel Kant.

Born on August 31, 1739, in Halberstadt, Eberhard was trained in
theology (1756–59) at the University of Halle, where he also studied
some philosophy and classical philology. This prepared him for a career
as preacher and theologian, which, after an initial position as private

---

[11] The biographical material on Eberhard is derived mainly from the *Allgemeine Deutsche
Biographie* (Leipzig, 1887), 5: 568–71.

tutor, he began pursuing in 1763, first in Halberstadt, then in Berlin. While in Berlin he came into contact with and was greatly influenced by the main figures of the *Aufklärung*, especially Friedrich Nicolai and Moses Mendelssohn. Under the influence of these men his theological position moved steadily away from orthodoxy. This culminated in the publication in 1772 of his *Neue Apologie des Sokrates, oder Untersuchungen der Lehre von den Seligkeit der Heiden* [New Apology for Socrates, or Investigation of the Doctrine of the Salvation of the Heathens], a book which was widely discussed at the time and went through several editions and translations. This work was occasioned by the polemic stemming from the condemnation of Marmontel's *Bélisaire* on the grounds that it contains the heretical doctrine of the salvation of the virtuous heathens. During the course of this work, Eberhard not only defends this principle against orthodox objections, but proceeds to launch a vigorous attack on the entire range of questionable orthodox dogmas, from the concept of supernaturally efficacious grace, which he saw as the denial of the significance of human effort, to the doctrine of the vicarious satisfaction, which he found to be morally repugnant, and including, in his eyes, the totally non-sensical doctrine of eternal punishments. Moreover, in connection with the latter point, he attacks the Leibnizian defense of the doctrine of eternal punishment as found in the *Theodicy* on the grounds that Leibniz is being insincere in his concession to orthodoxy.[12]

It was largely this latter point which drew him into conflict with Lessing, who at that time was engaged in a vigorous polemic with the whole movement of theological rationalism or neology to which Eberhard belonged. Also, interestingly enough, in this polemic Eberhard found himself accused by Lessing, as he was later to be accused by Kant, of misunderstanding Leibniz. Lessing formulated these charges in a pair of essays, *Leibniz von den ewigen Strafen* [Leibniz on Eternal Punishments] and *Des Andreas Wissowatius Einwürfe wider die Dreieinigkeit* [Andreas Wissowatius' Objections Against the Trinity], both of 1773. In these essays Lessing not only attacks Eberhard's general analysis of religious dogmas, but also defends Leibniz against the charges of insincerity in terms of the distinction between the esoteric and the exoteric meaning of his doctrine.[13] Eberhard responded to Lessing's attack in the second part of *New Apology for Socrates* (1774), which was written while he held a preaching position in Charlottenburg.

---

[12] For a discussion of this work and of Eberhard's role in the theological polemic of the *Aufklärung*, see H. E. Allison, *Lessing and the Enlightenment* (University of Michigan Press, 1966), esp. pp. 40–42.

[13] *Lessing and the Enlighenment*, pp. 83–95.

After this, Eberhard's main interests turned from theology to philosophy. The first fruits of his efforts in this direction was the *Allgemeine Theorie des Denkens und Empfindens* [General Theory of Thinking and Sensing] (1776, second edition, 1786), which was greatly influenced by Mendelssohn and which was awarded the prize of the Berlin Academy. In it he attacked the psychological sense of innateness which he claimed to have found in Leibniz's *New Essays*. Largely as a result of this he was called to Halle (1778) where he became professor of philosophy. He apparently proved to be quite popular as a teacher and exerted considerable influence on the young Schleiermacher. While a professor, he published several handbooks on various aspects of philosophy, based largely on his lectures. These included: *Sittenlehre der Vernunft* [Ethics of Reason] (1781); *Theorie der schönen Künste und Wissenschaften* [Theory of Fine Arts and Sciences] (1783); *Vernunftlehre der natürlichen Theologie* [Rational Doctrine of Natural Theology] (1787), which Kant himself used in connection with his lectures on the philosophy of religion; *Allgemeine Geschichte der Philosophie* [Universal History of Philosophy] (1788); and *Kurzer Abriß der Metaphysik mit Rücksicht auf den gegenwartigen Zustand der Philosophie in Deutschland* [Short Sketch of Metaphysics with regard to the Present Condition of Philosophy in Germany] (1794), all of which present a fairly standard Leibniz-Wolffian position. During this period he also published a variety of works dealing with such topics as aesthetics and the German language. His last work, *Der Geist des Urchristenthums* [The Spirit of Original Christianity] was published in 1808, one year before his death.

Eberhard's concern with the *Critique* dates back to its first appearance, and he apparently continually criticized it in his lectures. With the publication of the second edition in 1787, however, he evidently felt it necessary to make this opposition known to a wider public. Thus, together with several other Wolffians, but mainly with J. G. Maaß and J. E. Schwab, he founded in 1788 a journal, the *Philosophisches Magazin*. The general purpose of the journal was to provide an organ through which Eberhard and his collaborators could launch a full-scale attack on the Kantian philosophy and its defenders from the Wolffian standpoint. More specifically, its initial intent was to oppose the *Allgemeine Literatur-Zeitung*. This latter journal was founded in Jena in 1785 by Kant's friend and ally, J. G. Schulze, and its purpose was to defend the critical philosophy, which, as we have already noted, was at the time under attack from all directions. Schulze and Reinhold, although joined by a host of lesser names, assumed primary responsibility for this defense, so that Kant himself could be left free to complete the critical philosophy. In order to gain a wider public, however, Eberhard's journal did not concern itself exclusively with Kant and his defenders, but devoted at least some space in each issue to other topics, some even of a completely non-philosophical nature.

The first volume of the *Philosophicsches Magazin* appeared in four issues in 1788–89. It boldly asserted the basic superiority of the Leibnizian over the Kantian position, claiming that whatever is true in Kant is already found in Leibniz, and that wherever Kant differs from Leibniz he is wrong. This was immediately rebutted by the *Allgemeine Literatur-Zeitung*, with reviews, first by Rehberg and then by Reinhold, the latter, as we shall see, making use of material provided by Kant. Eberhard and his collaborators responded to these reviews and raised some significant new objections in the second volume of the *Philosophisches Magazin* which appeared in 1790. That same year, *On a Discovery* appeared in response to the first volume. After this, Eberhard published two more volumes of the journal in 1791 and 1792. These addressed themselves largely to the continuing defenses of the critical philosophy issuing from the Kantian camp, and included a not altogether successful attempt by Eberhard to reply to the objections raised by Kant in his essay. Although there are some interesting further criticisms of Kant's philosophy of mathematics, especially as interpreted by disciples such as Schulze, much of the discussion consists of a rehash of previous arguments. Finally, the *Philosophisches Magazin* was succeeded by the *Philosophisches Archiv* which appeared in two volumes in 1793 and 1794. Here Eberhard and his collaborators continued their attack on Kant, engaged in a counter attack on Schulze, who in the second part of his *Prüfung der Kantischen Critik der reinen Vernunft* [Examination of the Kantian Critique of Pure Reason] (1792) issued an extended critique of the Eberhardian position, and gradually turned their attention more toward Reinhold, who by that time had set out on a path of his own. Eberhard's own contributions to this last stage of the debate are found chiefly in a series of "Dogmatic Letters," where in distinguishing between the "objective dogmatism of Leibniz" and the "subjective dogmatism of Kant," he develops a critique of the Kantian notion of the thing in itself which anticipates some of the objections later raised against Kant by Schelling and Hegel.[14] Here again, however, this line of attack is already implicit in the charges of subjective idealism which Eberhard raises against Kant in the very beginning of the controversy.

Kant, for his part, was particularly upset by Eberhard's attack. As both the correspondence with Reinhold and the actual text of *On a*

---

[14]This is claimed by Hans Vaihinger, *Commentar zur Kant's Kritik der reinen Vernunft* (Stuttgart, Berlin, Leipzig, 1892), II: 540. Vaihinger also gives (pp. 534–40) a brief history of the whole debate between Eberhard and the Kantians, which he poignantly characterizes (p. 529) as "die Peripetie des Kantianismus."

Discovery clearly shows, he not only viewed it as a misguided, albeit rhetorically effective assault on the whole significance and originality of the critical enterprise, but he came to regard Eberhard as a dishonest man who deliberately distorted the teachings of the *Critique* in order to sway an ignorant public. Thus, despite the pleadings of Reinhold and despite the urgency of completing his labors on the *Critique of Judgment*, he decided to break his long standing vow not to enter into any direct controversies with his critics. The result was Kant's only full-scale explicitly polemical work, and many of the considerations which led Kant to produce such a work can be found in his correspondence from the years 1786 to 1789.

It appears that Kant, who, as we have already noted, made use of Eberhard's *Vernunftlehre der natürlichen Theologie* in his lectures on the philosophy of religion, was first informed of the latter's activities against him by his correspondent Ludwig Heinrich Jacobi. Writing from Halle, Eberhard's home base, on July 17, 1786, Jacobi tells Kant of his own modest efforts to popularize and clarify the critical philosophy, and as evidence of the need for such work he cites Eberhard's claim that the *Critique of Pure Reason* is incomprehensible and his consequent efforts to discourage students from reading it.[15] This news was confirmed by Kant's long time friend, Johann Christoph Berens, who, writing from Berlin on December 5, 1787, reports to Kant on the reception of the *Critique* in the various parts of Germany which he has visited, and notes that "Professor Eberhard fears the moral consequences of your teaching, and feels that you should have followed the old views."[16]

Kant next learned of Eberhard's activities against him in another letter from Jacobi. Writing again from Halle, on February 28, 1789, he tells Kant that he has just received the third issue of the first volume of the *Philosophisches Magazin*, and he notes that "Eberhard speaks therein almost entirely alone, and the entire issue is directed against the *Critique*." He goes on, however, to add:

> The reasoning therein is for the most part correct, and the bulk of the propositions which it affirms are true and may be justified. The strangest thing, however, is the assertion that the *Critique* affirms the opposite. The point in which there is a real conflict concerns only (1) the universality of the sensible forms, and (2) the universality of the concepts of the understanding; both of which are here strongly affirmed. Nevertheless, as is already known a priori, the grounds are derived completely from the subject. It demonstrates what no one denies, viz., that we proceed correctly in thinking *noumena* through the categories, but not that we can know any real predicate thereof.[17]

[15] AK X: 459.
[16] *Ibid.*, pp. 507–508.
[17] AK XI: 5.

A somewhat more accurate assessment of the situation was provided by Reinhold, who, writing on April 9, 1789, first informs Kant of a portrait (of Kant) which he is having sent to him for his birthday, and then proceeds to notify him of the disastrous effect on public opinion already created by Eberhard's misrepresentation of the critical philosophy. He asserts that this misrepresentation must not be allowed to go unanswered, but requests that Kant not waste his precious time and energy by personally entering into the controversy. He recommends instead that Kant make public a simple and direct statement to the effect that Eberhard and his followers have not correctly interpreted the teachings of the *Critique*, and thus that their refutations are beside the point. In this context he also asks Kant to note briefly, if possible, some of the principle areas of misunderstanding in his next letter so that he can make use of them in a published rebuttal.[18]

Kant did not reply to Reinhold until May 12 (see Appendix A for a translation of the complete text of the letter), and he excuses this delay on the grounds that he had to go to the public library to find the first three issues of Eberhard's journal. From this it appears quite clear that until this time Kant did not have any first-hand knowledge of Eberhard's criticisms, but was relying completely on information provided to him by his correspondents. Now, however, after actually having read Eberhard's criticisms for the first time, he notes bitterly to Reinhold: "*That Mr. Eberhard, like many others, has not understood me, is the least one can say* (for that would be partly my fault). But, as the following remarks will show, he actually sets out to misunderstand me, and to make me incomprehensible." Kant then proceeds to discuss certain specific passages from Eberhard, largely dealing with the latter's formulation and interpretation of his analytic-synthetic distinction. These closely parallel statements which are contained in the published text of *On a Discovery* and they shall be considered in the context of a systematic analysis of Kant's position.

This is followed exactly one week later by a second letter to Reinhold (also translated in Appendix A). Here Kant develops in considerable detail the criticisms suggested in the first letter, underlines his convictions concerning Eberhard's lack of honesty, and gives Reinhold leave to use these remarks in whatever manner he sees fit. He still, however, declines because of his work on the *Critique of Judgment*, and the "infirmities of age" to personally engage in the controversy.

Following Kant's instructions, Reinhold replied on June 14, that he plans to include the material submitted to him by Kant in a review of the third issue of Eberhard's journal. He also expresses, however, an intention to initially make use only of the material which Kant pro-

[18] *Ibid.*, pp. 17–18.

vided in his first letter, and to "keep the rest in reserve," in anticipation of the inevitable counter-attack by the Eberhardian forces.[19]

It was apparently around this time that Kant changed his mind concerning the decision not to personally enter into a controversy with Eberhard. Thus, in his letter to Reinhold of September 21, he informs his disciple that he is in fact preparing a short essay against Eberhard, which he shall finish that Michaelmas and send to him as soon as possible. Moreover, he also expresses a desire to see the first issue of the second volume of the *Philosophisehes Magazin* which had already appeared but which, as usual, was not yet available in Königsberg. Thus, he asks Reinhold to see to it that a copy be sent to him from Berlin.[20]

Once again, however, Kant changed his mind. Thus, we find him writing to Reinhold on December 1, reporting favorably on his initial reading of the latter's new work, *Theorie des Vorstellung-Vermögens* [Theory of the Faculty of Representation]; lamenting about the difficulties of old age, especially in regard to concentration on difficult topics, which he offers as an excuse for not having given Reinhold's work more careful attention, and notifying him that he is preparing a substantial work on Eberhard, which he expects to send him by Easter, together with the long-awaited *Critique of Judgment*.[21] This work, of course, turned out to be *On a Discovery*, and it thus seems that, in the space of less than three months, the initially projected brief essay had assumed the proportions of a small book. Moreover, for once Kant's estimation of the time required to complete a project was accurate, as the work was published on April 20, 1790.

Kant's interest in Eberhard and the *Philosophisches Magazin*, however, did not end with the publication of *On a Discovery*. He also studied a least the second volume of the journal, and we thus find him writing to Schulze, first on June 29 and then again on August 2, 1790, telling him of his continued displeasure with Eberhard's activities, and enclosing some materials which Schulze is instructed to use in his review of the second volume in his Jena journal.[22] This material consisted of two sets or sheets of objections to Eberhard's contributions to the second volume, which Kant included with his first letter, and a discussion of three essays by the mathematicisn A. G. Kästner, which he sent together with the second letter. This Kant material was first uncovered and published by Wilhelm Dilthey in the *Archiv für Geschichte der Philosophie* 14 (1890).[23] Kästner's essays, entitled respectively

---

[19]*Ibid.*, pp. 59–63.

[20]*Ibid.*, pp. 88–89.

[21]*Ibid.*, pp. 111–12.

[22]*Ibid.*, pp. 183–84.

[23]For the history of these materials and their discovery, see W. Dilthey, "Neue Kanthandschriften," *Kant-Studien* III (1899): 367 ff.

"What is the Meaning of Possible in Euclid's Geometry?" "On the Mathematical Concept of Space", and "On Geometrical Axioms," appeared in the fourth issue of the second volume, and dealt with basic issues in the philosophy of mathematics from a more or less Leibnizian perspective. In sharp contrast to his treatment of Eberhard, Kant treats Kästner with great, although not completely sincere, respect. His purpose, as he reveals to Schulze, is to show that Eberhard can derive no support for his position from Kästner's work. Thus he emphasizes that, unlike Eberhard, Kästner does not confuse the sensible with the intelligible, and space as an a priori intuition with an image. Moreover, he even goes so far as to claim, obviously for purely tactical reasons, that Kästner's position is in essential agreement with the *Critique*.

Schulze's review appeared in September 1790. In it he made use of, and developed the criticisms of Eberhard submitted by Kant, and presented the remarks on Kästner almost verbatim. He also added analyses of his own of other portions of the second volume of the *Philosophisches Magazin*. This includes an important response to Maaß' criticism of the analytic-synthetic distinction, which Kant, in his concern with Eberhard, neglected. However, although Kant did not write this response, he most certainly approved of it, and it can thus safely be regarded as genuinely Kantian. Thus, both because of its incorporation of material actually supplied by Kant, and Schulze's own contributions, the review constitutes an important supplement to *On a Discovery* (accordingly, relevant selections from it are translated in Appendix B).

Finally, there are additional references to Eberhard in Kant's correspondence, especially with Beck. Thus, in a letter dated September 1, 1791, we find Kant suggesting that Beck address himself to some of Eberhard's criticisms in his proposed commentary on the *Critique*,[24] and in a subsequent letter of December 4, 1792, he dismisses the view of Eberhard and Garve that the idealism of the *Critique* is basically the same as that of Berkeley.[25] This latter reference is especially worthy of note in light of the fact that Kant almost completely ignores this aspect of Eberhard's critique in *On a Discovery*.

This continued attention to Eberhard is no doubt partly due to a purely personal reaction to what Kant felt to be a perverse attack and a deliberate falsification of his position. This feeling, which, as we shall see, was not entierly justified, is clearly revealed on every page of *On a Discovery*, as well as in the correspondence with Reinhold and Schulze. It gives the essay a personal, polemical tone which is lacking in Kant's other writings. This attention, however, was also partly due to a growing concern of the aging Kant to clearly define his philosophy vis-à-vis

[24] AK XI: 289-92.
[25] *Ibid.*, pp. 394-96.

the Leibnizian, and thus to establish once and for all its originality and its role in the history of thought. Paradoxically enough, this concern seems to have developed just at the time when some of Kant's erstwhile disciples such as Reinhold and Fichte were developing critical doctrines in radically new directions, which Kant himself refused to acknowledge. Seen in this context, *On a Discovery* is not merely an occasional piece, but the first step in an attempt to arrive at a definitive formulation and defense of the basic principles of the critical philosophy. The next major step was undoubtably Kant's decision in 1793 to enter the essay competition sponsored by the Berlin Academy of Sciences on the topic "What progress has metaphysics made in Germany since the time of Leibniz and Wolff?" Unfortunately, Kant never completed this prize essay ("On the Progress of Metaphysics"), but the unfinished drafts contain a further articulation and extension of the line of argument found in *On a Discovery*.[26]

[26] For an analysis of the content and history of this projected work, see H. J. de Vleeschauwer, *La déduction transcendentale dans l'oeuvre de Kant* (Paris, 1937), III: 455–90.

II

THE EBERHARDIAN ATTACK

Eberhard describes the basic purpose of the *Philosophisches Magazin* in the prefatory statement to the first issue: "Report on the Purpose and Organization of the *Philosophisches Magazin*, together with some Considerations on the Present Conditions of Philosophy in Germany." This report reflects perfectly the standpoint of the *Aufklärung*, with its emphasis on the popularization of philosophical issues. It points out that as the result of the spread of enlightment and the efforts on behalf of its disseminators to express their thoughts in a popular idiom, a general philosophical culture, or at least a more wide-spread concern with speculative issues, has emerged. Thus, for the first time in Germany, philosophy has ceased being merely an affair of the schools and has become instead a real force in the intellectual life of the people.

It is within this context that Eberhard proposes to consider the *Critique of Pure Reason*. Its author, he reflects, desired to initiate a philosophical revolution, and in this he was not disappointed. As a matter of fact, he writes:

The success surpassed anything which the most sanguine hope of the warmest enthusiasm could have expected. The *Critique of Pure Reason* and the philosophy contained therein made a sensation such as has not been seen in the philosophical world for a long time. It did this, however, with different people in different ways. Some, who were even confused concerning the organization of their system, for which they had to first collect, examine, and combine the materials, found here the greatest part of their system rejected in a lump, and saw themselves to be relieved of a great labor. Others, who had already come to doubt the usefulness of their system, found their doubt confirmed, and also found with this confirmation the peace of certainty. Finally, others, who only derive their knowledge from the latest books, and for whom the most recent is always the truest, followed blindly. Most, however, were stupefied by the boldness of the undertaking, the confidence in its execution, as well as the subtlety of the investigation and the newness of the terminology. Moreover, only a few have been able to recover from this stupor.[1]

[1] *Philosophisches Magazin* I: 4–5.

The avowed purpose of the *Philosophisches Magazin* is thus to enable more people to recover from the stupor induced by the *Critique of Pure Reason*. It proposes to do this by a careful, impartial analysis and by a point by point comparison of its crucial theses with the corresponding theses in the Leibniz-Wolffian metaphysics. The result, as Eberhard later claims in a passage which was to become the starting point of Kant's reply, is the demonstration of the following truth:

> The Leibnizian philosophy contains just as much of a critique of reason as the new philosophy, while at the same time it still introduces a dogmatism based on a precise analysis of the faculties of knowledge. It therefore contains all that is true in the new philosophy and, in addition, a well-grounded extension of the sphere of the understanding.[2]

Eberhard thus challenges, in the name of Leibniz, the Kantian opposition between dogmatism and criticism, as well as the pretensions of the latter to having alone satisfactorily answered Humean scepticism. "Already before Locke's work on the human understanding appeared," he writes, "Leibniz had forestalled any arbitrary limitation of the extent of human knowledge by means of a complete account of the sources of our concepts."[3] It is thus Leibniz, not Kant, who first provided the critical antidote to Hume. Moreover, he did so in such a manner that he was able to escape all of the disastrous consequences resulting from the limitation of knowledge to the phenomenal realm. It is thus armed with the basic principles of Leibnizian rationalism, albeit often interpreted in an essentially Wolffian fashion, that Eberhard proposes to engage in a systematic onslaught on the *Critique of Pure Reason*.[4] As Kant himself noted ironically, however, the procedure of the *Philosophisches Magazin* is anything but systematic. Not only does Eberhard have a tendency to jump from point to point and to repeat himself incessantly, but the polemic with Kant is often interrupted by articles of a totally non-philosophical nature. Eberhard's polemic can thus be more profitably approached topically rather than chronologically. Viewed in this light, it can be divided into four main areas: (1) a critique of Kant's doctrine concerning the limits of knowledge, especially the doctrine of transcendental illusion; (2) the positive justification of knowledge claims concerning the non-sensible reality; (3) a critique of the Kantian conception of sensibility, and the interpretation of the synthetic a priori status of mathematics which is intimately related to this conception; (4) the attack on the originality and philo-

[2]*Ibid.*, p. 289.
[3]*Ibid.*, p. 19.
[4]Eberhard summarizes the Leibnizian doctrine which he deems most relevant in 13 propositions (*ibid.*, pp. 20–22) that are, however, largely ignored in his subsequent discussion.

sophical significance of Kant's distinction between analytic and synthetic judgments. In some of these points, he is joined by his colleagues, most notably J. G. Maaß, and since the latter's criticisms are not only often considerably more to the point than Eberhard's, but were also later taken up by Eberhard, we shall consider the most important of these within the context of our analysis.

1

The Limits of Knowledge

Eberhard categorically rejects Kant's central claim that our knowledge is limited by the sensible conditions under which alone objects can be given to the mind in intuition, and thus cannot reach beyond possible experience to a non-sensible (noumenal) reality. This, according to Eberhard, again arguing in the name of Leibniz, only defines the limits of our sensible or intuitive knowledge. It does not, however, at all affect the possibility of a purely rational, non-intuitive knowledge of "true things" or things in themselves. Such knowledge requires that reason have a content of its own, independently of that which is provided by sensibility in intuition. Eberhard will proceed, allegedly following Leibniz, to argue precisely this, but before he can do it, he must first address himself to the Kantian thesis that this very belief is an example of transcendental illusion.

This occurs mainly in an essay entitled "On Logical Truth or the Transcendental Validity of Human Knowledge." Here as elsewhere, Eberhard approaches the problem from a historical perspective. Until the advent of the *Critique*, he suggests, philosophy had believed itself able to presuppose the "logical truth" or "transcendental validity" of its rational knowledge. These terms, which Eberhard regards as synonymous, are roughly equivalent to Kant's notion of objective reality, i.e., correspondence to possible objects or states of affairs. Eberhard's point is that philosophers in the rationalistic tradition had assumed that metaphysical reasoning, which is based on genuine first principles, and which deduces its conclusions from these principles in accordance with the laws of logic, yielded results which were not only internally consistent, but also provided a true description of the nature of reality. This is certainly true enough, and he illustrates it by reference to Leibniz, for whom, it is alleged, the completion of metaphysics required nothing more than the first principles of human knowledge. Given the "logical truth" or "transcendental validity" of these principles, which for Leibniz were contradiction and sufficient reason, one can conclude that everything that follows logically from these principles likewise possesses such truth. It is therefore only a question of combining these truths

with one another and with their first grounds "according to the principles of syllogistics."[5]

All of this, however, was called into question by Kant's doctrine of
transcendental illusion. This doctrine, as we have seen, contends that
pure reason, when unguided by experience, not only can, but inevitably
and naturally does, lead itself by perfectly logical means to illusory
conclusions. In his examination of this doctrine, Eberhard ignores
Kant's application of it in the "*Paralogisms*" and "*Antinomies*," but
emphasizes the fact that Kant himself admits the naturalness of this
illusion and the "subjective certainty" involved in the procedure of
rationalistic metaphysics. As Eberhard interprets Kant: "We find ourselves completely compelled to transfer this connection of our concepts
to the objects. This is, to be sure, in his opinion an illusion, but none
the less unavoidable. . . ."[6]

Eberhard's actual "refutation" of Kant on this point amounts to
little more than the bare assertion of the legitimacy of the move from
naturalness to truth. His claim is, in effect, that it is absurd to regard
reason, which is the source of truth and the only basis for distinguishing
between truth and illusion, as itself a source of illusion. Such a view, he
suggests, would lead to a hopeless scepticism. "For what is truth," he
reflects, "if not the agreement with the necessary laws of reason and
understanding."[7] In so far as metaphysics proceeds in accordance with
these laws, it can be assured of its "logical truth," i.e., the agreement of
such knowledge with its object, and need not be concerned either with
the requirement to locate this object in intuition or with the danger of
falling into illusion. From the Kantian standpoint, however, it is obvious that such an argument simply begs the question raised by the
Critique. Kant, after all, does not raise general objections against the
"soundness of reason," nor does he call into question the laws of logic,
which, as we shall see, are essentially what Eberhard means by the
"necessary laws of reason and understanding". Rather, his point is that
logical consistency is, to be sure, a necessary, but not a sufficient condition of truth, at least in regard to synthetic judgments, i.e., judgments
which claim to relate to an object or to possess "objective validity."[8]
Such judgments, as he shows at length in the *Transcendental Dialectic*,
can be perfectly consistent, and still not refer to any object. Thus, in so
far as he does not really deal with this claim, Eberhard failed to address
himself to the argument of the *Critique*, but instead simply reaffirmed
the old rationalistic position which Kant called into question.

[5] *Ibid.*, pp. 150–51.
[6] *Ibid.*, pp. 151–52.
[7] *Ibid.*, p. 154.
[8] Cf. *Critique of Pure Reason*, A151/B190-A153/B193.

On the basis of this reaffirmation, Eberhard proceeds to express his confidence in the future of metaphysics, a science to which he claims to have devoted a large portion of his life. "Even if a considerable portion of this realm would have to be abandoned," he reflects, "an even more considerable area would remain."[9] (It is in this connection that he speaks of the "uncontested, fertile fields of ontology" which Kant treats with bitter irony.) He argues in regard to metaphysics: "We can always continue to work for its extension, we can always seek to enrich it with new truths, without first having to concern ourselves with the transcendental validity of these truths." Moreover, he continues, in a passage which Kant attacked in a particularly pointed fashion:

In this way have the mathematicians completed the delineation of entire sciences without saying a single word about the reality of their object. This may be illustrated by a notable example, by an example that is too pertinent and instructive not to be allowed to be cited here. Apollonius and his interpreters have constructed the entire theory of conic sections without anywhere teaching the way in which the ordinates on the diameters of these curved lines can be applied, despite the fact that the reality of the entire theory rests on this. If this application were not possible, the construction of the conic section could not be accomplished, and it would remain uncertain if there were a subject to which the properties demonstrated in all of the beautiful problems of the theory pertains.[10]

Eberhard's immediate concern, however, is not with mathematics but with metaphysics. He recognizes that, in order to really refute Kant and vindicate the claim that metaphysics yields genuine knowledge of a super-sensible reality, he must not merely affirm, but actually demonstrate the "logical" or "transcendental" validity of the basic principles of such reasoning. These, following Leibniz, he takes to be the principles of contradiction and sufficient reasoning, and he defines these as principles of the *form* of our knowledge. Whatever is in accord with these rules of reason, he claims, is true. The only question is: "If objects thought in accordance with this form are just as true and certain, or if everything in the objects is as we conceive it according to these laws, or finally, if, according to Kant's language, these laws have a transcendental validity."[11]

What this amounts to is the necessity of providing a demonstration of the principle of sufficient reason. This must be done, he points out, because philosophy, unlike mathematics, cannot rest content with undemonstrated axioms. Moreover, since the only higher principle available for such a demonstration is the principle of contradiction, it must be derived therefrom. Now, such a demonstration was not attempted

[9] *Philosophisches Magazin*, I: 157.
[10] *Ibid.*, pp. 158–59.
[11] *ibid.*, p. 160.

by Leibniz. For him, the principle of sufficient reason, as the principle of existential and hence contingent truths, was viewed generally as coordinate with the principle of contradiction, which is the principle of possibility and hence of necessary truths.[12] It was, however, attempted by Wolff and Baumgarten,[13] and Eberhard's demonstration essentially follows this model, although he does give the argument a new, and as Kant points out, not very felicitous twist. The demonstration is as follows:

Either everything has a reason or not everything has a reason. In the latter case, something could be possible and conceivable, the reason for which is nothing. —If, however, one of two opposite things could be without a sufficient reason, so likewise could the other be without a sufficient reason. If, for example, a portion of air could move towards the east, and the wind could blow towards the east without the air in the east becoming warmer and more rarified, then this portion of air would be just as able to move to the west as to the east. The same air would therefore be able to move at the same time in two opposite directions, to the east and to the west and, consequently, to the east and not to the east; that is to say, it could at the same time be and not be, which is contradictory and impossible.[14]

The "transcendental validity" of this principle is thus claimed to follow as an immediate consequence of the principle of contradiction. If two contradictory predicates are both possible in relation to a subject, Eberhard reflects, "there must be a reason" (so muß Etwas seyn) why the one rather than the other pertains. This reason is the ground of the truth of a true proposition; for it is the ground "whereby one can know why something is, and why it is so and not otherwise."[15] To deny this would be to admit that one and the same subject could have two contradictory predicates at the same time, and this is clearly absurd. Thus, the principle of sufficient reason is allegedly established by means of an argument of the *reductio* form, and the only remaining question, at least about the form of knowledge, concerns the principle of contradiction itself. In regard to this Eberhard writes:

I must somewhere remain standing with a first truth wherein the chain of all remaining truths is anchored. This first truth cannot receive its certainty from any other truth in the chain; otherwise it would not be the first. What moves us then to accept it? Nothing other than the consciousness that I cannot think anything contradictory. If I try to, I feel that the one operation of my power of representation destroys the other. Whatever therefore is something, whatever therefore is thinkable, must not contain a contradiction. It cannot be at the same time A and not A.

---

[12]Cf. Leibniz, *Monadology* §§33-36; *Correspondence with Clarke*, 2nd letter, §1; *Theodicy*, §44.

[13]Christian Wolff, *Philosophia prima sive Ontologia* (Halle, 1776), sect. 66-70, A. G. Baumgarten, *Metaphysica* (Halle, 1739), §20.

[14]*Philosophisches Magazin* I: 163-64.

[15]*Ibid.*, p. 164.

Can I now apply that to every object? Can there be anything apart from me wherein there is something contradictory, something the predicate of which is at the same time A and not A? I see that it cannot be in my thought, and, to be sure, not because it is a fully indeterminate A which is cancelled and destroyed by a just as indeterminate not A. It must therefore hold not merely of my thought, it must have a universal validity. I must be able to transfer it from my representations to objects. The principle of contradiction is therefore an objective principle; the principle of reason (*der Satz des Grundes*), if it receives its certainty from it, must be one also.[16]

This particular argument, which Kant, interestingly enough, does not address himself to, is typical of Eberhard and of his style of arguing. It really can be reduced to the claim that the principle of contradiction has objective validity because we cannot conceive of an object which violates it. This Kant would certainly grant, but would proceed to point out that it does not for that reason cease being a merely logical principle determining our *concepts* of things, and therefore become a metaphysical principle extending our knowledge of the *nature* of things. Kant's whole critique of Leibnizian rationalism is predicated on the claim that it erroneously identifies our concepts of things with the things themselves. It is because of this identification that it is led to the illusory belief that it can gain genuine knowledge of these things by a mere analysis of their concepts.[17] Here as elsewhere, however, Eberhard seems to simply ignore rather than deal with this distinction, and this fact underlies his entire critique of the doctrine of transcendental illusion.

2
The Content of Knowledge

Having allegedly established the transcendental validity of the principles of the form of our knowledge, Eberhard's next step is to consider the question of its content or matter. Reasoning in accordance with the principle of sufficient reason will, after all, not take us very far unless there is something to reason about, some content that can be cognized through that principle. Eberhard must come to grips with Kant's claim that the only possible material for human knowledge is provided by sensibility, and is therefore subject to its formal conditions, space and time. The demonstration of the possibility of a purely rational knowledge of things in themselves, and thus of the possibility of a metaphysics of the Leibnizian style, depends on the refutation of this doctrine. Hence, in opposition to this doctrine Eberhard will endeavor to show:

[16] *Ibid.*, pp. 165–66.
[17] This is the central topic of the "Amphiboly of Concepts of Reflection" in the *Critique*.

(1) Kant's forms of knowledge are only forms of sensible knowledge, not at all of rational knowledge (*Verstandes Erkenntniß*); (2) they are therefore only the simplest concepts of this sensible knowledge; (3) the simplest concepts of rational knowledge are unimageable (*unbildlich*) and super-sensible; (4) this rational knowledge is *in abstracto* merely symbolic and *in concreto* only intuitive, and the simplest *intuitive mark* thereof is representation.[18]

Here, as throughout his analysis, Eberhard seems to equate Kant's distinction between intuition and concept with the Leibnizian distinction between intuitive and symbolic knowledge. The problem, however, is that he uses these notions neither in their genuinely Kantian nor Leibnizian senses. The *locus classicus* for this distinction in Leibniz is his "Reflections on Knowledge Truth and Ideas" (1684), where, after distinguishing between clear and distinct, adequate and inadequate knowledge, he introduces the distinction between intuitive and symbolic knowledge. As the passage makes perfectly clear, our knowledge can be regarded as intuitive only in so far as the mind possesses a fully determinate, i.e., distinct idea. In instances of symbolic or "blind" knowledge this is not the case, and the mind substitutes a sign or word for the idea itself. Moreover, the vast majority of our knowledge, not only in algebra and arithmetic, but nearly everywhere else, is symbolic. This, Leibniz claims, is because "we cannot, when an idea is very complex, think at once of all of its constituent characters." Only when this is possible, however, do we have intuitive knowledge. Moreover, Leibniz concludes: "Only intuitive knowledge can give us distinct, primitive ideas, whereas we can have only symbolic knowledge of complex ideas."[19]

Eberhard, on the other hand, although he uses Leibnizian terminology, equates intuitive knowledge with sensible and imageable (*bildlich*) knowledge, and non-intuitive or symbolic with non-sensible or abstract knowledge; and in so doing he not only obviously differs from his alleged authority, Leibniz, but also succeeds in completely distorting Kant's doctrine. This conception does, however, have the advantage of making it relatively easy to explain the possibility of knowledge of the non-sensible. In the above passage, he begins by affirming that space and time are merely forms of sensible knowledge; thereby leaving open the possibility of a non-sensible knowledge not subject to these conditions. Such a knowledge would be non-intuitive, which, as we have seen, means only that it does not involve images, but it would be none the less genuine and refer to a true object. Moreover, the basis for affirming such an object, which would constitute the "first elements of all sensible knowledge," is the "need to provide a ground for these

[18] *Philosophisches Magazin* I: 168.
[19] Leibniz, *Selection*, ed. Philip P. Wiener (New York: Charles Scribner's Sons, 1951), p. 285.

images (space and time) which lies outside the sphere of sensible knowledge."[20] Thus, against Kant's claim that "thoughts without content are empty," Eberhard proposes to show that understanding or reason has a specific content of its own, viz., the "real essence" of things which provides the "objective grounds" of the images of space and time. These objective grounds are reached by reasoning from our sensible experience in accordance with the principle of sufficient reason.

Eberhard proposes to establish this in regard to both space and time. Beginning with time, which presents fewer difficulties, he contends:

Concrete time, or the time which we feel, is nothing other than the succession of our representations; for even the succession of movement may be reduced to the succession of representations. Concrete time is therefore something composite; its simple elements are representations. Since all finite things are in a continual flux, these simple elements can never be sensed; inner sense can never sense them separately; they are always sensed together with something which precedes and follows. Furthermore, since the flux of alterations of all finite things is a continual, unbroken flux, no sensible part of time is the smallest, or a fully sensible part. The simple elements of concrete time therefore lie completely outside the sphere of sensibility. This is not opposed to the observation of previous metaphysics, and Leibniz philosophized in regard to this in his usual profound manner. The understanding therefore raises itself beyond the sphere of sensiblity as it discovers the unimageable simple without which the sensible images, even in respect to time, are not possible. It recognizes, therefore, to begin with, that something objective pertains to the image of time, these indivisible elementary representations, which together with the subjective grounds, which lie in the limits of the finite mind, give to sensibility the image of concrete time. For on account of these limits these representations cannot be simultaneous, and on account of the very same limits, they cannot be distinguished in the image.[21]

What is true of concrete time holds also of abstract time. By the latter Eberhard means simply the concept of time formed by abstraction from the concrete time of experience with its unbroken flux. The elements of this time are indivisible moments, and these moments, he claims, "relate to abstract time just as undetermined unities relate to abstract number." On this basis he concludes:

It is therefore a double error if one takes the elements of time for empty representations, for representations which have no objects, and, indeed, because they lack the form of intuition. For the elements of concrete time do not lack the intuitive aspect, it is the representation itself (p. 160); the elements of abstract time have, to be sure, nothing immediately intuitive, they have it, however, *mediately* in the concrete, from which the abstract time is derived.[22]

Since space is likewise a form of intuition, it is subject to a similar analysis: "The first elements of the composite with which space arises,

[20] *Philosophisches Magazin* I: 168.
[21] *Ibid.*, pp. 169–70.
[22] *ibid.*, pp. 170–71.

are, just as the elements of time, simple and beyond the sphere of sensibility. They are beings of the understanding, unimageable, they cannot be intuited under any sensible form, they are, nevertheless, undeniably true objects."[23] Thus, once again, Eberhard contends against Kant that merely because something is not an object of sensible knowledge, it does not follow that it is unknowable. Starting with the empirically given, and proceeding in accordance with the principle of sufficient reason, it becomes possible to demonstrate the objective reality of the simple, non-sensible grounds of both space and time. Moreover, not only the existence, but also the actual nature of those simple substances, out of which body as appearance is composed, can be demonstrated. This nature is:

The enduring of which the accidents are determinations, force, which contains their ground. This abiding, this substantial, lies, to be sure, beyond the sphere of the senses, the understanding cannot form any intuitive representation of it. It must, however, exist if the fundamental laws of reason possess an objective worth, logical truth or transcendental validity. If, therefore, no form of intuition underlies it, this proves only that it is not knowable through the senses; for only for them are the forms of intuition necessary conditions of knowledge, not at all for the understanding.[24]

By this process of reasoning Eberhard arrives at simple substances, understood with Leibniz as forces. Such substances are the "true things" or things in themselves which underlie our sensible representations or phenomena. In this way he claims to have answered Kant and to have provided a cogent example of metaphysical reasoning. The full articulation of this position, however, requires an analysis of the nature of the understanding, its content and its relation to sensibility. This is undertaken in an essay in the third issue, appropriately titled "On the Field of Pure Understanding." Here the basic point is that sensible and hence intuitive knowledge is directed towards particulars, presented either through the senses or the imagination in the form of images, while non-intuitive, conceptual knowledge, or knowledge through the understanding, is concerned with universals or "universal things" (allgemeine Dinge). These universal things, which allegedly provide the content for our non-sensible representations, turn out to be the genera and species whereby the particular things apprehended by the senses are distinguished from one another according to their essences and properties. "These are, to be sure," he notes, "not actual when separated from the particulars, but they are actual, the higher genera and species mediately, the lowest species immediately in the particular thing contained under them."[25]

[23] Ibid., p. 171.
[24] Ibid., pp. 173–74.
[25] Ibid., pp. 270–71.

But how does the mind arrive at these general concepts through which the non-sensible is cognized? Here, Eberhard remarks in a note of triumph, the answer is so simple that he wonders how Kant could have failed to notice it. It is nothing more than abstraction, understood essentially in the way in which Locke described the process in the *Essay*, i.e., a separating out and consideration of that which is common to several particulars. What remains as a result of this process are general features pertaining to all objects of a particular kind and, ultimately at the highest level of abstraction wherein we encounter "categories" or "ontological concepts", features pertaining to all objects or, in Kant's terms, "an object in general." "In this way," Eberhard writes, "the understanding rises from lower to higher concepts, and thus from the sensible to the intelligible."[26] Furthermore, this sensible or intuitive origin also serves to guarantee the objective validity of these concepts. In proceeding by way of abstraction, the understanding keeps its contact with the real. It only loses the features pertaining to individuals in their particularity, what Eberhard calls the imageable or intuitive features, but it keeps the unimageable yet still conceivable features pertaining to all reality. This is the same point which Eberhard expressed in a previously cited passage and elsewhere in terms of the distinction between being immediately and mediately intuitive. The former characterizes sensible concepts; the latter, since they are derived from sensible concepts through abstraction, the non-sensible or general concepts. Our non-sensible concepts have therefore as much claim to validity as our sensible ones, and the limits of our imagination, i.e., our ability to represent particular individuals, does not determine the limits of our reason. Finally, this line of argument, which reads more like a critique of Berkeley or Hume than of Kant, is clinched by an illustration that proved to be of particular interest to Kant.

I must here make use of an example, the appropriateness of which will only become apparent later. The senses and imagination of man are not capable of forming an exact image of a thousand-sided polygon, i.e., an image whereby it could, for example, be distinguished from one with nine hundred and ninety-nine sides. Nevertheless, as soon as I know that a figure has a thousand sides, my understanding can ascribe different predicates to it, which are all attributes of a figure with that number of sides. I know, for example, that its cube root is ten, that its quadratic root is not rational, I know whether or not it is a figurate number, etc. Here, therefore, is a case wherein the understanding knows a great deal about an object without the senses and the imagination being able to form a determinate image of it. How then can it be demonstrated that the understanding can neither affirm nor deny anything of things in themselves because the imagination can form no image thereof, or because we do not know all the determinations which pertain to its individuality?[27]

[26]*Ibid.*, p. 271.
[27]*Ibid.*, pp. 272–73.

As the passage makes clear, Eberhard's whole argument seems to turn on the equations of the sensible with the imageable, and the non-sensible, non-imageable with the conceptual. It is in light of these equations that he proceeds to demonstrate that we have conceptual knowledge of general truths that as such cannot be represented in images. Moreover, since his non-sensible objects are regarded as things in themselves or noumena, the demonstration of the possibility of conceptual knowledge is viewed as equivalent to the demonstration of the possibility of knowledge of things in themselves. Now, given this conception of the sensible and its relation to the non-sensible, the move from the one to the other is completely non-problematic and finds its paradigm in mathematical reasoning. The problem, however, as Kant will point out, is that this move does not yield the non-sensible in the Kantian sense, and therefore does not show that the non-sensible *in this sense* is knowable, which was precisely the thesis that Eberhard claimed to have established in his refutation of Kant.

3

The Sensible Conditions of Knowledge

Eberhard does, however, consider Kant's theory of sensibility and the correlative notion of appearance in great detail and in a number of separate places. His basic concern is to show that Kant misunderstands Leibniz on this point, and that, when properly understood, the Leibnizian doctrine is far superior to the Kantian. In this connection he also attacks the Kantian theory of pure or a priori intuition, and on the basis of this analysis he enters, in the second volume, into an interesting attack on Kant's philosophy of mathematics. He does not address himself to the central arguments of the *Transcendental Aesthetic* until later in the controversy, but such an analysis is provided in the first volume by his colleague J. G. Maaß, and this forms an intrinsic part of the Eberhardian polemic.

Kant's misunderstanding of Leibniz: Eberhard's basic charge, namely, that Kant misunderstood the Leibnizian conception of sensibility, and therefore also of appearance, is formulated in an essay entitled: "On the Essential Distinction between Knowledge through the Senses and through the Understanding." This polemic takes the form of a commentary on a passage from the *Transcendental Aesthetic*, and in order to aid in the comprehension of the argument, we shall cite the passage in full:

The concept of sensibility and of appearance would be falsified, and our whole teaching in regard to them would be rendered empty and useless, if we were to accept the view that our entire sensibility is nothing but a confused representation of things, containing only what belongs to them in themselves, but doing so under an aggregation of characters and partial representations that we do not consciously distinguish. For the difference between a confused and a clear representation is merely logical, and does not concern the content. No doubt the concept of 'right', in its commonsense usage, contains all that the subtlest speculation can develop out of it, though in its ordinary and practical use we are not conscious of the manifold representations comprised in this thought. But we cannot say that the common concept is therefore sensible, containing a mere appearance. For 'right' can never be an appearance; it is a concept in the understanding, and represents a property (the moral property) of actions, which belong to them in themselves. The representation of a body in intuition, on the other hand, contains nothing that can belong to an object in itself, but merely the appearance of something, and the mode in which we are affected by that something; and this receptivity of our faculty of knowledge is termed sensibility. Even if that appearance could become completely transparent to us, such knowledge would remain *toto coelo* different from knowledge of the object in itself.

The philosophy of Leibniz and Wolff, in thus treating the difference between the sensible and the intelligible as merely logical, has given a completely wrong direction to all investigations into the nature and origin of our knowledge. This difference is quite evidently transcendental. It does not merely concern their (logical) form, as being either clear or confused. It concerns their origin and content. It is not that by our sensibility we cannot know the nature of things in themselves in any save a confused fashion; we do not apprehend them in any fashion whatsoever. If our subjective constitution be removed, the represented object, with the qualities which sensible intuition bestows upon it, is nowhere to be found, and cannot possibly be found. For it is this subjective constitution which determines its form as appearance.[28]

Eberhard begins his assault by asserting that the distinction as found in Leibniz and Wolff is *both* transcendental and logical. By the claim that it is transcendental he means that sensibility and understanding are, indeed, distinguished in regard to their objects. This claim is justified by the repetition of the assertion that the objects of the senses are representations of particulars, known by means of images, while the objects of the understanding are non-intuitive, general ideas and necessary truths. It is further understood that this is not only compatible, but actually essentially connected with their logical difference, i.e., the difference in regard to clarity and distinctness emphasized by Kant. This follows because, given the nature of the human intellect, only general truths can be known distinctly, while the objects of sensible knowledge can only be grasped indistinctly, since they have non-sensible grounds. Furthermore, similar arguments can be raised against Kant's claim that the philosophy of Leibniz and Wolff fails to distinguish between the objects of these faculties in terms of their origin and content. Both parts of this claim are dismissed as false. First of all, it distinguishes between them in regard to their origin: "For it says: sensibility receives its idea through sensation; the understanding, through

---

[28] *Critique of Pure Reason*, A44/B61–62.

abstraction and combination by reason." Secondly, it distinguishes between them in regard to content: "For it says: the ideas of the understanding are general and non-intuitive, the ideas of sensibility particular
and intuitive."[29]

Having thus repudiated the charge that the philosophy of Leibniz
and Wolff falsified the concept of sensibility (a charge which Kant, in
his correspondence with Reinhold, erroneously denied having made
[see Appendix A]), Eberhard turns to the closely related concept of
appearance. Here again Kant's account is shown to be in error. This
error lies in the claim that the Leibnizian philosophy considers everything an appearance that is unclearly or obscurely represented. Rather,
he points out, it only regards that which is unclearly or obscurely
represented *through the senses* as appearance. For example, body is an
appearance for Leibniz, because it is represented obscurely through the
senses, and this in turn is because the senses are incapable of grasping
the simple substances (monads) of which it is composed. Kant's reference to the concept of right is therefore beside the point; for though
this concept may be indistinct, it is by no means sensible. Moreover, the
claim that the character of an appearance in the Leibnizian philosophy
is based solely on the form of clarity and not on its origin and content
is equally unfounded. Its origin is indicated in its definition, i.e., as
something obscurely represented through the senses, and its content by
the fact that it is an intuitive idea and the representation of a particular
thing.[30]

Kant, however, not only misunderstands the Leibnizian notion of
appearance, but his own conception is thoroughly confused. It is defined, according to Eberhard, as a modification of sensibility, but sensibility is defined in turn as the capacity to be modified, and this, he
reflects, is obviously circular.[31] Moreover, not content with this apparently easy victory, he endeavors to examine the Kantian notion somewhat more carefully in order to decisively establish the superiority of
the Leibnizian one. In so doing, however, he attacks Kant from two
directions which are rather difficult to reconcile with one another. On
the one hand, Kant is accused of idealism. This charge is introduced in a
number of scattered places in the first volume, but never really discussed in a systematic fashion. It basically amounts to the familiar
contention that Kant is a subjective idealist in the manner of Berkeley
because he denies that appearances have objective grounds, i.e., are
grounded in things in themselves.[32] On the other hand, he tries at the

[29] *Philosophisches Magazin* I: 296–97.
[30] *Ibid.*, p. 297.
[31] *Ibid.*, pp. 298–301.
[32] *Ibid.*, pp. 369–71.

same time to show that, even on Kant's assumptions concerning the nature of appearance, it is possible to gain through these appearances some knowledge of things in themselves.

The starting point of this latter argument is the reflection that Kant himself acknowledges that appearances are grounded in things in themselves, and this directly contradicts the idealism charge. Furthermore, it involves an extreme realistic reading of Kant's doctrine of the thing in itself. Eberhard is arguing in effect that the differences between two appearances encountered in experience are grounded in the differences in the underlying things in themselves. We are not able to distinguish these grounds in experience, but it is on their basis that we can alone distinguish between the appearances or sensible representations. Hence, one object is perceived as red, another as blue, because of a difference in their "real essence," which is equated with the thing in itself. So construed, the doctrine leads directly to the Leibnizian position. According to Leibniz, Eberhard argues, a representation may be said to be clear but not distinct, and thus obscure, when it enables the mind to distinguish one object from another, but does not suffice to apprehend the true nature of these objects nor the grounds of their distinction. But this is precisely what Kant, together with Leibniz, must acknowledge to occur in sense experience. Thus, Eberhard concludes, Kant must concur with the Leibnizian doctrine that we do represent things in themselves in sense experience, however obscurely, and that appearances must be regarded as representations of things in themselves.[33]

This further serves to support the Leibnizian principle, constantly reiterated by Eberhard, that appearances have both subjective and objective grounds. The former, as suggested by the above analysis, are the limits of the subject, i.e., his inability to distinctly perceive the elements of the composite, and the objective grounds, as one might suspect, are the simple grounds or non-sensible elements. Therefore, not only can we have, even in experience, some obscure awareness of these objective grounds, but to the extent to which our knowledge is based on these grounds, and freed from the subjective limits imposed by sensible conditions, it becomes certain, and to the extent to which it is affected by these subjective limits, it is subject to illusion or at least distortion. Sensibility is thus not a positive source of knowledge, but merely a function of finitude which serves to limit human knowledge. This central thesis of classical rationalism is illustrated by an appeal to some of the standard examples of perceptual illusion, all designed to show that the source of this illusion lies in subjective limits, by which Eberhard means simply limits in the capacity of the various sense

[33] *Ibid.*, pp. 298–303.

organs. He concludes these considerations with a general statement of his rationalitic position:

The grounds of rational knowledge are purely objective; the grounds of sensible knowledge are also subjective. The first contains, insofar as it is rational knowledge, truth, the other contains, insofar as it is sensible knowledge, illusion. The similarity of the former with its object is obvious; the similarity of the latter with its object is concealed, and all the more concealed, the more subjective grounds modify the representation of the object. The truths of rational knowledge are necessary and eternal, those of sensible knowledge contingent and temporal. . . . Since, finally, all illusion is grounded in the limits of the power of representation, it can now be seen that only that can be true which is not grounded in the incapacity of the power of representation, and that everything not grounded therein, but grounded instead in the object, must be true.[34]

As with Leibniz, a purely rational knowledge is the ideal. It characterizes the knowledge possessed by the divine mind which is not in any way limited by sensible conditions. Human knowledge, however, is so limited, and thus falls victim to illusion or distortion. Nevertheless, to the extent to which the mind can overcome these limitations, and this, for Eberhard, seems to be fairly considerable, it shares in the divine knowledge, thereby gaining certain knowledge of necessary truth. This whole conception of knowledge is quite explicitly theocentric, and stands in sharp contrast to the Kantian emphasis on the finite, human subject with its cognitive capacities. It is not, however, until the first volume of the *Philosophisches Archiv* that Eberhard really calls attention to this, pointing out that the key to the Leibnizian position lies in the fact that it seeks the source of knowledge in the divine understanding, while the critical philosophy appeals only to the human understanding and thereby falls into numerous contradictions.[35]

Having repudiated the Kantian theory of sensibility, Eberhard turns to the notion of pure or a priori intuition. His initial concern is with the alleged innateness of such intuitions, with this innateness being viewed as a necessary consequence of their apriority. He thinks, however, that the traditional doctrine of innateness is not available to Kant, because he recognizes no being who can implant them in the mind ("the representation of an infinte being is empty"). But, Eberhard continues, even if Kant does regard these intuitions as innate, this will not suffice. This argument is based on the interpretation of intuitions as images, and consequently the view that space and time (for Kant) are sensible images. Given this assumption, Eberhard feels that he has only to point

---

[34] *Ibid.*, pp. 304–5.

[35] *Philosophisches Archiv* I, part 4: 49, 89; Wilhelm L. G. Eberstein, *Versuche einer Geschichte der Logile und Metaphysik bey der Deutschen von Leibniz bis auf gegenwärtige Zeit*, 2 vols. (Halle, 1794 and 1799; reprinted by Culture et Civilisation, Brussels, 1970), II: 215–16; Vaihinger, *Commentar zur Kant's Kritik*, p. 539.

out that an innate or a priori image is an absurdity—in his terms, a *qualitas occulta*. From this he concludes that not the images themselves, but only their subjective grounds can be innate; and these subjective grounds, as we have already seen, turn out to be the limits of the subject.[36]

This leads Eberhard to the question of just what Kant means by these "forms of intuition" or "forms of sensibility." There are, he suggests in light of the above analysis, two possible interpretations: either "forms of intuition" refer to the limits of the subject and his power of knowledge, as a result of which the manifold is perceived in terms of the images of space and time, or the "forms" refer to those images in general themselves. Eberhard does not decide between these two possible interpretations, nor does he think it necessary to do so; for in either case, "his theory is either partially or completely contained in the Leibnizian."[37] Eberhard does not bother to explain what he means by this, but his claim seems to reduce to the assertion that, no matter which of the alternatives Kant accepts, he will be forced to admit an essential tenet of the Leibnizian position, viz., that the limits of the subject and the images of space and time which are its products serve only to render obscure our representations of the things in themselves that underlie our sensible experience.

Kant's theory of mathematics: In the second volume Eberhard applies this line of thought to Kant's theory of mathematics, and in the process anticipates many of the objections which have been raised against this theory by logicists such as Couturat.[38] The first step in this attack is a further critique of the notion of a priori intuition in general and the claim that space and time are examples thereof. Once again, equating intuition with image, Eberhard rejects the possibility of an a priori intuition of space (the argument applying *mutatis mutandis* to time) on the essentially Cartesian grounds that since all images are determinate, we cannot have an image of the infinite. Furthermore, this very determinateness, and hence particularity, of all images is held to render absurd the very idea of an a priori or general image.[39] Having thus repudiated the Kantian conception of intuition, Eberhard next proceeds to show that intuitions do not play the crucial role in mathematical demonstration which Kant suggests. This is argued in terms of the basic rationalistic principle, shared by Kant, that experience, or

[36]*Philosophisches Magazin*, I: 387–89. See also Appendix C, wherein this whole argument is outlined.

[37]*Ibid.*, p. 391.

[38]Louis Couturat, "La Philosophie de mathématics de Kant," *Revue de Métaphysique et de Morale* 12 (1904): 321–83.

[39]*Philosophisches Magazin* II: 84–90.

empirical (i.e., sensible) representations can serve as the subjective condition for the recognition (in Platonic terms the "occasion"), but not as the ground or source of necessary truths. In the course of his attack, Eberhard applies this line of argument first to geometry and then to arithmetic and algebra.

The analysis of geometry centers around its axiomatic basis. It is generally agreed, Eberhard claims, that definition is the first principle of demonstration; for it alone determines the possibility of affirming or denying a predicate of a concept. This, however, is apparently denied by Kant, for whom geometry is based on axioms rather than definitions. Eberhard's task is thus to clarify the relation between axioms and definitions in geometrical demonstration. This is done in a Leibnizian fashion by distinguishing between primitive and derived axioms. The former are completely identical propositions and are recognized as such. The latter are not recognized as such, however, because they contain sensible or intuitive elements. Nevertheless, since these elements are due merely to the limits of the finite understanding, the latter are, in principle, reducible to the former, viz., they are identical for the divine intellect which is not subject to these limits. They are not reducible, however, for the finite understanding, whose power of representation is limited. Thus, while it is admitted that geometrical concepts do necessarily contain sensible or intuitive elements, it is also claimed that, since these elements are only a consequence of the finitude of the human understanding, their necessity is conditioned and subjective rather than objective. Intuition, in other words, is not the ground of the necessity of geometrical truth, but only a necessary condition for the cognition of this truth by the finite understanding.[40]

Moreover, these same considerations are even more obviously applicable to arithmetic. Thus, in attacking Kant's famous analysis of "$7 + 5 = 12$," Eberhard first points out that the fingers or points, to which Kant refers, serve only as aids in calculating the sum, and not as the ground of the certainty of the proposition. He then notes that this appeal to intuition would seem to be most necessary in dealing with large sums, although this is precisely where it is lacking. Finally, he provides a demonstration of the proposition in question based on the definition of 12 as $11 + 1$. This demonstration closely parallels one provided by Leibniz in the *New Essays*,[41] and proceeds by means of a progressive reduction to identity:

$$7 + 1 = 8. \text{ per Def.}$$
$$8 + 1 = 9. \text{ per Def.}$$

[40] *Ibid.*, pp. 156–70.
[41] Leibniz, *New Essays concerning Human Understanding*, Book IV, Chaps. 7 and 10.

9 + 1 = 10. per Def.
10 + 1 = 11. per Def.
11 + 1 = 12. per Def. 1 + 1 + 1 + 1 + 1 = 5.[42]

This is followed by a consideration of the notion of characteristic or symbolic construction, which Kant briefly introduces in the *Transcendental Doctrine of Method*.[43] Eberhard views this as a possible second basis for the alleged syntheticity of arithmetic and algebra, and in this context he claims that the introduction of this notion involves a radical change in Kant's position. The syntheticity of geometry, he believes, was justified by Kant on the grounds that an intuition must be *added* to the concept; so that the concept itself contained an imageable or sensible element (whereas Kant himself always speaks of constructing or exhibiting a concept in intuition, which means providing an intuition *corresponding* to the concept.) But since arithmetical and algebraic concepts obviously do not have these intuitive elements, Eberhard thinks that Kant was forced to justify the syntheticity of these sciences on the grounds that their concepts are presented through symbols (*Zeichen*), which assume the function of intuitions. Such an expedient is of no avail, however, as the mere fact that a judgment contains symbols of concepts does not suffice to make it synthetic; for otherwise any formally expressed judgment would *ipso facto* become synthetic.[44]

Finally, Eberhard turns to the attempt to explain the synthetic nature of arithmetic by means of the introduction of an intuition of time. This was, of course, attempted by Kant in the *Prolegomena*, where in contrast to both editions of the *Critique*, he suggested that the intuition of time plays a role in arithmetic analogous to that played by space in geometry. Thus, while geometry is based upon the pure intuition of space, arithmetic is there said to achieve its concept of number by the successive additions of units in time.[45] Now, although apparently abandoned by Kant, this line of thought was taken up by and developed in some detail by Schulze,[46] and it is against him that Eberhard addresses his remarks. Here his strategy is simply to point out that the appeal to succession will not suffice to explain the syntheticity of arithmetic for two obvious reasons: (1) succession is a subjective feature of the finite mind (in contemporary terms, "psychological") rather

[42] *Philosophisches Magazin*, II: 174. Cf. Couturat, "Mathématics de Kant," pp. 338–42 makes exactly the same points.

[43] *Critique of Pure Reason*, A717/B745.

[44] *Philosophisches Magazin*, II: 174–78. Cf. Couturat, "Mathématics de Kant," pp. 355–56.

[45] *Prolegomena*, p. 283 (Beck translation, p. 30).

[46] Johann Schulze, *Prufung der Kantischen Critik der Reinen Vernunft* I, part 1 (Königsberg, 1789), pp. 219–30.

than a characteristic of the object (number); and (2) since all human thought is successive, this argument would serve to make all judgments synthetic.[47]

The Transcendental Aesthetic: All of the proceeding discussion relates to, but does not directly meet the argument of the *Transcendental Aesthetic*, wherein Kant presents his theory of sensibility. This task, as we have already noted, was left to Eberhard's colleague, J. G. Maaß. Thus, in order to complete the attack on Kant's position, Maaß addresses himself specifically to the main thesis of this section of the *Critique*, viz., the claim that space and time are forms of outer and inner sense respectively, and as such are merely subjective, and do not correspond to anything in the realm of things in themselves. In response to this he alleges that even if we accept Kant's contention concerning the subjectivity of space and time, this does not justify the conclusion that they do not pertain to things in themselves, or more generally, that there is nothing in the things in themselves corresponding to them. Kant's argument is based on a false dichotomy: either space and time are merely subjective forms, or they are (or at least pertain to) things in themselves. This, however, neglects a third possibility, viz., that they may be both subjective forms and still pertain to things in themselves. This is in fact the Leibnizian view, and it is essentially what Eberhard was claiming with the contention that space and time have both objective and subjective grounds. Unlike Eberhard, however, Maaß is not concerned with relating Kant to Leibniz. His criticism of Kant's doctrine is purely internal, and his concern is simply to show that Kant's failure to acknowledge this third alternative is inconsistent with the doctrine of the unknowability of things in themselves. This latter doctrine, he maintains, forbids Kant from moving from the claim that space and time are forms of sensibility to the claim that they do not pertain to things in themselves; for to know that things in themselves are not in space and time is, after all, to know a good deal about them.[48]

Maaß was not the first to voice this objection. Credit for this goes to another opponent of the *Critique*, Hermann Andreas Pistorius, and in the nineteenth century it was reiterated by Adolf Trendelenburg in his famous controversy with Kuno Fischer. Moreover, like Trendelenburg and unlike Pistorius, who articulated two possible versions of the third hypothesis, Maaß remained ambiguous as to its precise nature. The two possibilities suggested by Pistorius but not distinguished by Maaß, are: (1) that space is objective and subjective at the same time, i.e., that

---

[47]*Philosophisches Magazin* II: 178-79. Cf. Couturat, "Mathématics de Kant," pp. 349-50.
[48]*Philosophisches Magazin* I: 119-23, 360 ff., 470-72.

things in themselves actually are in space; and (2) that the a priori forms of space merely correspond to an analogous relation in the things in themselves. Furthermore, as Hans Vaihinger points out in his discussion of this whole dispute, these two versions of the third hypothesis, articulated by Pistorius, correspond to two possible interpretations of the Leibnizian doctrine of monads. According to what Vaihinger calls the metaphysical (really idealistic) interpretation, monads are regarded as "metaphysical points," purely intelligible substances without any materiality. As such, monads cannot strictly be said to be in space, and the purely conceptual relations governing the monads are only analagous to the spatial relations between phenomena. Leibnizian monads can also be viewed, however, from the standpoint of the philosophy of nature (realistically), and from this point of view, although the monads are still immaterial, their combination yields the objective material world, and they can be regarded as parts or elements of that world, and thus as located in space.[49] Now Kant, as we shall see, tends to interpret the monadology in the metaphysical or idealistic sense. Eberhard, however, with his claims that space and time have objective as well as subjective grounds (which would correspond to the idealistic interpretation), and that they are composed of simple, non-sensible elements (the realistic interpretation), not only fails like Maaß to distinguish the two senses in which the Leibnizian or third hypothesis can be construed, but actually seems to move from one formulation to the other, without noting any difficulties in such a procedure—a strategy for which he was to be severely rebuked by Kant.

Much of the balance of Maaß's essay is devoted to specific application of his basic line of thought to the central arguments of the *Transcendental Aesthetic*. His treatment of the first two arguments of the "Metaphysical Exposition of the Concept of Space" provides a clear illustration of his method. In the first argument Kant, it will be recalled, claims that space is not an empirical concept derived from outer experience on the grounds that it must already be presupposed if one is to refer sensation to something outside himself. This has been appropriately called the "Platonic argument" because of its similarity to the argument of the *Phaedo*, wherein it is claimed that it is only because of our prior awareness of the idea of equality that we can become aware of the approximations of equality found in experience.[50] Against this, Maaß again accepts Kant's premises and denies the conclusion. A representation A, he reasons, may indeed underlie or be presupposed by

[49] Vaihinger, *Commentar zur Kant's Kritik* II: 146–47.

[50] Cf. Gottfried Martin, *Kant's Metaphysics and Theory of Science*, trans. P. C. Lucas (Manchester University Press, 1955), p. 30.

another representation B, and thus not be derivable from it. It does not follow from this, however, that it precedes it and is a priori; for he suggests, once again introducing a third hypothesis, it is also possible that they are correlative, i.e., that neither can be given without the other. Moreover, on this assumption, the concept of A could only be obtained by abstraction from the complex AB, and it would therefore by an empirical concept.[51]

The second or "Aristotelian argument"[52] suffers a like fate. This is often presented as a complement to the first, intended to eliminate precisely that weakness which Maaß found in the first. Here Kant argues for the a priority of our representation of space on the grounds that "we can never represent to ourselves the absence of space, though we can quite well think it as empty of objects". From this he concludes: "It must therefore be regarded as the condition of the possibility of appearances, and not as a determination dependent upon them. It is an a priori representation, which necessarily underlies outer experiences."[53]

However, this argument, Maaß claims, fails like the first one to establish the a priority of space, and for essentially the same reason, viz., it neglects a third alternative. One cannot reason from the fact that we can think A without B, but not B without A, to the conclusion that A is a necessary condition for B. Both may be conditioned by a third ground C. On this assumption, which is, of course, the Leibnizian view with all of its ambiguity, the features which Kant's argument attribute to space can be accepted without having to deny that our concept of space is empirical, first acquired by abstraction from the relations of outer objects present in experience.[54]

Maaß is here arguing from a Leibnizian perspective, but unlike Eberhard, who was generally concerned with defending Leibniz, Maaß concentrates on pointing out internal difficulties in the Kantian position. In the present essay, he obviously did an admirable job of just that, as he touched on most of the classical objections that are continually raised against this position of the *Critique*. It is therefore lamentable that Kant, who devoted all of his attention to Eberhard, did not see fit to reply to this analysis of his argument.

4

The Analytic-Synthetic Distinction

The heart of Eberhard's polemic, and the aspect to which Kant devoted the most attention, is contained in the essay "On the Distinction

---

[51] *Philosophisches Magazin*, I: 124.
[52] Martin, *Kant's Metaphysics*, p. 32.
[53] *Critique of Pure Reason*, A24/B38-39.
[54] *Philosophisches Magazin*, I: 126-29.

of Judgments into Analytic and Synthetic." Here Eberhard concentrates on the distinction as initially formulated in the Introduction of the *Critique*, that is, on the formulation in terms of a distinction between merely explicative (analytic) judgments, which are called such because they "add nothing through the predicate to the concept of the subject," but rather function merely in "breaking it up into those constituent concepts that have all along been thought in it, although confusedly ... ," and *ampliative* (synthetic) judgments, which "add to the concept of the subject a predicate which has not in any wise been thought in it, and which no analysis could possibly extract from it."[55] Eberhard finds a lack of clarity in this formulation, which he proposes to remedy with a fresh analysis. This analysis shall: (1) demonstrate the confusion in Kant's account; (2) show that the distinction does not have the importance that Kant attributes to it; and (3) show that, when the distinction is properly drawn, it becomes obvious that we have knowledge of things in themselves.

This Eberhardian formulation turns on a distinction between different kinds of predicates:

In all universal affirmative judgments the predicate is either one (*einerlei*) with the subject or it is not; and if it is one with it, either entirely or only partially. In the first case, the predicate contains all of the determinations of the subject by means of which it can always be distinguished from all other things. Now this identity may be undeveloped, as in the proposition: all triangles are triangles; all bodies are bodies; or it may be developed through a definition, as in the proposition; all triangles are three-sided figures; all bodies are extended things which have motive and inertial force. These are entirely identical, or as some have named them, *empty* judgments. The predicate, however, can also be one with only one or some, but not all of the determinations of the subject. These are *partially identical* judgments, as the judgments: all triangles are figures; all bodies are extended.[56]

In all of these judgments, Eberhard points out, the predicate is either the essence of the subject itself (the entirely identical judgments) or a part of the essence of the subject (the partially identical judgments). These constitute the two species of analytic judgments and, in light of this distinction, Eberhard presents a definition of analytic judgments which he claims to be more precise than Kant's. They are judgments:

... in which the predicate is either the essence of the subject itself, or one of its essential parts. For this says in the predicate nothing more than what was really contained in the concept of the subject, although not so clearly, and with such a distinct consciousness, more specifically, in which the predicate is the definition of the subject or a mark of this definition.[57]

This formulation, it is claimed, removes the vagueness inherent in the Kantian notion of being thought or contained in the concept of the

[55] *Critique of Pure Reason*, A7/B11.
[56] *Philosophisches Magazin* I: 312–13.
[57] *Ibid.*, p. 313.

subject. This vagueness is due to the fact, allegedly overlooked by Kant, that there are also judgments which assert attributes of the subject. These attributes are determined by the essence of the subject and thus stand in necessary connection with it. But since they are not themselves part of the essence, one cannot say that they are contained in it. Rather they are grounded in this essence in accordance with the principle of sufficient reason. Thus, Eberhard concludes: "There are a priori judgments or necessary truths in which the predicates are attributes of the subject, that is, determinations which do not belong to the essence of the subject, but have their sufficient reason in this essence."[58] These judgments correspond to Kant's synthetic a priori judgments. Both mathematical and metaphysical judgments belong to this class. Kant's synthetic a posteriori judgments, on the other hand, are those in which the predicate expresses accidental conditions or relations of the subject. Veridical instances of the former constitute, together with the entirely and partially identical judgments, the class of necessary truths, and of the latter, the class of contingent or temporal truths.

Thus, Eberhard interprets this basic Kantian distinction in terms of the Leibnizian theory of predication. Different forms of judgment are determined by the ways in which the predicate is related to the concept of the subject. A given predicate may express either the essence or part of the essence of the subject, an attribute, an accident, or a relation thereof. From this perspective it is no wonder that Eberhard fails to see a great deal of originality in the Kantian distinction. It turns out to be nothing more than the old distinction, already clearly delineated by Wolff and Baumgarten, between identical and non-identical judgments, the former resting on the principle of contradiction, the latter on the principle of sufficient reason. All that Kant really did was to give this familiar old distinction a new name.[59]

Kant, however, not only changed the name, but also confused the issue. For if we grant that synthetic judgments are those in which the predicates are affections of the subject, in the case of necessary truths these affections being attributes, a new distinction arises; viz., between predicates known a priori and those known a posteriori. Now Kant, according to Eberhard, seemed to understand by synthetic judgments merely those which express "the not absolutely necessary truths . . . and those in which the necessary predicates can only be known a posteriori by the human understanding."[60] By this perplexing reference to necessary truths known a posteriori, which, as might be expected, was

[58] *Ibid.*, p. 314.
[59] *Ibid.*, pp. 316–18.
[60] *Ibid.*, p. 318.

sharply attacked by Kant, Eberhard seems to be referring to mathematics. The point apparently being alluded to in a highly oblique way is Kant's insistence on the necessity for intuition in all mathematical judgments. Since Eberhard equates intuition with image, and since he, as we have seen, rejects the whole notion of an a priori intuition, he can conclude that, according to Kant's doctrine, mathematics is, indeed, a science which provides knowledge of necessary truths a posteriori! This interpretation is confirmed in the next sentence, wherein Eberhard claims that Kant only counted experiential and mathematical judgments as synthetic. So construed, however, his notion of synthetic or ampliative judgments is obviously too narrow. As an example, he cites the metaphysical proposition: "*All that is necessary is eternal, all necessary truths are eternal truths.*" This, he notes, "is obviously a synthetic proposition, and yet it can be known a priori, and yet it contains no empirical judgment."[61]

Nevertheless, despite this suspicion expressed above, Eberhard confesses some uncertainty as to which of these two conceptions of synthetic judgments Kant advocates. By this he evidently meant to ask whether Kant would also count as synthetic those judgments in which the connection between the predicate and the concept of the subject can be known a priori (no doubt in accordance with the principle of sufficient reason), or merely, as just suggested, only those in which it can be known a posteriori (through intuition or experience). The basic problem, according to Eberhard, is that both can legitimately be claimed to extend our knowledge. Thus, Kant must either make his definition somewhat more precise, or he must show that the human understanding is not able to acquire knowledge of the former kind of predicate.[62]

Eberhard proceeds to further underline the alleged inadequacy of the Kantian theory by presenting a complete classification of kinds of judgments. This is held to be already implicit in Aristotle, but is actually based on the previous considerations together with some material taken from the logician Jacob Bernoulli.

I. Universal judgments, in which the subject is the higher generic concept to which the predicate is attached. *Undetermined Judgments, iudicia indefinata, Bernoulli.*

    1. Judgments in which the predicates are characteristics which belong to the essence of the subject. *Essential judgments, analytic judgments, Kant.*

---

[61] *Ibid.*, p. 319.
[62] *Ibid.*, pp. 319–20.

a. The entire essence, or the higher concept under which the sub-ject belongs, together with the difference from the lower concept, therefore the entire definition, *entirely identical judgments, iudicia totaliter identica.*

b. The higher concept without the difference from the lower con-cept, *partially identical judgments, iudicia partialiter identica.*

2. Judgments in which the predicate is an attribute of the subject: *non-essential, synthetic a priori, Kant.*

a. In which the predicate is a proper attribute (*attributum proprium*), *reciprocal judgments, iudicia reciprocabilia.*

b. In which the predicate is a common attribute (*attributum com-mune*), *non-reciprocal judgments, iudicia non reciprocabilia.*

II. Universal judgments in which the predicate is known through expe-rience, and in which the subjects are individuals, contained under a higher concept, *determined judgments, iudicia definita, Bernoulli. Gen-eral synthetic judgments a posteriori, Kant.*[63]

After this elaboration of the theory of predication, Eberhard turns to what he takes to be the serious points at issue: viz., whether meta-physics contains synthetic judgments (Kant is held to have denied this), and if so, whether such judgments yield knowledge of things in them-selves. Now, given the definition of synthetic judgments presented above, he finds it difficult to see how their presence in metaphysics could be denied. As an example he cites the judgment, "all finite things are alterable and the infinite thing is unalterable." Moreover, he con-tinues, if this can be demonstrated a priori, then it is a synthetic a priori judgment, and from this it follows:

... that our pure rational knowledge also contains synthetic propositions. Thus, a pure science of reason is possible, and our previous metaphysics is such a science. For it not only contains truths of reason which rest on the principle of contradic-tion, but also those which rest on the principle of sufficient reason.[64]

Furthermore, Eberhard continues, unless one understands synthetic a priori judgments in this sense, which is the sense in which they are to be found, although not under that name, in Wolff and Baumgarten, "their truth (agreement with the object) is not conceivable." This leads once again to the raising of the charge of subjective idealism against the *Critique.* Here his argument is based on the analysis of the nature of a true synthetic judgment for Kant. Such a judgment must, if it is true, agree with its object. The nature of this agreement, however, remains a mystery for the critical philosophy, and this is because it characterizes the object of cognition as appearance. Since appearances, for Kant, are

[63] *Ibid.*, pp. 322–23.
[64] *Ibid.*, p. 326.

nothing more than representations in us, the claim that synthetic judgments are true reduces to the claim that "representations agree with representations," which is a mere tautology.[65] Thus, contrary to the teaching of the *Critique*, the possibility of synthetic judgments, both a priori and a posteriori, can only be understood if such judgments are taken as referring to things in themselves.

Eberhard concludes this discussion with a statement epitomizing his whole attitude towards the analytic-synthetic distinction:

If, therefore, one wishes to bring the distinction between analytic and synthetic judgments into metaphysics, if the distinction is to have a sense, then it can only be grounded in the difference of the mode of determination of the predicate through the subject, and the principle of truth in analytic judgments can only be the principle of contradiction, and in synthetic judgments the principle of sufficient reason. Since, however, everything is true which is in accordance with these principles, this distinction is completely useless for determining the logical truth of a judgment. Hence, the question as to whether a proposition is analytic or synthetic is, in regard to its logical truth, irrelevant; for both types can be logically true. It is, however, obvious that the entire distinction makes no sense if it is not formulated in terms of the grounds of division found in the Leibnizian dogmatism. For in the theory of critical idealism synthetic judgments can have no objects outside of the representations; for they cannot relate to anything which is actual apart from the representations, and their logical truth thus consists merely in the agreement of a representation in us with the same representation in us. Thus, critical idealism presupposes a theory which reduces the entire discussion to a play with words. The final result is: either appearances are grounded in true things which are actual outside the representations, and there is a knowledge of these things in themselves, namely, through the understanding, in which case dogmatism is justified, or they are mere appearances, mere representations. Then, however, synthetic judgments are not conceivable; for their truth consists in the agreement of a representation with itself.[66]

Finally, in this context we must at least briefly consider another essay by Maaß, entitled "On the Highest Principle of Synthetic Judgments in Relation to the Theory of Mathematical Certainty." This title is somewhat of a misnomer, as the essay does not really have very much to do with the problem of mathematical certainty. The bulk of it is devoted to a reiteration and defense of points already raised by Eberhard, e.g., the interpretation of the analytic-synthetic distinction in terms of the essence-attribute distinction. Moreover, since it only appeared in the second volume of the *Philosophisches Magazin*, it was naturally not discussed by Kant in *On a Discovery*. It was, however, as we shall see, discussed by Schulze in his review of the second volume, and Schulze's remarks (translated in Appendix B) are of considerable

---

[65] *Ibid.*, pp. 328-29.
[66] *Ibid.*, pp. 321-22.

importance for an understanding of Kant's formulation of the analytic-synthetic distinction. Most importantly, however, Maaß, as in his earlier essay on the *Transcendental Aesthetic*, here succeeds in formulating some objections to Kant's position which not only go considerably beyond anything suggested by Eberhard, and which the latter adopted in his subsequent treatments of the issue, but which again anticipate some of the subsequent and now "classical" objections to Kant's theory.[67]

Like Eberhard, Maaß attacks Kant's formulation of the analytic-synthetic distinction on the grounds of its alleged vagueness. But whereas for Eberhard this vagueness concerned the Kantian answer to the question as to just what *kinds* of judgments are synthetic, a point on which Kant seems to be relatively clear, for Maaß it concerns the criterion for deciding *in any given instance* whether a particular judgment is analytic or synthetic. Maaß pursues this theme in his character-istically relentless manner, beginning by citing Kant's most explicit for-mulation of the distinction in the Introduction of the *Critique*:

In all judgments in which the relation of a subject to the predicate is thought (I take into consideration affirmative judgments only, the subsequent application to negative judgments being easily made), this relation is possible in two different ways. Either the predicate B belongs to the subject A, as something which is (covertly) contained in this concept A; or B lies outside the concept A, although it does indeed stand in connection with it. In the one case I entitle the judgment analytic, in the other synthetic. Analytic judgments (affirmative) are therefore those in which the connection of the predicate with the subject is thought through identity; those in which this connection is thought without identity should be entitled synthetic.[68]

In commenting on this passage, Maaß first notes the tremendous importance which Kant attributes to the distinction thus formulated, and then proceeds to point out that it is far too indeterminate to do the job which Kant intends it to do. This is because on the basis of this formulation it would be in many, if not all cases impossible to decide whether a given judgment was analytic or synthetic. Apart from ex-plicitly identical judgments or tautologies, the same judgment which for one person is synthetic, would be analytic for another. The problem, of course, is the psychological or, in Maaß's terms, figurative (*bildliche*) fashion in which this crucial distinction is formulated. One person may simply "think more on a given concept" than another, and thus for him a judgment would be analytic, while for another person, with a less

[67]Cf. Lewis White Beck, "Can Kant's Synthetic Judgments Be Made Analytic?" and "Kant's Theory of Definition," both reprinted in L. W. Beck, *Studies in the Philosophy of Kant* (Indian-apolis: Bobbs-Merrill Co., 1965).

[68]*Critique of Pure Reason*, A6–7/B10, *Philosophisches Magazin* II: 187–88.

determinate concept, it would be synthetic, involving a predicate which was not part of his original concept.[69]

Moreover, Maaß continues, the situation is hardly improved if one turns to Kant's second formulation, i.e., to the distinction between explicative (analytic) and ampliative (synthetic) judgments, which was the primary target of Eberhard's attack. Here again we run into precisely the same problem: whether a given judgment serves to extend one's knowledge or merely to clarify what one already knows is a contingent, psychological matter, depending upon the extent of a given individual's knowledge at a particular time. On this basis the distinction remains completely relative and of no real philosophical significance.[70]

If, therefore, Maaß reflects, transcendental idealism is to provide an essential and not merely a relative distinction between analytic and synthetic judgments, if it is to avoid the conclusion that one and the same judgment can be both analytic and synthetic, and if it is to be possible to determine in each instance to which category a given judgment belongs,

... then a universal rule must be provided, whereby it is in each case possible to determine whether or not the predicate B lies in the subject A; whether or not it can be thought through identity; whether or not it is a merely explicative, or an ampliative judgment.[71]

Maaß then proceeds to consider possible candidates for such a rule which might serve to firm up the Kantian distinction. The first candidate is the view which contends that the question as to what lies or is contained in a given concept is determined by the fundamental representation (*Grundvorstellung*), understood in the temporal sense (*der Zeit nach*). On this basis the essential features of a given concept are its temporally prior ones, those which are to be found in its initial formation, and a judgment which predicates any or all of these characteristics or marks of the concept in question is analytic, while one which predicates other characteristics is synthetic.[72] Such an empirical, psychological approach, however, obviously does not suffice to save the Kantian distinction. For one thing, the marks contained in the initial concept of a given object vary from individual to individual, and are thus entirely relative. Moreover, if the concept in question is sensible, it is impossible to determine which marks belong to our initial conception and which were only added later, as we cannot be sure of our first impressions. Secondly, since our capacity for knowledge is limited, our initial con-

[69] *Philosophisches Magazin* II: 188–89.
[70] *Ibid.*, pp. 188–189.
[71] *Ibid.*, p. 190.
[72] *Ibid.*, p. 191.

ception of an object is not likely to contain very much of what is essential to it, and thus of what might properly be said to be contained in its concept. By way of illustration, Maaß cites as examples the judgments "the grass is green" and "a body has a color." On the above criteria, such judgments would have to be regarded as analytic since they express temporally primitive characteristics of our conceptions, and this contradicts Kant's explicit claim that judgments of experience are one and all synthetic.[73]

Maaß next turns to the theory of definition as a more promising approach to the problem. The key question, as we have seen, is how do we know that the predicate B belongs to the concept of the subject A, and Maaß's answer is: only through the definition of A. Only by means of a definition, he argues, can we determine with certainty what is contained in a concept. We can say that a judgment is analytic if the predicate B either gives the definition of the subject A or some characteristic found in that definition. If it does not do so, then it is synthetic.[74]

Even this, however, will not quite do. The problem is that there are two kinds of definitions: real and nominal. The former, he contends, expresses the essence of the subject, and the latter determinations derived from the essence. Now, if it be the case that every judgment in which the predicate was a definition or a characteristic of the definition of the subject was analytic, then this would obviously hold also for nominal definitions. On this basis, however, we would have to regard many judgments as analytic which for Kant were synthetic. This is especially true of mathematical judgments; for insofar as their predicate is an attribute of the subject, it can be used in a nominal definition, thereby generating an analytic judgment. For example, the judgment "the sum of the angles of a triangle are equal to two right angles" would be analytic, because a triangle can be nominally defined as a figure, the sum of the angles of which is equal to two right angles.[75]

Thus, Maaß arrives at the conclusion that only a real definition can serve as the basis for an analytic judgment in the Kantian sense. But since a real definition has been itself defined as one which expresses the essence of the subject, we find ourselves suddenly back in the Wolffian camp. Hence, we have a return to the distinction, emphasized by Eberhard, between being *contained* in the concept of a subject, and being *determined* through it. Only the essence or essential characteristics of a subject can be said to be contained in its concept. If the former, then the judgment expressing this is completely identical; if the latter, then it is partially identical. These are, of course, the two species of analytic

[73] *Ibid.*, pp. 191–93.
[74] *Ibid.*, p. 194.
[75] *Ibid.*, pp. 194–96.

judgment referred to by Eberhard. Determinations, on the other hand, which are grounded in the subject (in accordance with the principle of sufficient reason) are attributes, and their relation to the subject is expressed in non-identical, i.e., synthetic judgments.[76] This is precisely the way in which Eberhard formulated this distinction, but whereas he did so more or less straightforwardly, Maaß argues, in effect, that it is only such a conception of the analytic-synthetic distinction that can save it from the hopeless relativism and triviality which is suggested by Kant's vague formulation. Once again, therefore, we are led to the conclusion that whatever is good in the *Critique* is already contained and, indeed, in a more satisfactory form, in the philosophy of Leibniz and Wolff.

This sustained attack on the analytic-synthetic distinction is the culmination of the Wolffian assault on the critical philosophy. Implicit in it are all of the points previously discussed, viz., the rejection of the notion of transcendental illusion and the affirmation of the possibility of genuine knowledge from mere concepts, without the necessity of any appeal to intuition or experience; the consequent affirmation of the possibility of knowledge of things in themselves; and the rejection of the Kantian theory of sensibility and its role in cognition. From this standpoint, judgments are regarded as synthetic, and thus ampliative, whenever the connection between the subject and predicate is based on the principle of sufficient reason, and this occurs whenever the predicate is an attribute rather than the essence or part of the essence of the subject. This whole analysis presupposes, of course, the "transcendental validity" of the principle of sufficient reason, and it leads to the result that all non-identical judgments are synthetic. On this assumption, it is easy to claim that we have non-identical, i.e., synthetic, judgments expressing necessary truths, and that these can be justified without any appeal to intuition or possible experience, i.e., simply by showing that the predicate is "grounded in" (deducible from) the concept of the subject. By this means Leibnizian dogmatism is reinstated in the face of the critical attack. The problem, however, is that, on the one hand, this use of the principle of sufficient reason completely begs the question which concerned Kant and, on the other hand, this simple equation of synthetic with non-identical judgments involves a complete misunderstanding of the Kantian position. However, although the latter point involves a misunderstanding, it is one which is suggested by some of Kant's best known formulations of the distinction. An examination of Kant's response to this line of criticism, and his consequent attempt to reformulate this distinction and the associated doctrines is therefore crucial for an adequate understanding of the critical philosophy. It is to this examination that we now turn.

[76] *Ibid.*, pp. 196–97.

III

KANT'S RESPONSE

Because of its polemical intent, *On a Discovery* follows the order of argumentation set out by Eberhard. Thus, the work is divided into two main parts, corresponding to the "two acts" into which Kant believes that the Eberhardian "play" is divided. The first part deals with the alleged objective reality of those concepts to which no corresponding sensible intuition can be given, including an analysis of the principle of sufficient reason and the concept of the simple. The second deals with the distinction between analytic and synthetic judgments, and the problem of the possibility of synthetic judgments a priori. The work concludes with a brief and somewhat ironical discussion of Leibniz, the intent of which is to suggest that the Leibnizian philosophy is really in essential agreement with the *Critique*. This reverses the actual order of the *Critique*, where Kant begins with the distinction between analytic and synthetic judgments and the question of the possibility of synthetic judgments a priori, and then proceeds to explain that the conditions which explain the possibility of such judgments also imply their limitation to possible experience. Our analysis, which is intended to uncover the logical structure of Kant's argument, shall follow the more natural order of the *Critique*. Accordingly, we shall: (1) consider the analytic-synthetic distinction, together with the problem of the synthetic a priori; (2) provide an analysis of Kant's theory of sensibility; (3) conclude with brief discussions of Kant's doctrine of the limits of knowledge, his actual refutations of Eberhard, and his treatment of Leibniz.

1
The Analytic-Synthetic Distinction

Kant begins the second part of his essay with a reiteration of the basic critical principle that the possibility of synthetic judgments a priori must be resolved prior to any engagement in metaphysical speculation. Any philosophy which neglects this principle is characterized as a dogmatism. Eberhard, however, had challenged this thesis, and yet at the same time had affirmed the "critical" nature of his position, or rather the Leibnizian position in the name of which he wrote. Before proceeding with a justification of the critical principle, Kant must therefore present a preliminary analysis of the nature of dogmatism in order to show that Eberhard did not understand what the *Critique* meant by the term.

The situation is complicated by the fact that Kant uses the term in several distinct senses in the *Critique*. The most basic refers to "dogmatism in metaphysics." Such dogmatism is characterized as the procedure whereby philosophy "confidently sets itself to this task (metaphysics) without any previous examination of the capacity or incapacity of reason for so great an undertaking."[1] This is contrasted with scepticism—and with criticism—as the method of the *Critique*. In the *Antinomies* and elsewhere, Kant also speaks of a "dogmatism of pure reason." This expression is used to characterize the thesis position in the *Antinomies*, or the portion which presupposes "intelligible beginnings."[2] Unlike the former, this kind of dogmatism makes special claims, viz., "That the world has a beginning, that my thinking self is of simple and therefore indestructible nature, that it is free in its voluntary actions and raised above the compulsion of nature, and finally that all order in the things constituting the world is due to a primordial being, from which everything derives its unity and purposive connection . . . ."[3] Dogmatism in this sense is contrasted not with criticism or scepticism, but with empiricism. Finally, in the *Transcendental Doctrine of Method*, Kant divides all apodictic propositions into *dogmata* and *mathemata*.[4] A synthetic proposition, derived directly from concepts, is there characterized as a dogma, in contradistinction to one derived from the construction of concepts, which is a *mathema*. In this context then, the dogmatic employment of reason is contrasted with its mathematical employment, i.e., its employment in the construction of concepts.

Now in his half disclaimer, half justification of dogmatism, Eberhard actually addresses himself to the first-mentioned and main sense in which it is found in the *Critique*. Moreover, in charging Eberhard with misunderstanding his teachings on this point, Kant actually introduces a new conception, or at least new formulation of the old conception of

---

[1] *Critique of Pure Reason*, BXXX, B7.
[2] *Ibid.*, A 466/B499.
[3] *Ibid.*
[4] *Ibid.*, A736/B764.

the nature of dogmatism.[5] This becomes apparent in the key footnote (227), where after giving a definition of dogmatism in the main text which is in essential agreement with the *Critique*, viz., "the general trust in its (metaphysics) principles, without a previous critique of the faculty of reason itself. . . ," he points out in the note that a dogmatism originates with respect to the super-sensible when a priori principles, which express necessary conditions of the possibility of experience and are thus confirmed in experience, are extended beyond experience and held to be valid of non-sensible objects. As Kant shows in the *Antinomies*, such an employment leads to a conflict of reason with itself, and thus to scepticism. Here, however, the main point is that this describes the precise sense in which Leibniz and Eberhard are held to be dogmatists. In view of this conception, it is not enough to have demonstrated one's metaphysical principles, as Eberhard claims to have done (after all, it is precisely the possibility of providing cogent demonstration of contradictory claims that is established in the *Antinomies*), or even, like Leibniz, to have engaged in a prior investigation of the faculty of knowledge. Rather, in order to escape the charge of dogmatism, it is necessary to first establish through "mature criticism . . . the possibility and general conditions of a priori knowledge" (227). This, however, the Leibnizian philosophy fails to do, and it is therefore justly called a dogmatism.

Thus, Kant returns to the claim of the *Critique* that the indispensable starting point for any scientific metaphysics is an investigation of the possibility of synthetic judgments a priori. As a preliminary to this, however, he must first present the distinction between analytic and synthetic judgments. This presentation is intended to be a simple reiteration of the formulation of the *Critique* and the *Prolegomena*. But as we shall see in the course of our analysis, Kant seems to change, or at least to sharpen, this earlier formulation in response to Eberhard's criticism. In so doing he succeeds in making explicit a line of thought which was only implicit in the Introduction of the *Critique of Pure Reason*.

The distinction in general: In the *Critique*, it will be recalled, the initial formulation of the distinction is in terms of the manner in which the relation between the subject and predicate is thought in two kinds of judgments: "Either the predicate B belongs to the subject A, as something which is (covertly) contained in this concept A; or B lies outside the concept A, although it does indeed stand in connection with it." In the former case, the judgment is analytic, in the latter, synthetic. Moreover, as Kant proceeds to add, apparently by way of

---

[5]H. J. de Vleeschauwer, *La déduction transcendantale dans l'oeuvre de Kant* (Paris, 1937), pp. 403–4.

clarification: "Analytic judgments (affirmative) are therefore those in which the connection of the predicate with the subject is thought through identity; those in which this connection is thought without identity should be entitled synthetic." This formulation is supplemented by a further, and allegedly equivalent characterization of the two kinds of judgment as explicative and ampliative respectively. In terms of this characterization, explicative (analytic) judgments add nothing through the predicate to the concept of the subject, "merely breaking it up into these constituent concepts that have all along been thought in it, although confusedly." Ampliative (synthetic) judgments, on the other hand, "add to the concept of the subject a predicate which has not been in any wise thought in it, and which no analysis could possibly extract from it. . . ."[6] In the *Prolegomena* the formulation is essentially the same as the second version in the *Critique*, although it also points out that the distinction in question concerns the *content* of judgments, not their *origin* or logical form.[7]

The initial formulation in *On a Discovery* essentially follows that of the second version of the *Critique* and the *Prolegomena*. Synthetic judgments are defined as those "through the predicate of which I attribute more to the subject of the judgment than I think in the concept to which I attach the predicate. This predicate, therefore, extends my knowledge beyond what is contained in that concept." Analytic judgments, on the other hand, "serve merely to more clearly represent and assert what is already thought and contained in the given concept" (228). The emphasis is therefore placed on the respective functions of the two kinds of judgments, not, as the initial formulation of the *Critique* suggests, on the logical relation between subject and predicate. Analytic judgments function merely to explicate a given concept, to make clear what is already implicit in this concept; while synthetic judgments in some manner or other actually extend our knowledge beyond this given concept.

In light of this conception, Kant proceeds to repudiate Eberhard's interpretation of the distinction in terms of judgments which assert the essence, or part of the essence, of the subject (analytic judgments in Eberhard's terms) and of those judgments in which the predicates are attributes of a subject (synthetic judgments in Eberhard's terms). This repudiation is essentially nothing more than a development of the objections which Kant had already raised in his letter to Reinhold of May 12th.

---

[6] *Critique of Pure Reason*, A6–7/B10–11.

[7] *Prolegomena*, 266; L. W. Beck, *Studies in the Philosophy of Kant*, (Indianapolis: Bobbs-Merrill, 1965), p. 14.

These objections fall into two parts. First of all, he points out, both in the letter to Reinhold and in *On a Discovery*, that the essence-attribute distinction is completely beside the point. Such is the case because "it is clear that, if one has not already given a criterion for a synthetic a priori proposition, the statement that the predicate is an attribute in no way illumines its distinction from an analytic proposition." Such a characterization, as Kant proceeds to point out, serves only to show that the predicate "can be derived as a necessary consequence from the essence" and, consequently, that the connection is known a priori. The crucial question, however, as to "whether it is derived analytically according to the principle of contradiction or synthetically according to some other principle remains thereby completely undetermined" (229). The problem is that the means whereby the predicate is necessarily connected with the essence is not explained, and simply calling it an attribute hardly solves this problem. Moreover, if one does take this line, then the problem simply reappears in terms of the necessity of distinguishing between analytic and synthetic attributes, i.e., between those which can be derived from the essence of the subject according to the principle of contradiction and those which, although necessarily connected with it, cannot be so derived.

Kant illustrates this by means of the judgment: every body is divisible. Divisibility, he points out, does not form part of the essence of the concept of body. This might also be expressed by saying that it does not form part of the definition of body. It can nevertheless be derived as a logical consequence from part of that essence or definition, viz., extension. On Eberhard's criterion divisibility therefore must be regarded as an attribute of body, and the resulting judgment is synthetic. As Kant points out, however, its connection with the concept of body is none the less analytic. Despite that fact that the connection between subject and predicate is indirect or mediate (divisibility not forming part of the essence of body), it is still purely logical, i.e., based on the principle of contradiction, and the resulting judgment is therefore analytic. Moreover, this is to be contrasted with a genuinely synthetic judgment, such as, "substance is permanent." Once again the predicate can be characterized as an attribute of the subject, but this time the predicate (permanence) cannot be derived analytically from the concept of the subject. This is because, as Kant claims elsewhere, the pure concept, or unschematized category of substance, signifies only a logical relation of that which is always subject and never predicate, and thus includes nothing concerning temporal duration.[8] It was precisely

---

[8] *Critique of Pure Reason*, B149, B288.

on this point that the synthetic nature of the First Analogy turned. Thus, Kant concludes the first part of his assault with the reflection:

It is therefore apparent, first of all, that the hope of explaining synthetic propositions a priori through propositions which have attributes of their subject as predicate is destroyed, *unless one adds to this that they are synthetic*, and thus perpetuates an obvious tautology (231).

The second and perhaps central aspect of Eberhard's argument, turns on the alleged role of the principle of sufficient reason or ground (*Grund*) in synthetic judgments. Just as the law of contradiction is the principle of analytic judgments (which Kant himself acknowledges), so the latter functions as the principle of synthetic judgments. In this manner the originality of the Kantian position is undermined and his doctrine is completely encompassed within a Leibnizian perspective. Kant must therefore also address himself to Eberhard's use of this principle in the explanation of synthetic judgments a priori. He had already criticized Eberhard's formulation and demonstration of this principle in the first part of the essay, and we shall consider this in some detail in the sequel. We are now concerned only with the basic point which Kant developed in the earlier criticism and which he applies in the present context. This point is that the principle of sufficient reason, and with it the very notion of ground, can be taken either in a logical or in a real sense, and that Eberhard not only confuses the two, but that his whole argument rests on this confusion.

Taken in its logical sense, the principle of sufficient reason states that every proposition must have a reason. This is a logical or formal principle of knowledge. As such it follows from the principle of contradiction, and is thus itself an analytic proposition. A logical ground is therefore merely the ground of the connection between the predicate and the concept of the subject in a judgment. Taken in its real, material or transcendental sense (Kant seems to use all of these inter-changeably), the principle of sufficient reason asserts that "every thing must have its reason." This is a synthetic proposition, and as such not only cannot be derived from the principle of contradiction, but itself stands in need of a justification. It therefore can hardly serve as the principle of synthetic judgments. Finally, as Kant suggests in his letter to Reinhold of May 12th, the notion of a real ground can be construed in a twofold sense. It can refer either to the *formal* ground of the intuition of an object, illustrated by the example of the sides of a triangle serving as the grounds of its angles, or it can refer to the *material* ground of the existence of the thing, i.e., the cause.

Now it is obvious from the above that in so far as Eberhard appeals to the principle of sufficient reason in order to explain the possibility of synthetic judgments a priori, he necessarily construes it in a logical sense. For if he had taken it in the material sense, he would have had to admit that, far from serving as a principle capable of explaining the possibility of synthetic judgments, it is itself a synthetic judgment, and stands in need of an explanation. The problem, however, is that the appeal to this principle was expressly designed to provide an extra-logical principle of judgments, or at least one which is independent of the principle of contradiction; and this function certainly cannot be performed by the principle of sufficient reason construed in the logical sense. But Eberhard, as Kant sees it, tries to hide all this from the reader by claiming that in synthetic judgments, or judgments deter-mined according to the principle of sufficient reason, the predicate (attribute) is not part of the essence of the subject (essence here taken to be the logical essence or concept), but is nevertheless "grounded" therein. Thus, the attribute is held to be necessarily connected with the essence, but not identical with it, or immediately derivable from it. Since, however, the ground in question can only be a logical ground, we are no further along than before. Once again we see that the fact that the judgment is not identical (either completely or partially) and the connection of the predicate with the concept of the subject is not immediate does not effect its purely logical, and hence analytic, status.

The nature of Kant's quarrel with Eberhard is clearly illustrated by his discussion of the latter's attempt to provide examples of synthetic judgments a priori taken from metaphysics. Eberhard had presented two such examples, and in each case Kant proceeds to show that they are obviously analytic because they concern merely the logical relation between concepts. The examples are: "Everything which is necessary is eternal, all necessary truths are eternal truths" (235); "All finite things are alterable, and the infinite thing is unalterable" (236). The ana-lyticity of the first is established by pointing out that eternality, as applied to the notion of truth, does not refer at all to temporal dura-tion, but to the knowability of a proposition a priori, and this is "com-pletely identical" with its knowability as a necessary truth. Kant's treat-ment of the second proposition is considerably more detailed and more directly related to his general criticism of Eberhard's position. The argument turns essentially on the connection between alterability and temporality: "Only that is alterable which cannot exist other than in time." Existence in time, however, is, for Kant, not necessarily con-nected with the concept of a finite thing in general, but only with a thing qua object of sensible intuition (appearance). Eberhard, however, for obvious reasons, wishes to affirm this proposition independently of any reference to sensible intuition. This implies that the connection between alterability and finitude, and their opposites, is to be understood "in accordance with their mere concept" and therefore logically. Then, however, the proposition is analytic, affirming only the connection between the concept of a finite being and alterability, in the sense of incomplete determination, and between their opposites, an infinite being and complete determination or immutability.

From all this we can see that Kant's main charge against Eberhard's treatment of the distinction between analytic and synthetic judgments, and this applies equally to the latter's alternative formulation in terms of the distinction between identical and non-identical judgments, is that he is endeavoring to equate the analytic-synthetic distinction with a distinction between two kinds of logical relations of concepts, i.e., direct containment (full or partial identity) and mediate containment or implication, which is covered by the vague term "ground." In response to this, Kant admits, in effect, that if this were what was meant by the distinction, then its claims to originality and philosophical significance would certainly be spurious, as such a formulation sheds absolutely no light on the nature of synthetic judgments in general, much less on the possibility of the a priori variety. The basic error in this kind of approach is that it remains within the confines of formal or, in Kant's terms, general logic. But as he had explicitly affirmed in the *Critique*:

The explanation of the possibility of synthetic judgments is a problem with which general logic has nothing to do. It need not even so much as know the problem by name. But in transcendental logic, it is the most important of all questions; and indeed, if in treating of the possibility of synthetic a priori judgments we also take account of the conditions and scope of their validity, it is the only question with which it is concerned.[9]

Despite this explicit statement, however, Kant's overall approach to this distinction seems to be far from consistent. Thus, in the initial formulations in the *Critique*, which, as we have noted, formed the basis for the attacks of Eberhard and Maaß, Kant does formulate it in terms of the question as to whether or not the predicate is contained in the concept of the subject, and thus whether or not its connection with this concept is "thought through identity." Such a formulation certainly suggests Eberhard's interpretation, especially in light of the fact that Kant fails to distinguish in the *Critique*, although he does elsewhere, between identical and analytic judgments.[10] Furthermore, important

---

[9]*Ibid.*, A154/B193.
[10]Most clearly in the *Progress of Metaphysics*, AK, Vol. XX, p. 322. Cf. Vleeschauwer, *Déduction Transcendentale*, p. 406.

support for the Eberhardian interpretation was provided by Schulze, who explicitly asserts that all analytic judgments are identical and distinguishes only between complete and partial identity.[11]

Nevertheless, this situation is considerably rectified by the analysis in *On a Discovery*. Here, in response to the objections stemming from the Leibnizian camp, Kant makes it quite clear that the crucial question underlying the whole analytic-synthetic distinction is not the logical question concerning the relation between the predicate and the concept of the subject in the judgment (whether or not the relation is "thought through identity"), but the transcendental or material question as to whether or not the predicate stands in a real relation to the object. Synthetic judgments assert such relations, while analytic judgments merely assert logical relations between concepts.

This sharp opposition between the logical and the real, the formal and the transcendental, is a central feature in the critical philosophy, and comes especially into play in the critique of Leibnizian panlogism. In this guise, its roots go deep into the pre-critical period, first appearing in the *Nova Dilucidatio* of 1755, wherein, following Crusius, Kant already distinguishes between the real and logical sense of the principle of sufficient reason.[12] In the Inaugural Dissertation of 1770 we find the general distinction between the real and logical use of the intellect, and it is in this form that it reappears in the *Critique*, albeit with the assertion of the limitation of the real use to objects of possible experience. In this critical form, which is developed in *On a Discovery*, the logical refers to the purely conceptual. Thus, a logical relation is one which holds between concepts, a logical predicate is simply any concept which is predicated of another, and a logical essence is merely the sum total of the partial concepts making up a given concept. Rules governing logical relations are purely formal, as they abstract from the content of thought. Real relations, on the other hand, concern precisely the content of thought. They hold between things thought about, or between concepts and things. Moreover, just as a real ground is the ground of a thing, and a real essence the essence of a thing, so a real predicate is a determination of the thing.[13] From this we can clearly see that the defining characteristic of synthetic judgments is that they relate concepts or predicates to objects, while analytic judgments are merely concerned with logical relations between concepts (the predicate and

[11] Johann Schulze, *Prufung der Kantischen Critik der Reinen Vernunft* I, part 1 (Königsberg, 1789), p. 30.

[12] AK I: 391 ff. English translation by F. E. England in *Kant's Conception of God* (London, 1929), pp. 220 ff. See also England's own discussion of the issue, pp. 21–41.

[13] *Critique of Pure Reason*, A598/B626.

the concept of the subject). This also makes it easy to see why this distinction does not belong to general logic. It is Kant's firm and oft-expressed conviction that general logic abstracts from the question of the relation between knowledge and its object and concerns itself merely with the form of thought. It is therefore obvious that such a logic can have nothing to say concerning the relation between a concept and an object, although it can, of course, have a good deal to say concerning the identity or non-identity of the predicate with the concept of the subject.

Furthermore, the notion of real relation provides the basis for understanding the sense in which synthetic judgments extend our knowledge. Maaß, as we have seen, had pointed out some of the misleading, psychologistic implications of this notion of extending one's knowledge. For example, it might appear that the question as to whether a given judgment extends one's knowledge, and is therefore synthetic, is a function of how much a particular individual is able to clearly think in a given concept. In the discussion of the analytic-synthetic distinction in his *Lectures on Logic*, however, Kant anticipates this criticism by distinguishing between a *formal* and a *material* extension of knowledge.[14] Analytic judgments are admitted to extend our knowledge in the first sense, i.e., they often lead to an awareness of some previously unrecognized implications of our concepts, and this, as a matter of fact, is precisely the service which Kant often claims that metaphysicians of the Leibnizian school have rendered to philosophy. Nevertheless, this is sharply distinguished from a material extension of our knowledge which occurs in synthetic judgments. This always involves the relation of a predicate to an object referred to by the subject expression, not to a pre-given concept of the subject. But this is equivalent to saying that it establishes a *real relation* to the object, not a merely *logical relation* to the subject concept. Such a judgment therefore extends (in the material sense) our knowledge of the object and at the same time establishes the objective validity, applicability, or real possibility of the predicate concept.

It is likewise obvious from this why Kant claimed that all existential judgments are synthetic, and why the problem of objective validity only arises in respect to synthetic judgments. Kant asserts the former within the context of his famous refutation of the ontological argument on the grounds that existence is not a "real predicate," i.e., one which determines a thing. In an existential judgment, we "go beyond the given concept," not in the sense of increasing it with further determinations

---

[14]*Logik*, § 36, AK IX: 111.

(existence), but in the sense that we posit an object corresponding to it, or assert its objective validity.[15] In analytic judgments, on the other hand, there is neither any existential reference nor question of objective validity. This is, of course, not to deny that analytic judgments can be true in the sense that they affirm logical relations which hold of the world, e.g., it is in fact true that there are bodies (which is not affirmed in analytic propositions), and that all bodies are extended. The point, however, is that the latter and all analytic judgments, abstract from any existential reference. Their concern is merely with the content of a given concept and not with the question of whether or not the concept refers to a possible object. As a result, perfectly true (non-contradictory) judgments can be formed concerning empty concepts, i.e., concepts which have logical, but not real possibility.

Finally, we can see that these same considerations point to the misguided nature of a frequent objection to Kant's distinction. This is the contention that the distinction (in terms of the question of whether the predicate is really contained or thought in the concept of the subject) applies only to categorical judgments.[16] On this basis it is often said to be impossible to classify other forms of judgment, e.g., hypothetical or disjunctive, as either analytic or synthetic. As we have seen, however, Kant's distinction, at least as developed in *On a Discovery*, does not at all concern the logical form, but rather the content of a judgment, so that this objection is completely beside the point.

The Synthetic A Priori: These general considerations concerning the nature of the distinction between analytic and synthetic judgments should put us in a better position to understand the problems involved in the explanation of the possibility of synthetic judgments a priori. The "critical problem" arises from a reflection on the fact that certain synthetic or objectively valid judgments are held to be necessarily true. As such, however, these judgments cannot be based on experience, for experience can never yield strict necessity or universality. Furthermore, since the connection between concept and object is not learned from experience, the concept itself, which in the synthetic judgment is predicated of the object, must be non-empirical or a priori. This follows from the fact that if the predicate concept were empirical, then its relation to the object could be derived from experience, and the ensuing judgment would not be a priori.

Now this requirement that synthetic judgments a priori involve a priori concepts may not seem obvious at first glance. For one thing,

---

[15] *Critique of Pure Reason*, A598–599/B626–627.

[16] Louis Couturat, "La Philosophie de mathématics de Kant," *Revue de Métaphysique et de Morale* 12 (1904): 324.

analytic judgments, which are always a priori, can be formed on the basis of empirical concepts; for another, Kant distinguishes between merely a priori and pure a priori propositions, the former involving empirical concepts and the latter no admixture of anything empirical.[17] The former difficulty, however, can be remedied by the reflection that analytic judgments abstract from the question of objective reference, and hence from the origin of the concept. Just as analytic judgments can be formed about real or empty concepts, so too they can be formed about either empirical or a priori ones. The second difficulty is overcome by the realization that even "impure" a priori propositions involve a priori concepts as predicates. In Kant's own example, "every alteration has a cause," the emphasis is placed on the fact that alteration is an empirical concept. As the argument of the Second Analogy shows, however, the a priori character of the proposition is based on the a priori character of the predicate concept (causality). The problem thus concerns the necessary relation between the concept (causality) and the feature of the empirical world to which the subject expression (alteration) refers.

This, however, suggests that the problem of explaining the possibility of synthetic judgments a priori is identical with the problem of explaining how our a priori concepts can relate to objects or have objective validity. This latter problem, which is given considerable attention in *On a Discovery*, was first explicitly raised by Kant in a famous letter to Marcus Herz, of February 21, 1772. There, reflecting on what he takes to be a basic weakness or omission in the argument of his Inaugural Dissertation, he asks:

What is the ground of the relation of that in us which we call "representation" to the object? If a representation is only a way in which the subject is affected by the object, then it is easy to see how the representation is in conformity with this object, namely, as an effect in accord with its cause, and it is easy to see how this modification (*Bestimmung*) of our mind can *represent* something, that is, have an object. Thus the passive or sensuous representations have an understandable relationship to objects, and the principles that are derived from the nature of our soul have an understandable validity for all things insofar as those things are supposed to be objects of the senses. In the same way, if that in us which we call "representation" were active with regard to the object, that is, if the object itself were created by the representation (as when divine cognitions are conceived as the archetypes of all things), the conformity of these representations to their objects could be understood. Thus the possibility of both an *intellectus archetypi* (on whose intuition the things themselves would be grounded) and an *intellectus ectypi* (which would derive the data for its logical procedure from the sensuous intuition of things) is at least intelligible. However, our understanding, through its representations, is not the cause of the object (save in the case of moral ends), nor is the object (*Gegenstand*)

[17] *Critique of Pure Reason*, B3.

the cause of the intellectual representations in the mind (*in sensu reali*). Therefore the pure concepts of the understanding must not be abstracted from sense perceptions, nor must they express the reception of representations through the senses; but though they must have their origin in the nature of the soul, they are neither caused by the object (*Object*) nor bring the object itself into being. In my discussion I was content to explain the nature of intellectual representations in a merely negative way, namely, to state that they were not modifications of the soul brought about by the object.[18]

This formulation is often contrasted with the genuinely critical problem of the synthetic a priori; the latter, as Kant himself tells us in the *Prolegomena*, being suggested to him by Hume's analysis of the causal principle. The interpretation of Norman Kemp Smith is typical. He sharply distinguishes between this problem and the critical problem on the grounds that, in the letter to Herz, Kant was still concerned with establishing the possibility of a transcendent metaphysics in the style of Leibnizian rationalism or, more precisely, with the question of the relation between our a priori representations and things in themselves. Under the influences of Hume's criticism of the causal principle, however, Kant came to realize that the possibility of physics as well as metaphysics was at stake. He was therefore led to his Copernican revolution, from the standpoint of which the initial problem was transformed into the problem of the possibility of synthetic judgments a priori.[19] It is thus acknowledged that the problem raised in the letter to Herz helps to prepare the ground for the realization of the problem of the *Critique*, but it is nevertheless held to be quite distinct from it.[20]

There is admittedly a good deal of truth in this manner of viewing the situation. In both the Dissertation and the letter to Herz, Kant was concerned with the problem of accounting for the possibility of knowledge of a super-sensible reality or realm of things in themselves. Moreover, this conflicts with the central theme of the *Critique of Pure Reason*, viz., that the human mind can know only appearances and not things in themselves. Nevertheless, it should also be kept in mind that this critical limitation of knowledge to appearances concerns the *solution* to the problem, not the problem itself. The problem of the explanation of the objective validity of our a priori concepts arose, as we have seen, within an essentially Leibnizian perspective, and it was quite naturally seen in terms of the relation between these concepts and a non-sensible reality. Hume's sceptical reflections, to be sure, changed

---

[18] AK X: 30. The translation quoted in the text is by Arnulf Zweig, *Kant's Philosophical Correspondence, 1759–99* (Chicago: University of Chicago Press, 1967), pp. 71–72.

[19] Norman Kemp Smith, *A Commentary to Kant's Critique of Pure Reason*, 2nd ed. (New York, 1962), p. 206, 219 ff.

[20] Robert Paul Wolff, *Kant's Theory of Mental Activity* (Cambridge, Mass.: Harvard University Press, 1963), pp. 22–25, 30–32.

the direction of Kant's concern from the non-sensible to the empirical. The problem, however, still remained of accounting for the applicability of non-empirical or a priori concepts to objects of experience; and *this* is equivalent to the problem of explaining the possibility of synthetic judgments a priori.

The first chapter of the *Transcendental Deduction* provides decisive evidence for the equivalence of these problems in Kant's mind. There we find Kant reflecting that "among the manifold concepts which form the highly complicated web of human knowledge, there are some which are marked out for pure a priori employment, in complete independence of all experience; and their right to be so employed always demands a deduction." But since empirical proofs cannot suffice to justify this kind of employment, he concludes: "We are faced with the problem how these concepts can relate to objects which they do not yet obtain from any experience."[21] Kant, of course, goes on to claim that this can only be explained if it can be shown that "only through the representation is it possible to know anything as an object,"[22] and thus that the objects in question must be appearances rather than things in themselves. For our present purposes, however, the key point is that in the *Transcendental Deduction*, the very heart of the *Critique*, this is presented as the "critical problem" and thus as identical, by implication at least, with the better known formulation: how are synthetic judgments possible a priori.

Rather than two distinct issues, the one more or less "pre-critical," with certain lingering vestiges in the *Critique*, the other "genuinely critical"; we really have two distinct formulations of one and the same problem. We shall later attempt an explanation of why the problem took this two-fold form for Kant, and we shall then suggest that it reflects Kant's constant concern to define the critical philosophy in relation to both Leibnizian rationalism and Humean scepticism. For the present, however, it suffices to note that it is only in light of this equivalence that Kant can defend the transcendental, non-logical nature of the analytic-synthetic distinction, and thus refute the objections stemming from the Wolffian camp.

Moreover, the recognition of the equivalence of these two problems has important consequences for the interpretation of Kant's conception of syntheticity. More specifically, it points to the nature of the connection between synthetic judgments, intuitions, and sensibility. It is, of course, one of the basic tenets of the *Critique* that it is only through intuition that the mind can come into immediate relation with an

---

[21] *Critique of Pure Reason*, A85/B117.
[22] *Ibid.*, A92/B125.

object. Objects are given to the mind through intuition, they are thought through concepts.[23] It is therefore only in so far as a concept can refer to intuition that it can relate to an object or have objective validity. As both Frege and Hintikka have already noted, the notion of intuition in Kant is broader than that of sensibility, and is defined generically as an individual or particular idea (*Repraesentatio Singularis*).[24] For the human mind, however, intuition is always sensible; an object only being intuitable through sensibility, the faculty of receptivity. From this it would seem to follow that the problem of synthetic judgments a priori is really the problem of how a priori or non-empirical concepts can relate to sensible intuitions and through them to objects. This in turn suggests that there is a close relation between the problem of the synthetic a priori and the problem of the schematism. It is therefore not surprising to find Kant writing to Reinhold concerning Eberhard's claim that he (Kant) has not provided a principle of synthetic judgments:

But that principle is unequivocally presented in the whole *Critique*, from the chapter on the schematism on, though not in a specific formula. It is this: all *synthetic judgments* of *theoretical reason* are possible only by the relating of a given concept to intuition. (Appendix A.)

Although there is no reference to the schematism in *On a Discovery*, probably because it was not discussed at all by Eberhard, the basic thought expressed in the above passage is constantly reaffirmed in the text. One of the clearest expressions of this is to be found in a passage which refers to the *Transcendental Analytic* as a whole:

One can now see from what I have just presented as the succinct result of the analytic portion of the critique of the understanding, that this expounds with all necessary detail the principle of synthetic judgments in general, which follows necessarily from their definition, viz., *that they are only possible under the condition that an intuition underlies the concept of their subject*, which, if the judgments are empirical, is empirical, and if they are synthetic judgments a priori, is a pure intuition a priori. (241)

The interesting feature of this passage is that it not only asserts the connection between synthetic judgments and intuition, but also between synthetic judgments a priori and pure or a priori intuition. Previously we had seen that such judgments require pure concepts; now we see that they require pure intuitions as well. A synthetic judgment a

---

[23]*Ibid.*, A68/B92–93.

[24]Gottlob Frege, *The Foundations of Arithmetic*, German text with English translation by J. L. Austin, 2 rev. ed. (Evanston, Ill., 1968), p. 19; and Jaakko Hintikka, "On Kant's Notion of Intuition (Anschauung)," in *The First Critique, Reflections on Kant's Critique of Pure Reason*, ed. Terence Penelhem and J. J. MacIntosch (Belmont, California: Wadsworth Publishing Co., 1969), pp. 38–53.

priori thus relates pure concepts to pure intuitions, and the question of the possibility of such a relation brings us back once again to the problem of the schematism in the *Critique*. Unfortunately, this line of thought is not fully articulated in *On a Discovery*, but it is in the already mentioned *Progress in Metaphysics*, wherein Kant continues his polemic with Leibnizian rationalism. In the latter work, he writes:

> Knowledge is a judgment from which a concept arises which has objective validity, i.e., to which a corresponding object in experience can be given. All experience, however, consists of the intuition of an object, i.e., an immediate and singular representation, through which the object is given to knowledge, and of a concept, i.e., a mediate representation through a mark which is common to several objects, through which it is therefore thought.—One of these two modes of representation alone cannot constitute knowledge, and if there is to be synthetic knowledge a priori, there must also be a priori intuitions as well as concepts.[25]

The analysis in *On a Discovery*, however, not only develops the connection between synthetic judgments and intuition, but also between synthetic judgments and synthesis. This latter point emerges in connection with the discussion of the second model in terms of which Eberhard endeavored to interpret the distinction between analytic and synthetic judgments. This is the distinction, borrowed from Bernoulli, between identical and non-identical judgments. In response to this attempt to deny the originality and significance of his distinction, Kant points out that the identical-non-identical distinction "does not provide the least clue as to the possible mode of connection of such representations a priori." In contrast to this, the notion of a synthetic judgment "immediately brings with it a reference to an a priori synthesis in general . . . ," and this, Kant continues,

> must naturally suggest the investigation which is no longer logical but already transcendental: whether there are not concepts (categories) which express nothing but the pure synthetic unity of the manifold (of any intuition) with regard to the concept of an object in general, and which underlie a priori all knowledge thereof. Moreover, since this concerns merely the thought of an object in general, the question also arises as to whether the manner in which the object must be given (namely, the form of its intuition) must not likewise be presupposed a priori for such synthetic knowledge. Then the attention directed to this point would have inevitably transformed that logical distinction, which otherwise can be of no use, into a transcendental problem. (244–45)

Syntheticity and concept formation: These considerations, linking synthetic judgments rather intimately with the notions of intuition and synthesis, also serve to suggest the connection between such judgments and acts of concept formation. This is pointed out by Vleeschauwer in

[25] AK XX: 266.

his discussion of *On a Discovery*. Starting with the fact that synthe-ticity does not refer to the logical form of the judgments, he suggests instead that it refers to the formation of the concept of the subject.[26] While analytic judgments merely explicate what is contained in a given concept, therefore presupposing an already constituted or determined concept, the act of synthesis involved in a synthetic judgment issues in the formation or determination of the concept itself. This determina-tion occurs because in a synthetic judgment the predicate concept is not predicated of (or in a negative judgment excluded from) an already constituted or given subject concept, but rather of the intuition, or totality of intuitions, referred to by the subject expression. The subject concept is therefore the outcome rather than the starting point of such a judgment.

This line of interpretation finds strong confirmation in Kant's *Lectures on Logic*. In the Introduction to these lectures, Kant distin-guishes sharply between *making a concept distinct* and *making a distinct concept*. The former occurs through the analysis of a given con-cept. Against the "logicians of the Wolffian school," however, he points out that this does not cover all cases of distinct concepts. Analysis gives distinctness or brings to consciousness only those marks or partial con-ceptions which have already been thought in the concept. It does not do so, however, "in reference to those marks which first pertain to the concept as parts of the entire possible concept." This latter kind of distinctness is defined as "synthetic distinctness," thereby emphasizing that it is the outcome of a synthetic process. As Kant proceeds to point out,

when I make a distinct concept I begin from the parts, and move from there to the whole. There are as yet no marks present; I first obtain these through synthesis. From this synthetic process, then, results synthetic distinctness, which actually extends my concept through that which is added to it as marks in intuition (pure or empirical). [27]

Hence we see quite explicitly that Kant does indeed regard a distinct concept as the product of a synthetic activity. As the result of this activity, it stands in relation to intuition, and thus to an object. It is for this reason that Kant calls it a "possible concept," meaning thereby a concept of a possible object. Prior to such a synthesis, Kant claims, there are no marks present. This means simply that there are no concep-tions which relate to an object, or serve as the ground of the cognition of an object (a task which he had previously assigned to marks).[28]

[26] Vleeschauwer, *Déduction transcendantale*, pp. 410–11.

[27] *Logik*, Introduction, Section VIII, AK IX: 63; English translation by T. K. Abbott, *Kant's Introduction to Logic* (London: Vision Press, 1963), pp. 53–54.

[28] *Ibid.*, p. 64.

These marks or partial conceptions only obtain this status through a synthesis wherein they become part of a total concept of an object. If we view this in light of Kant's discussion of synthesis in the *Critique*, we see that these would-be marks are mere intuitions, and as such they only relate to an object by being brought under a rule or general concept. The result of this activity is the determinate concept or empirical knowledge of an object.[29] On this interpretation, then, a synthetic judgment (at least of a posteriori variety) is the linguistic expression for the intellectual activity (synthesis) through which the mind acquires empirical knowledge, and this is the point that Kant was apparently trying to suggest in *On a Discovery* by underlining the connection between synthetic judgments and synthesis.

Concepts and Judgments: As has been pointed out by the French philosopher Roger Daval, this whole approach involves a break with the traditional i.e., Aristotelian conception of the relation between concepts and judgments.[30] This conception, which was shared by Leibniz and Eberhard, is based on the principle of the priority of the concept over the judgment. On this view, cognition starts with two pre-given concepts (the subject and predicate), and the judgment expresses the union, or lack thereof, of these two concepts. From the Kantian standpoint, however, the situation is far more complex and involves a reciprocity; as there is a sense in which the judgment is prior to the concept, as well as one in which the concept is prior to the judgment.

This reciprocity is clearly evident in the brief, but important, analysis of judgment, contained in the section of the *Critique* entitled "The Logical Employment of the Understanding,"[31] which functions as a part of the "Metaphysical Deduction." This section is not without its ambiguities, largely because it treats of judgment in general without distinguishing between the analytic and synthetic variety. (The judgment offered in illustration, "all bodies are divisible," is a classic example of an analytic judgment.) Such a procedure might seem to be appropriate for an analysis of the "logical employment of the understanding," in contradistinction to the "real employment"; for logic, as we have seen, abstracts from the relation between knowledge and its object, and thus does not concern itself with the distinction between analytic and synthetic judgments. The problem, however, is that within the framework of this logical analysis Kant succeeds in articulating two central critical theses, viz., that understanding is judging and that judgment involves the reference of concepts to intuitions (a claim which

---

[29] Cf. *Critique of Pure Reason*, B141–142.

[30] Cf. Roger Daval, *La métaphysique de Kant* (Paris, 1951), pp. 62–67.

[31] *Critique of Pure Reason*, A66/B91–A69/B94.

Kant elsewhere makes only in regard to synthetic judgments). These theses not only underlie Kant's conception of the relation between concepts and judgments, but also his whole polemic with Leibnizian rationalism.

All of this is implicit in the characterization of judgment as "the mediate knowledge of an object", or "the representation of a representation of it". Here judgment, as discursive or conceptual thought, is being contrasted with intuition, which alone stands in immediate relation to objects. This leads to the by now familiar conclusion that judgment can only yield knowledge of objects by referring concepts to intuitions, and this is what is meant by "mediate knowledge of an object." In judging, as Kant goes on to claim, I come to know an object through a general concept which holds of many representations (intuitions), and "among them of a given representation that is immediately related to an object." This essentially involves a synthetic activity whereby the manifold of representations are unified ("thereby much possible knowledge is collected into one"). It is for this reason that judgments are also described as "functions of unity amongst our representations." But to unify our representations in this manner is precisely to form a concept, and thus the concept through which "much possible knowledge is collected into one;" and through which the mind obtains a "mediate knowledge" of an object, again emerges as a result of the act of judgment. This last point is even more forcefully expressed in the next section, "The Pure Concepts of the Understanding, or Categories," which constitutes the "Metaphysical Deduction" proper. There Kant asserts: "Before we can analyze our representations, the representations must themselves be given, and therefore as regards *content* no concepts can first arise by way of analysis."[32] Analysis presupposes synthesis, both in a logical and a temporal sense; and this in turn implies that it is only possible to form an analytic judgment, or to analyze the content of a given concept, after this concept has been formed by a synthetic activity or judgment.

Nevertheless, although Kant claims that no concept can first arise through analysis, he does not hold that all concepts are the result of judgment or synthesis. This is because judgment, as a unifying activity, itself stands in need of principles or rules, i.e., concepts. Concepts are thus not only viewed by Kant as the result of synthesis or judgment, but also as the rules which determine this activity. In this sense, concepts precede judgment. But this in turn leads to the need to distinguish between two orders of concepts, or at least, if one is to avoid an infinite regress, to acknowledge a set of concepts which function as the

---

[32] *Ibid.*, A77/B103.

ultimate forms or rules of judgment and never as the products thereof. These would be the pure concepts of the understanding, which in the language of *On a Discovery* express: "nothing but the pure synthetic unity of the manifold (of any intuition) with respect to the concept of an object in general, and which underlie a priori all knowledge thereof." Thus, the necessity for affirming a class of pure concepts as "rules of rules"[33] emerges from a consideration of Kant's conception of the relation between concepts and judgments, and this consideration casts a good deal of light on his not altogether successful attempt to derive these concepts from an analysis of the table of judgments of formal logic.

Our present concern, however, is not with the problems involved in the "Metaphysical Deduction," but with the Kantian notion of syntheticity. It is in this context that we can now consider the Kant-inspired response of Schulze to the criticism first raised by Maaß and later reiterated by Eberhard, as well as by countless numbers of subsequent critics. This objection, it will be recalled, centered around the alleged variability of the distinction between analytic and synthetic judgments. The basic claim was that this was an inadequate principle of division because, in the case of any given judgment, it is impossible to determine with certainty whether it is analytic or synthetic. This, according to Maaß, is due to the fact that whether a judgment is analytic or synthetic depends on just how much or how little happens to be thought in the concept of the subject, and this is highly variable. Thus, the judgment "gold is yellow" could be analytic at one time for the person who happened to define gold as a "yellow metal" and synthetic for another person at another time.

The Kantian response, as formulated by Schulze, consists of two steps, both of which are closely related to the previous discussion. First of all, Schulze points out that Maaß confuses a situation in which one and the same judgment or proposition can be regarded as either analytic or synthetic, which for Kant is absurd, with one in which the same sentence can be viewed as expressing two distinct propositions. As Lewis White Beck has suggested, this claim is largely based on Kant's notion of the "fixity of a concept." In light of this doctrine, which seems to be an essential tenet of Kantianism, Beck notes:

A concept cannot be arbitrarily widened through the accumulation of information. It can be replaced by another called by the same name; but of any given concept it can be decided what is implicit in it to be explicated in analytical judgments and what does not lie in it at all. [34]

[33] Cf. Robert Paul Wolff, *Kant's Theory*, pp. 121–31.

[34] Lewis White Beck, "Can Kant's Synthetic Judgments Be Made Analytic?", *Philosophy of Kant*, p. 83.

Schulze expresses this thought by pointing out that, in order to determine the content of a judgment expressed by a given sentence, it is necessary to determine what is signified by the subject and predicate terms ("what should be thought under the subject as well as the predicate"). If different things are thought under these terms, then we are dealing with different concepts, and if this is the case, with different propositions. The fact that one of these is analytic and the other synthetic has no bearing at all on the firmness of the Kantian distinction. Furthermore, in light of this point, Schulze concedes to Maaß the possibility of creating analytic judgments by packing the concepts of the subject so as to include in it, by definition, all of the desired predicates. He points out, however, that this trick (*Kunststück*) is of absolutely no avail. This is because such an arbitrarily concocted definition is purely nominal, and thus avoids the crucial issue which, as we have already suggested, concerns the concept of the subject itself. It is thus encumbent upon the formulator of a definition, which is intended to change a synthetic into an analytic judgment, to justify the attribution of the additional marks to the concept of the subject. Such an attribution is equivalent to the formation of a new concept, and it is the objective reality of this new concept which must be established. Thus, Schulze writes:

... first prove that any one of its marks really belongs to a possible object, and then, when you have done that, prove that the other marks belong to the same thing that the first one belongs to without themselves belonging to the first mark. (Appendix B.)

The demand is thus to show that the definition in question is real and not merely nominal, i.e., that the expression refers to a possible object. But this, as we have seen, is equivalent to showing that it stands in relation to intuition. In so doing, however, as in all cases of real definition, one has formulated a synthetic judgment.[35] Thus, as Beck has also pointed out in his analysis of this passage, all that has been accomplished by this attempt to render a synthetic judgment analytic, through a change in the definition of the subject, is to shift the locus of syntheticity to the formation of the subject concept itself.[36] If our previous analysis is correct, however, this is precisely where the emphasis should have been placed all along. Such an emphasis brings to the fore those points which we have suggested are crucial for an understanding of Kant's notion of syntheticity, viz., that it involves the relation of concepts to intuitions; that it involves an activity of synthesis;

[35] *Reflexionen zur Logik*, 2994, 3003, AK XVI: 606, 610. See also Beck, "Kant's Theory of Definition", *Philosophy of Kant*, pp. 64-65.

[36] Beck, "Can Kant's Synthetic Judgments Be Made Analytic?", *Philosophy of Kant*, p. 84.

and that this activity can be viewed as a process of concept formation or determination.

The consequence which Schulze draws from this is essentially a reiteration of the point that Kant emphasized both in *On a Discovery* and the correspondence with Reinhold: "The entire dispute as to how much or how little should be contained in the concept of the subject has not the least effect on the merely metaphysical question: how are synthetic judgments possible a priori, but belongs merely in the logical theory of definitions . . . ." We can thus see once again that for Kant the analytic-synthetic distinction is metaphysical (here equivalent to transcendental), and not logical, and therefore concerns, as Kant suggests in the *Prolegomena*, the content of judgments and not their logical form. But this means that it concerns that which is asserted in the two kinds of judgments. Synthetic judgments, at least those of theoretical reason, always assert that a concept refers to a possible object, and, according to Kant, the condition for such a claim being valid is that it refers the concept to intuition. Analytic judgments, on the other hand, predicate one given concept of another, and the reference of either concept to intuition is simply not taken into consideration or abstracted from. Thus, as was suggested previously, while analytic judgments may hold of the world, or be objectively valid, e.g., it is true that all bodies are extended, they need not so hold to be true, and in fact, are really *about* concepts and their logical relations, rather than about the relation between a concept and the world. [37]

Gram's Interpretation: It is interesting that much the same interpretation of the nature of syntheticity in Kant, albeit with only a passing reference to *On a Discovery*, has been developed by Moltke Gram in his recent book: *Kant, Ontology, and the A Priori*.[38] If, however, our analysis of *On a Discovery* is correct, it not only provides decisive evidence for Gram's interpretation, but also provides a means for resolving a fundamental contradiction which Gram claims to find in Kant's various accounts.

Gram formulates his interpretation in terms of a sharp distinction between two theories of predication which he finds at work in the *Critique*. The first is the "explicit theory," advocated by the "traditional interpretation." This closely follows Kant's formulation in the Introduction. Thus, it views the distinction between analytic and synthetic judgments in terms of the question of whether one concept is contained in the other. Perhaps the clearest statement of this position is

[37] This is denied by H. J. Paton, *Kant's Metaphysics of Experience* (London, 1936), I: 84. This denial is hardly supported, however, by A736/B764, which is the only passage to which he refers in support of his interpretation.

[38] Moltke Gram, *Kant, Ontology and the A priori* (Evanston, Ill., 1968).

Paton's: "We must presume that the distinction between analytic and synthetic judgments implies a difference in the relation of subject-concept to predicate-concept."[39] Gram examines this formulation from a basically Leibnizian perspective. In so doing he assumes that the Kantian theory is to be construed as a challenge to the Leibnizian claim that in every true proposition the predicate is contained in the concept of the subject. By such a procedure he arrives at and presents, albeit in a far more sophisticated fashion, many of the same objections which were raised against the distinction by Maaß and Eberhard. He therefore comes to the conclusion that, in terms of this "explicit theory" of predication, there is no real basis for denying that allegedly synthetic a priori judgments are "covertly analytic,"[40] a thesis which is really equivalent to the claim that they can be handled in the Leibnizian fashion suggested by Eberhard.

Gram, however, also finds a "hidden" or implicit theory at work in the *Critique*, and this turns out to be much the same as the one which Kant formulates in response to Eberhard's challenge. This theory asserts that in synthetic judgments concepts are predicated of intuitions, and not of other concepts. It thus not only introduces a new, radically un-Leibnizian theory of predication, but also upholds a semantic conception of intuition, wherein intuitions function as parts of the content rather than merely being objects of judgment.[41] The key issue to which Gram points is the meaning of the notion of intuition in Kant, a point which hardly seems to have been settled in the Kant literature, and which, as we have seen, is obviously the crucial issue in the debate between Kant and the Leibnizians.

In denying the constitutive role of intuition (*Anschauung*) in human knowledge, Eberhard systematically equated it with image (*Bild*). He treats it as something merely subjective, grounded in the limits of the finite subject. As we have seen repeatedly, given this interpretation he is able to consistently argue along traditional rationalistic lines that images or intuitions are merely occasions for the acquisition of knowledge and not the ground of its objective validity. Moreover, as we have also seen, it is largely in light of this conception that Eberhard proceeds to reject Kant's whole theory of mathematics, as well as the critical limitations of knowledge to appearances. It is therefore no surprise that Kant repudiated such an interpretation of his conception of intuition, and proceeded to accuse Eberhard of a deliberate deception or misinterpretation. An interesting point, however, which emerges from Gram's

[39] Paton, *Kant's Metaphysics*, I: 84.
[40] Gram, *Kant, Ontology*, p. 50.
[41] *Ibid.*, pp. 35–38.

analysis, is that Eberhard's account is not too far removed from some of the standard interpretations of the notion of intuition found in the Kant literature.

These standard interpretations, as Gram suggests, tend to view intuitions either as sensations or as objects referred to by concepts. The basic difficulty with the first view, which seems to be adherred to by both Kemp Smith and Paton,[42] is that it becomes impossible to see how intuitions, construed as sensations, can have the constitutive role in human knowledge which Kant attributes to them in the *Critique*, and even more explicitly in *On a Discovery*, wherein synthetic judgments are held to establish the objective reality of a concept by referring it to intuition. This latter point would seem to suggest the second interpretation, wherein intuitions are viewed as objects of synthetic judgments, i.e., the particular individuals to which concepts refer. Moreover, such an interpretation, which is sometimes adopted by Eberhard, does have a good deal of support in Kant's text, as appearances, the objects of experience, are often described as an organized manifold of representations (intuitions). Nevertheless, as Gram points out, this interpretation likewise fails, as it does not do justice to the representative function of intuitions or to the grounds whereby intuitions are distinguished from concepts. [43]

This issue is not discussed in any detail in *On a Discovery*, as Kant essentially relies on the teaching of the *Critique*. There are, however, certain key passages in the *Critique* to which Gram calls attention, and which serve to cast light, not only on the nature and function of intuitions for Kant, but also on the basis for Eberhard's misunderstanding. Interestingly enough, these passages are strategically located at the beginning of the major sections in the *Critique*. The first is at the beginning of the *Aesthetic*:

In whatever manner and by whatever means a mode of knowledge may relate to objects, *intuition* is that through which it is an immediate relation to them, and to which all thought as a means is directed. [44]

The second is at the beginning of the *Analytic*:

But beside intuition there is no other mode of knowledge except by means of concepts. The knowledge yielded by understanding, or at least by the human understanding, must therefore be by means of concepts, and so is not intuitive but discursive. Whereas all intuitions, as sensible rest on affections, concepts rest on functions. [45]

[42] Kemp Smith, *Commentary to Kant's Critique*, p. 79, Paton, *Kant's Metaphysics*, p. 97.

[43] Gram, *Kant, Ontology*, pp. 29–33.

[44] *Critique of Pure Reason*, A19/B33.

[45] *Ibid.*, A68/B93.

The third is at the beginning of the *Dialectic* where Kant provides a list of the various species of the genus representation (*Vorstellung*), which seems to correspond to the notion of "idea" in the broad Cartesian sense:

The genus is *representation* in general (*repraesentatio*). Subordinate to it stands representation with consciousness (*perceptio*). A *perception* which relates solely to the subject as the modification of its state is sensation (*sensatio*), an objective perception is *knowledge* (*cognitio*). This is either *intuition* or *concept* (*intuitus vel conceptus*). The former relates immediately to the object and is single, the latter refers to it mediately by means of a feature (*Merkmal*) which several things may have in common. [46]

The key features in the conception of intuition found in these and similar passages are: 1) its relation to sensibility; 2) its relation to individual objects; 3) its function as that to which thought as a means is directed; 4) its function, together with concepts, as a mode of knowledge. Eberhard, like many other critics, focuses exclusively on the first three features, ignoring the fourth, which is crucial for an understanding of Kant's notion of syntheticity. The first of these features, which has already been touched upon, establishes the connection between intuition and sensation, thus giving rise to the standard interpretation, as well as suggesting the view that intuitions can be regarded as images. This equation of intuitions with images is reinforced by the second feature, which regards intuitions as representations of individuals. The third feature is the basis for the doctrine that intuitions function as the objects of knowledge. Eberhard interprets intuitions in this manner when he claims that the *Critique* embodies a subjective idealism. The fourth feature, however, makes it clear that intuitions cannot be regarded solely, if at all, as objects of knowledge, but also, and primarily, as ways of knowing anything. ("Thoughts without content are empty, intuitions without concepts are blind.... Only through their union can knowledge arise.")[47] But knowing, for Kant, is judging, and intuitions therefore have, as Gram suggests, a semantic function as parts of the content of judgments. [48]

[46] *Ibid.*, A320/B376-77.
[47] *Ibid.*, A51/B75.
[48] This line of interpretation has recently been at least implicitly criticized, albeit without any reference either to Gram's work or to the problem of syntheticity, by Manley Thompson, "Singular Terms and Intuitions in Kant's Epistemology", *Review of Metaphysics*, Dec. 1972, Vol. XXVI, No. 2, pp. 314-343. Arguing largely on the basis of Kant's assertion that "intuitions without concepts are blind", and the characterization of an appearance as the "undetermined object of empirical intuition", Thompson contends that empirical intuition can provide at most the data for knowledge of existing objects. By this he means that they provide the mind with a "spatio-temporal somewhat", rather than with a determinate object. Moreover, since intuitions do not refer to determinate objects, we cannot construe singular terms as referring to intuitions, and this would seem to undermine the role in judgment which we have attributed to

This naturally gives rise to the question as to why Kant designated judgments in which concepts are related to intuitions as synthetic in the sense described in the Introduction of the *Critique*, and it is here that Gram's analysis becomes especially relevant. This analysis focuses on Kant's argument in the *Aesthetic* that space and time are intuitions rather than concepts, although it could also have called attention to some of the points raised in response to Eberhard and Kästner (see Appendix B). In both places Kant was concerned with the refutation of the Leibnizian claim which, as we have seen, became a central issue in the polemic with Eberhard. This is the claim that spatial and temporal relations are conceptual, although they are only perceived through the senses, and consequently that our ideas of space and time are general concepts, derived by a process of abstraction. In regard to space, the argument applying *mutatis mutandis* to time, Kant offers, in the *Critique*, two reasons for treating the representation as an intuition rather than a general concept. First of all, he points out: "We can represent only one space; and if we speak of diverse spaces, we mean thereby only parts of one and the same unique space."[49] Space is thus an individual. It has parts in it, as opposed to a universal or general concept which has instances under it. Secondly, "these parts cannot precede the one all-embracing space, as being, as it were, constituents out of which it can be composed; on the contrary, they can be thought only as in it. Space is essentially one, the manifold in it, and therefore the general concept of space depends solely on the introduction of limitation."[50]

As Gram quite correctly points out, the crucial distinction here is between two senses of limitation. "A concept limits another," he notes, "only by restricting the class of objects which falls under it. But one volume of space cannot limit another in this way. Space is limited by one of its parts only in that the part is included by a larger whole."[51] Moreover, this explains why the parts of space cannot precede the whole; for to assert that they can is to make the self-contradictory claim that a limitation, which presupposes the whole of which it is a

---

intuitions. Such a conclusion, however, which Thompson does not explicitly affirm, does not follow from his analysis. Our claim is not that singular terms refer to unconceptualized intuitions; a completely unconceptualized intuition could, for Kant, not even be brought to consciousness, and the empirical intuition of a not further determined "spatio-temporal somewhat" is itself the result of a synthesis according to pure concepts. Rather, our point is simply that the subject term in a synthetic judgment must refer to intuition in the sense that it must be taken as the linguistic expression for one or a plurality of conceptually determined "spatio-temporal somewhats". The subject of such judgments must therefore be an intuitive representation.

[49] *Ibid.*, A25/B39.

[50] *Ibid.*

[51] Gram, *Kant, Ontology* , p. 30.

limitation, nevertheless precedes that whole. But to say that space as a whole precedes its parts and is not limited or determined by them means to imply that space, unlike general concepts, cannot be reduced to or constructed out of its parts. This is precisely why Kant characterized it (and time) as an intuition. Such irreducibility therefore serves as the defining character of an intuition or representation of an individual.

Finally, it is precisely this feature of intuitions which explains their role in synthetic judgments, understood in the manner in which Kant describes them in the *Critique* and the *Prolegomena*. Since intuitions cannot be reduced to or constructed out of concepts, judgments in which the subject expression refers to intuitions cannot have a predicate which is "contained in the concept of the subject." They are therefore synthetic in the "logical sense," and thus the initial formulation of the notion of synthetic judgment is at least compatible with the thesis that such judgments predicate concepts of intuitions.

Nevertheless, even granting the compatibility of the two formulations, it remains the case that the initial formulations in the *Critique* and *Prolegomena* are extremely misleading and give rise to just the kind of misunderstanding evidenced by Eberhard and Maaß. It therefore seems encumbent upon anyone interpreting the analytic-synthetic distinction in the fashion here suggested to explain why Kant initially formulated it in such a misleading manner. Gram endeavors to explain this by appealing to an alleged incoherence in Kant's own position. This is held to be due to Kant's failure to distinguish between the two theories of predication previously described. Such a conclusion, however, is not really necessitated by the facts, as there are a number of considerations which may serve to explain why Kant initially presented the distinction in the way in which he did, and thus help to reconcile his "implicit" and "explicit" teachings.

First of all, we can note that Kant uses "concept" not only in a technical fashion, wherein it is opposed to intuition, but also in a loose sense in which it includes the latter notion. Thus, in the *Transcendental Deduction*, he speaks of "the concepts of space and time as forms of sensibility."[52] Furthermore, it should be recalled that the initial formulation in the *Critique* occurs before the introduction of the concept-intuition distinction, and thus one can hardly expect Kant to appeal to it at that point. Rather, it is reasonable to expect him to proceed just as he did, and to introduce the distinction in terms of his loose version of "concept."

[52]*Critique of Pure Reason*, A85, B118. It should also be noted that Kant continually refers to the "concepts" of space and time in the *Transcendental Aesthetic*.

Secondly, one can also justify the initial formulation of the distinction in terms of the relation between concepts on the grounds that the distinction encompasses more than merely judgments of theoretical reason. It is only in regard to such judgments that we can talk about concepts being related to intuitions. For Kant, however, there are also synthetic judgments a priori of practical reason, the classic example being the principle of morality itself: "An absolutely good will is one whose maxim can always have as its content itself considered as a universal law." This, as Kant points out in the *Fundamental Principles of the Metaphysics of Morals*, is synthetic because "we cannot discover this characterization of the maxim by analyzing the concept of an absolutely good will."[53] In this case, however, we are dealing with a connection between concepts which stand in no relation to intuition, and as Kant goes on to suggest, the positive concept of freedom functions as the ground of this connection. In so far as the notion of a synthetic judgment is broader than that of theoretical reason, and since it is only in regard to the latter that one can meaningfully speak of the relation of concepts to intuitions, Kant was forced to formulate the notion of syntheticity loosely in terms of the relation between concepts. Nevertheless, this should not obscure the fact that it is only in so far as concepts are related to intuitions that one can speak of "objective validity."

There is, however, another and perhaps deeper reason behind the ambiguity of the Kantian formulation. It is the fact that in the *Critique of Pure Reason* Kant was engaged in a two front war with both scepticism and rationalism, with Hume and Leibniz. The introductions to both the *Critique* and the *Prolegomena*, it will be recalled, were addressed primarily to Hume. It was David Hume, after all, who first awakened Kant from his "dogmatic slumbers" by means of his analysis of the causal relation, and thereby raised the question on which the whole fate of metaphysics hinged, viz., how are synthetic judgments possible a priori? But the causal relation, so construed, involved the alleged relation of necessary connection between two distinct concepts. The problem suggested by Hume took the form: how can I necessarily connect a given concept A, with another B, which is distinct from it? Such a formulation leads naturally to the conception of syntheticity contained in the Introduction of the *Critique*. This conception is explicitly presented as an answer to Hume's problem, and since the *Critique* has generally been read, at least amongst Anglo-American philosophers, as an "answer to Hume," this formulation has generally been taken as the basis for the interpretation of Kant's doctrine.

[53] AK IV: 447.

But the *Critique of Pure Reason* is addressed as much, if not more, to Leibnizian rationalism as to Humean scepticism. This was clearly recognized by Eberhard, and it forms the basis of his polemic. Hence, from this point of view, Kant's concern is not so much with the relation between distinct concepts (since for Leibniz the predicate of a true proposition is always contained in the concept of the subject), but rather with the conditions of the objective validity of our pure or non-empirical concepts. Moreover, as we have seen, it is *this* question which occupies the center stage in the *Transcendental Deduction*, the very heart of the *Critique* as well as of *On a Discovery*.

Nevertheless, since the Leibniz-inspired problem of objective validity and the Hume-suggested question of necessary connection are not so much two distinct issues as two formulations of, or perspectives on, one and the same problem, and since the immediate impetus to the critical turn was provided by Hume, it is quite understandable why Kant initially formulated the issue in the way in which he did. These formulations in the *Critique* and the *Prolegomena* are misleading in the sense that they do not allow one to see the whole picture, viz., the equal relevance of the Kantian position to the metaphysical claims of Leibnizian rationalism. Thus, an interpretation of Kant's conception of the distinction between analytic and synthetic judgments which focuses, as so many do, on these passages, is bound to be incomplete and one-sided. The key point, however, is that given the loose use of "concept," which is the only use that one could expect to find in the *Introduction*, this initial analysis is perfectly compatible with the concept-intuition interpretation of syntheticity. Moreover, as Kant makes quite clear in both the correspondence with Reinhold and in *On a Discovery*, the question of the nature and possibility of synthetic judgments, especially of the a priori variety, is not to be considered primarily in terms of the Introduction but in terms of the *Transcendental Analytic* as a whole (with special emphasis on the schematism chapter). The conclusion to which we are led, therefore, is not that Kant was confused on this issue, as Gram suggests, and that he failed to distinguish between two theories of predication (his entire account of syntheticity in *On a Discovery* is grounded in this distinction), but rather that the initial formulation in the *Critique* only reveals one dimension of the problem, and that this formulation must itself be reinterpreted in light of what follows, both in the *Critique* itself and in subsequent works such as *On a Discovery*. We can therefore readily concur with Eberstein when, in reviewing the whole Kant-Eberhard controversy, he notes: "How much labor could have been saved if only the concept of a synthetic judgment had been clearly enough explained . . . ,"[54] but we are not forced to conclude, as he also suggests, that there is any real inconsistency in the Kantian position.

2

Pure Intuition

This manner of viewing synthetic judgments may help to explain why Kant held that the analytic-synthetic distinction belongs to transcendental rather than general logic and that it concerns the content rather than the logical form of judgments, but it does not by itself explain the possibility of synthetic judgments a priori. Such judgments, as we have already seen, require both pure concepts and pure intuitions. Pure or non-empirical concepts are, of course, no problem for a Leibnizian rationalist, but pure intuitions are another matter. It is the notion of a priori intuition and all that it implies, together with the characterization of space and time as species thereof, which forms the very heart of Kant's polemic with Leibniz, and which is subject to the most elaborate criticism by both Eberhard and Maaß. The defense of this difficult and crucial doctrine therefore became a central concern of Kant (as well as Schulze), and this concern lead to a significant clarification and development of a line of argument which was already articulated in the *Aesthetic* and *Amphiboly* in the *Critique*, and the first part of the *Prolegomena*.

The key statement of the Kantian conception of sensibility vis-à-vis the Leibnizian conception is found in the passage from the *Aesthetic* which has already been cited in connection with Eberhard's polemic. There, it will be recalled, Kant was primarily concerned to emphasize the implications of his theory of sensibility in regard to the unknowability of things in themselves. We shall turn to this aspect of Kant's position later, but for the present our concern is with Kant's claims concerning the role of sensibility in human knowledge. Here the key point is that sensibility is given a constitutive role, that is, it does not serve to limit or to provide the occasion for a purely rational kind of knowing of essentially non-sensible objects, but is rather a necessary ingredient in knowing itself, determining the content of knowledge and therefore helping to define the nature of objectivity as it can alone be encountered by the human mind. This is why Kant was so insistent on the claim that the distinction between sensibility and understanding is transcendental rather than logical. This serves to emphasize both that

---

[54] Wilhelm L. G. Eberstein, *Versuch einer Geschichte der Logik und Metaphysik bey der Deutschen von Leibniz bis auf gegenwärtige Zeit*, 2 vols. (Halle, 1794 and 1799; reprinted by Culture and Civilisation, Brussels, 1970) II: 220.

each faculty plays an irreducible role in human knowledge and that it is only in terms of their combination that one can explain the possibility of a priori synthesis.

Such a doctrine stands in sharp contrast to Leibnizian rationalism. The latter position, with its orientation of knowledge towards the divine mind, views the sensible element in cognition as an imperfection due to finitude and, correlatively, sees a priori or ontological concepts as derivable by abstraction from sense experience. Since the predicate in every affirmative true proposition is contained in the concept of the subject, all truths can be regarded as ultimately analytic or reducible to identities, although contingent (synthetic) truths can only be so reduced by means of an infinite analysis, and thus only by God. Nevertheless, this reducibility in principle is enough to make the difference between human and divine knowledge ultimately one of form (clearness and distinctness) rather than of content. This is turn entails the conclusion that sensibility, as construed by the Leibnizian, determines merely the form (the inevitable lack of perfect clarity and distinctness) rather than the content of human knowledge. Sensibility for the Leibnizian tradition is thus closely linked with finitude and limitation, and Eberhard is perfectly consistent with the teachings of this tradition when he grounds sensible intuition in the "limits of the subject." For Kant, however, and this is the crucial point in his whole polemic with Leibnizianism, sensible cognitions are no more reducible, even in principle, to intellectual cognitions (or *vice versa*), than intuitions or representations of individuals are reducible to collections of general concepts. Thus, rather than the Leibnizian model of the finite mind as a "limited deity" whose reliance upon the senses serves merely to limit the clarity and distinctness of its knowledge, Kant presents a conception of mind wherein the very content of knowledge is determined by sensible as well as intellectual conditions, and the idea of a non-sensible, purely intellectual knowledge is no longer conceived as a standard in terms of which human knowledge is found wanting but as a merely problematic concept.

The affirmation of the irreducibly sensible nature of the content of human knowledge provides the basis for Kant's more or less systematic critique of Leibnizian rationalism in *The Amphiboly of Concepts of Reflection*, appended to the *Transcendental Analytic*. Here Kant criticizes the four central doctrines of the Leibnizian metaphysic: (1) the principle of the identity of indiscernibles, (2) the denial of any real opposition between things, (3) the doctrines of monads and the pre-established harmony, (4) the theory of space and time as ideal. Each of these doctrines is viewed as rooted in a basic error, viz., a comparison of things merely in terms of their concepts, abstracting from the features in terms of which they can alone be sensibly apprehended or experienced. Since Leibniz compared things in this manner, Kant points out, "He . . . naturally found no other differences save those only through which the understanding distinguishes its pure concepts from one another."[55] Otherwise expressed, he failed to distinguish between the subject proper and the concept of the subject or, in the language of *On a Discovery*, between the logical essence (the concept) and the real essence. The latter involves a thing's spatio-temporal relations which, although they cannot be derived from its concept, nevertheless determine its nature and serve as the basis of its identification as a particular individual.

This basic error is clearly at work in the famous principle of the identity of indiscernibles, and thus Kant's criticism of this doctrine can serve as a clear illustration of his attitude towards Leibnizian rationalism. Kant's tactic is to show that this principle is a logical consequence of Leibniz's intellectualistic presuppositions. The Leibnizian claim is simply that if two objects, e.g., two drops of water, had exactly the same quality and quantity, they would be the same object (numerically identical). According to Kant, however, such an analysis abstracts entirely from the fact that for such objects to be known they must be given to the mind under the forms of space and time. Hence, even if they are exactly alike, or qualitatively identical, the mere fact that they are located in two distinct portions of space or points of time is enough to insure their numerical distinctness. The principle of the identity of discernibles thus only works if one abstracts completely from the spatio-temporal features of objects, thereby treating them as mere noumena; it does not at all hold for determinate objects of experience.[56] But by arguing in this manner, Kant suggests, "Leibniz erected an intellectual system of the world," or "intellectualized appearances," which is joined together with the correlative error of Locke who "sensualized all concepts of the understanding," i.e., interpreted them as nothing more than empirical or abstracted concepts of reflection.[57]

This line of thought is reaffirmed in *On a Discovery* in response to Eberhard's criticism. Perhaps Kant's strongest statement in this regard occurs in conjunction with the charge of deliberate obfuscation of the issue:

One cannot exhibit more clearly than Mr. Eberhard does against his will the infinite difference between the theory of sensibility as a special mode of intuition, which has its a priori form determinable according to universal principles, and the

---

[55] *Critique of Pure Reason*, A270/B321.
[56] *Ibid.*, A281–83/B337–38.
[57] *Ibid.*, A271/B321.

theory which views this intuition as a merely empirical apprehension of things in themselves, which (as sensible intuition) is only distinguished from an intellectual intuition by the clarity of the representation. From the *incapacity*, the *weakness*, and the *limits* of the faculty of representation (the exact expressions which Mr. Eberhard uses) one can derive no extension of knowledge, no positive determination of the object. The given principle must itself be something positive, which constitutes the substrate for such propositions, although only subjectively, and which only has objective validity in respect to appearances. (220)

Here the emphasis obviously falls on the positive function assigned to sensibility in human knowledge. Sensibility provides the means whereby an extension of knowledge beyond what is contained in a given concept is possible, and therefore the means whereby synthetic judgments are alone possible. This, however, cannot be accounted for by the Leibniz-Eberhard conception of sensibility in terms of limitation or incapacity, and sensibility therefore must be viewed as a special, irreducible mode of intuition. Moreover, as the passage also suggests, this special mode of intuition is to be regarded as having an a priori form, and thus we find at least a suggestion of the connection between the positive function that Kant attributes to sensibility and its intuitions, and the notion of an a priori form thereof. Unfortunately, this crucial connection between the positive function of sensibility and the a priori status of its forms is not systematically developed in any single place in *On a Discovery*. There are, however, several passages, both in this work and in Schulze's review, which bear on this point, and which therefore help us to better understand the Kantian doctrine.

The first occurs in response to Eberhard's contention that concrete time and space, or our sensible representations thereof, are composed of non-sensible elements. Against this Kant points out that such a claim, which is grounded in reason, nevertheless contradicts the most evident demonstrations of mathematics. He further points out that this consequence cannot be escaped by distinguishing, as Eberhard does, between abstract and concrete time, and holding that the demonstrations of mathematics apply only to abstract space and time which are imaginary entities. Against this doctrine, which is quite similar to that of Berkeley, Kant brings forth two objections which he regards as decisive: (1) the fact that physics is based on geometry (on Eberhard's view, the physicist would fall into error when he followed the laws of geometry, and this is simply not the case); (2) it can be demonstrated that each body in space and alteration in time can be divided in precisely the same manner as the space and time which they occupy. This is essentially the problem which was already recognized in the Inaugural Dissertation and analyzed in the context of the Second Antinomy in the *Critique*, and Kant here resolves the "paradox" in his usual manner, i.e., by means of an appeal to the ideality of space and time:

In order to avoid this paradox, which is felt to arise here because reason, which requires the simple as the foundation of all composites, contradicts what mathematics establishes in regard to sensible intuition, one can and must admit that space and time are merely conceptual entities (*Gedankendinge*) and beings of the imagination. This is not to say that they are invented by the latter, but rather that they underlie all of its combinations and inventions. This is because they are the essential forms of our sensibility and the receptivity of our intuitions, through which all objects are given to us. Moreover, since these universal conditions of sensibility are likewise a priori conditions of the possibility of all objects of the senses as appearances, these appearances must therefore accord with them. (202–3)

The important feature in this passage is the explanation of the ideality or subjectivity of space and time in terms of their constitutive function in human experience and their a priori status. The ideality of space and time is here asserted by characterizing them as "conceptual entities" (*Gedankendinge*) or "beings of the imagination." This is at variance with the language of the *Critique* and strongly suggests a species of subjectivity which is more akin to Hobbes than to the *Transcendental Aesthetic*. Such an interpretation, however, is dismissed on the grounds that space and time are not to be construed as fictions of the imagination, but rather as the conditions of its operation, and, indeed, the essential forms and conditions of sensibility, through which objects are given to us in experience. Now this is the doctrine of the *Critique*, and here as well as there their ideality is justified in terms of their constitutive function. It is for this reason that the *Critique* regards them as "transcendentally ideal," and holds that this is consonant with their empirical reality.[58]

The basic Kantian claim is that both the a priority and the ideality of space and time follow from their function as conditions of experience. The connection between being a condition of experience and being a priori is analytic for Kant, as being such a condition is precisely what is meant by saying that a "concept," e.g., space or time, is a priori. While propositions are said to be a priori in so far as they are necessarily true, concepts or representations have this status in so far as they provide necessary conditions, and that which they necessarily condition is human experience.[59] But if something is a condition of experience, it is absurd to claim that it is derived from experience. For to claim that it is so derived would be to suppose that it is possible to have experience before and apart from one of its conditions, and this is obviously contradictory. Thus, in so far as a representation is shown to be a condition of experience, it is *eo ipso* shown not to have its origin in experience, and the only other possible option, at least according to Kant, is to

---

[58] *Ibid.*, A27–38/B43–44, A35–36/52–53.

[59] Cf. A. C. Ewing, *A Short Commentary on Kant's Critique of Pure Reason*, 2nd. ed. (London, 1950), p. 29.

view it as part of the cognitive machinery of the human mind, and in this sense as ideal. One of the main goals of the *Transcendental Aesthetic* was therefore to show against both Leibnizian rationalism and empiricists like Locke, Berkeley, and Hume, that space and time are such conditions of experience, and against the Newtonians that as such they are ideal or subjective in the transcendental sense.

This line of thought is developed in the second part of the essay in connection with the already discussed principle that synthetic judgments a priori require a priori intuitions. This leads directly to the question of where such a strange entity is to be found and how its possibility is to be explained. In response to this question Kant reflects:

> But now I am instructed by the *Critique* to remove all that is empirical or actually sensible in space and time, therefore to negate all things qua empirically represented, and I then find that space and time remain, each as an individual being, the intuition of which precedes all concepts of them and of the things in them. Given the nature of these original modes of representation, I can only regard them as merely subjective (but positive) forms of my sensibility (not merely as the deficiency of the clarity of the representations obtained through this sensibility), not as forms of *things in themselves*, therefore only as forms of objects of sensible intuition, and hence of mere appearances. (240)

This is further developed on the following page where, after having reaffirmed the connection between synthetic judgments a priori and a priori intuition, he goes on to add that the recognition of the need to acknowledge the existence of a priori intuitions itself provides "an insight into the true nature of our sensibility." This is allegedly because this need "can be demonstrated independently of the derivation of the representations of space and time, and thus serve as a basis for the demonstration of their ideality, even before we have deduced it from their inner nature." This is reminiscent of the analytic method of the *Prolegomena*, which arrived at the ideality of space and time by showing that this was a necessary condition for the possibility of synthetic judgments a priori, rather than by means of a consideration of the "inner nature" of space and time. However, although Kant here seems to suggest that this method possesses its own independent validity, this is clearly at variance with his basic doctrine that only the synthetic method can really establish such principles. Moreover, it is obviously inadequate, for as has been often pointed out in connection with the *Prolegomena*, it assumes the existence of synthetic knowledge a priori, and this is just the point at issue not only between Kant and Hume, but also between Kant and Eberhard.

Clearly then, if Kant's argument is to work, he must establish the status of space and time as conditions of experience. Once this is granted, their a priority and ideality follow as a matter of course, but it is precisely this status which is denied by Leibnizianism. Now Kant had argued for this in the *Critique*, particularly in the already mentioned "Platonic argument" in the *Transcendental Aesthetic*, which maintained that space (and *mutatis mutandis* time) was not an empirical concept which has been derived from outer appearances on the grounds that "in order that certain sensations be referred to something outside me . . . and similarly in order that I may be able to represent them as outside and alongside one another . . . the representation of space must be presupposed." This was, of course, challenged by Eberhard, who claimed instead that the clear representation of space was an empirical concept, derived from outer experience, although its "grounds" are innate in us. Unfortunately, since the actual attack on this particular argument was undertaken in the first volume of the *Philosophisches Magazin* by Maaß, Kant does not explicitly deal with this issue in *On a Discovery*. This situation is somewhat rectified, however, by the fact that Eberhard takes over Maaß's basic criticism in his essay: "On the Concepts of Space and Time in Relation to the Certainty of Human Knowledge" in the second volume, and that this criticism is answered by Schulze in his review of that volume.

Eberhard's argument, like Maaß's before him, turns on the claim that Kant's conclusion (the apriority of space and time) does not follow from his premise. This premise, according to Eberhard, proves only that we cannot have outer sensations without the representation of space (or successive sensations without the representation of time), but not that space (or time) has the kind of priority over these sensations claimed by Kant; for it still remains possible that the dependence is mutual, and that the two are correlative. This, it will be recalled, was precisely Maaß's third alternative, and in response to this Schulze, speaking for Kant, writes:

This is incorrect; for the premise also says that in order that certain sensations be referred to something outside me, and similarly, in order that I may be able to represent them as *outside* and *alongside* one another, the representation of space *must already be presupposed*. Now it follows from this, not merely that outer sensations *cannot be without* the concept of space, but that they first became possible through it, and therefore that they already presuppose it as something independent of them, i.e., as a representation a priori. (Appendix B)

Thus, the notion of correlation does not serve to explain the relation between outer sensations and the representation of space. The latter is logically prior to the former, and it functions as a condition of the possibility thereof. In this sense it is a priori. This is not to say, as Eberhard seems to suggest when he challenges Kant's doctrine, that a clear conception of space is not dependent upon experience and that we are somehow equipped with a determinate conception of space (or time) before we begin to experience, but rather that it functions as a formal condition (really a formal cause in the Aristotelian sense) of this experience, and thus cannot be regarded as derived from it.[60]

Moreover, much the same considerations underlie Kant's discussion of innateness in *On a Discovery*. Eberhard, it will be recalled, had raised the question whether Kant had meant, when he talked about the forms of sensible intuition, "the limits of the power of knowledge, by which the manifold is connected into the images of time and space, or these images in general themselves." He had further gone on to claim that whoever regards an image—i.e., space or time—as innate is dealing with a *qualitatem occultatem*; and therefore that innateness can only be appropriately predicated of their subjective grounds. In response to this, Kant writes emphatically:

> The *Critique* admits absolutely no divinely implanted (*anerschaffene*) or innate (*angeborne*) representations. It regards them all, whether they belong to intuition or to concepts of the understanding, as *acquired*. There is, however, an original acquisition (as the teachers of natural right formulate it), consequently also of that which previously did not exist, and therefore did not pertain to anything before the act. Such is, as the *Critique* shows, *first of all*, the form of things in space and time, *secondly*, the synthetic unity of the manifold in concepts; for neither of these is derived by our faculty of knowledge from the objects given to it as they are in themselves, but rather it brings them out of itself a priori. There must, however, be a ground in the subject which makes it possible for these representations to originate in this and no other manner, and which enables them to be related to objects which are not yet given. This ground at least is innate. (221–22)

This appeal to the notion of original acquisition in contradistinction to innateness marks a return to the language of the Inaugural Dissertation, where Kant likewise regarded space, time, and the pure concepts in this manner. He there maintained that these representations are abstracted or acquired from "the action of the mind in co-ordinating its sense according to unchanging laws," and that nothing is innate (there connate) "save the law of the mind."[61] His point was not to deny that our conceptions of space and time are derived and therefore in a sense acquired through experience, but rather to emphasize that the source of these representations is not the objects encountered in experience, but the action or structure of the mind in terms of which these objects can alone be encountered.

Kant makes essentially the same point in *On a Discovery*, except that the "action" or "law of the mind" is replaced by the "form of recep-

---

[60] For a further discussion of this issue see H. E. Allison, "Kant's Transcendental Humanism," *The Monist* 55 (April 1971): 2.

[61] Inaugural Dissertation, §15, English translation by G. B. Kerferd and D. E. Walford in *Kant's Selected Pre-Critical Writings* (Manchester: Manchester University Press, 1968), pp. 73–74.

tivity." He argues that the innate ground is not, as Eberhard suggests, the limits of the faculty of knowledge, rather, "It is the merely particular *receptivity* of the mind, whereby it reviews representations in accordance with its subjective constitution, when affected by something (in sensation)" (222). It is therefore only the formal ground or condition of possibility that can be regarded as innate, and not the actual representation of space (with the same holding for time and the pure concepts of the understanding). They can, however, only be acquired from experience because they constitute its formal conditions, and are thus due to the structure of the knowing mind. Thus, although not strictly speaking innate, they are none the less a priori, and Kant expresses this by characterizing each as an *acquisitio originaria*.[62]

In the last analysis, however, all of Eberhard's misunderstandings and misrepresentations of the Kantian conceptions of space and time come together in the repeated reference to them as images, which is itself a direct consequence of his equation of Kant's notion of intuition (*Anschauung*) with image (*Bild*). Given this equation, it naturally follows that if space and time are intuitions, they are also images. But such an interpretation quite obviously makes nonsense of the *Transcendental Aesthetic*. Thus, in regard to Eberhard's query as to whether he might hold the images of space and time, as opposed to their subjective grounds, to be innate, Kant retorts:

> For where have I ever regarded the intuitions of space and time, in which images are first of all possible, as themselves images (which always presuppose a concept of which they are the presentation, e.g., the undetermined image of the concept of a triangle, for which neither the relation of the sides nor of the angles are given)? He has committed himself so completely to the deceptive ploy of using the expression *"image"* instead of *"sensible"* that he cannot get away from it. (222)[63]

Kant's point here is quite simply that, although all images are sensible, not all that is sensible can be characterized as an image. Specific

---

[62] Kemp Smith, *Commentary to Kant's Critique*, pp. 90-93, points to the connection between the formulations of *On a Discovery* and the Dissertation. He also claims that both are at variance with the *Critique*, wherein both space and time are held to be actually innate. Kant, however, never makes such a claim in the *Critique*, and the distinction between the formulations of the *Critique* and *On a Discovery* to which Kemp Smith points does not really seem to be present.

[63] In the *Critique of Pure Reason* (A142/B182) Kant does, indeed, claim that "the pure image (*reine Bild*) of all magnitudes (*quantorum*) for outer sense is space; that of all objects of the senses in general is time." It may therefore seem somewhat strange that Kant so vehemently denies, both in *On A Discovery* and in his correspondence with Reinhold, ever having treated space and time as images. In the above passage, however, which is taken from the schematism chapter, the emphasis must be on "pure." Now "pure" is generally used by Kant as equivalent to "form." Thus, a "pure image" would not at all be a specific image, but rather the form, framework, or in Heidegger's term "horizon", within which images are alone possible. So construed, the disclaimer in *On a Discovery* is really in substantial if not verbal agreement with the analysis of the *Critique*. Cf. Martin Heidegger, *Kant and the Problem of Metaphysics*, translation by James S. Churchill (Bloomington: Indiana University Press, 1962), pp. 108-9.

images are for Kant the result of the activity of the imagination, and as the above passage suggests, they presuppose a concept. The concept, according to the *Critique*, functions as the rule of synthesis, determining the imagination in the generation of the image. Images, to be sure, can be formed of empirical intuitions or representations of particular individuals, but such images already presuppose time (as the form of inner sense) in which they are generated and space which determines their formal structure. But these forms in which images are alone possible are not themselves images. Moreover, in treating them as such, Eberhard is guilty of precisely the same error as in his defense of the Leibnizian conception of sensibility against the Kantian one, viz., the failure to recognize its positive, constitutive role in human experience, and thus its a priori, formal structure. This conception lies at the very heart of the *Critique*, although its significance only becomes fully apparent when the critical position is defined vis-à-vis Leibnizian rationalism.

But if they are not images, what then are pure intuitions in general and intuitions of space and time in particular? The preceding analysis, which was based essentially on materials taken from *On a Discovery*, emphasized the roles of space and time as conditions or forms of sensibility. This seems to suggest that the notion of pure intuition is to be taken in an essentially dispositional sense, i.e., as a capacity to be affected in a certain manner, rather than as an actual representation or content of consciousness. Such a reading is given further support by Kant's claim that only the formal ground of intuition is innate, while its actual content is acquired as a result of experience. The problem, however, is that, in the *Critique*, Kant not only regards space and time as forms of intuition or sensibility (which is consistent with the dispositional view), but also as formal intuitions or pure manifolds; further, he claims that one can explain the possibility of geometry only by viewing space in this manner. Moreover, he claims in *On a Discovery* that pure intuitions must underlie our pure concepts in synthetic judgments a priori, and this only makes sense if the notion of pure intuition is taken to refer to some kind of determinate content of consciousness rather than a mere disposition.

Kant thus seems to use the notion of pure intuition in a twofold sense, and this is made perfectly explicit in Schulze's response (taken almost verbatim from Kant) to Kästner's essay on geometry (see Appendix B). There the discussion is directed specifically to space rather than to the notion of pure intuition in general, and the key point is the sharp distinction drawn between the space of the metaphysicians, which is given as a single, infinite magnitude, and the space or spaces of the geometrician, which are limited and constructed in accordance with concepts. The point of this distinction is to explain, in light of Eberhard's criticism, the infinity of space. This infinity turns out to rest on the fact that all determinate spaces (the spaces of the geometrician) must be viewed as parts of the one, all inclusive, and hence infinite space (the space of the metaphysician). The metaphysical status of this infinite space is of no concern to the geometrician, but for the philosopher it is said to consist merely in the "*pure form of sensible representation of the subject as an a priori intuition*". This clearly corresponds to the dispositional sense of pure intuition, while the space of the geometrician, with its determinate content, e.g., triangularity, corresponds to the other sense. In the two senses of space we can therefore find the two senses in which Kant uses the notion of pure intuition.

Pure intuitions, taken in the second sense, must therefore be distinguished both from images and from forms of sensibility or forms of intuition. Pure intuitions are distinguished from images on the grounds that they are a priori and first make images possible. They are distinguished from the forms of sensibility or forms of intuition on the grounds that they are actual representations, capable of functioning as the subject in synthetic judgments a priori. They must thus be both universal and necessary on the one hand and particular and determinate on the other. The universality and necessity is required in order for them to be pure or a priori, and the particularity of determinations in order for them to be intuitions. But if this is indeed the case, then it would seem that our analysis has served only to confirm Eberhard's criticism, and thus to show that this notion of pure intuition is inherently contradictory.

There is, however, another technical notion in the *Critique* which is subject to a similar dialectic. This is the notion of a "transcendental schema." Kant introduces this conception in the notoriously obscure chapter, "On the Schematism of the Pure Concepts of the Understanding," in order to explain the applicability of the categories or pure concepts to appearances. The problem is generated by the total heterogeneity of such concepts and appearances. Because of this heterogeneity, Kant thinks:

Obviously there must be some third thing, which is homogenous on the one hand with the category, and on the other hand with the appearance, and which thus makes the application of the former to the latter possible. This mediating representation must be pure, that is, void of all empirical content, and yet at the same time, while it must in one respect be *intellectual*, it must in another be *sensible*. Such a representation is the *transcendental schema*.[64]

[64] *Critique of Pure Reason*, A177/B138.

Now although he rejects as incoherent this particular formulation of the meaning and function of a transcendental schema, with its appeal to a "third thing" or "mediating representation" which is neither purely sensible nor purely intellectual, Gram has suggested that transcendental schemata can be construed as pure intuitions. Only such an interpretation, he thinks, can make sense out of the notion of a transcendental schema, and explain the role of the schematism chapter in the argument of the *Critique*. This chapter, he claims, endeavors to answer two closely related yet distinct questions: (1) What are the referents of the pure concepts? and (2) How can we claim that all appearances must fall under these concepts? Schemata, construed as pure intuitions, are held to provide the referents, not for the pure but for the schematized concepts (categories), and since pure intuitions function as the form of all empirical intuitions (appearances), it is easy to see why all appearances must conform to these concepts.[65] Moreover, in support of Gram's thesis, we can note that only on such an interpretation does the schematism chapter assume the significance which Kant granted to it in his letter to Reinhold in regard to the explanation of the possibility of synthetic judgments a priori; for only on this interpretation does it help to establish the connection between pure concepts and pure intuitions which are expressed in such judgments.

The theses that pure intuitions are transcendental schemata will not help us in the least, unless, however, the notion of schema in general and transcendental schema in particular can be explained independently of the notion of pure intuition. Furthermore, the problem is complicated by the fact that Kant defines "schema" in various and apparently incompatible ways. Basically, however, the schema of a concept can be regarded as the essential or generic features of the objects falling under that concept, i.e., a sort of outline or "monogram" of their defining characteristics.[66] This is distinguished both from the concept itself, which is here construed as the rule for the construction of the schema, and the image or representation of a particular object falling under that concept. These features are included in Kant's definition of the schema of a concept as the "representation of a universal procedure of imagination in providing an image for a concept."[67] The emphasis here must be placed on "representation." Strictly speaking, the concept itself is the procedure or rule of the imagination, and the schema its sensuous realization, defining the essential features of any object falling under that rule. In the language of the correspondence with Reinhold, the schema

---

[65] Gram, *Kant, Ontology*, pp. 83–129.

[66] Cf. Paton, *Kant's Metaphysics*, II: 35–36.

[67] *Critique of Pure Reason*, A140/B179–80.

can be said to be the formal ground of the intuition of the object. It is thus a particular representation which fulfills a generic or universal function, and it is schemata taken in this sense which, as we shall see, play a significant role in geometrical demonstration.

There are special difficulties, however, with the notion of a transcendental schema or a schema of pure concepts; for on the one hand, such concepts, unlike mathematical concepts, refer to all objects of possible experience rather than to any specific class thereof, and on the other hand, such concepts, owing to their purity, "can never be brought into any image whatsoever."[68] Just as the schema of the concept of a triangle must express the universal, necessary features of all triangles, so the schemata of the pure concepts of the understanding must express in a sensuous form, not reducible to an image, the universal, necessary characteristics of all objects of experience. These, however, could only be the essential characteristics of the forms or conditions under which objects are given to the mind, viz., space and time. But these characteristics are precisely the content of pure intuition or, rather, are themselves pure intuitions, qua contents or objects of consciousness. Such representations are both necessary and universal in that they apply to and condition all possible instances of spatio-temporal objects and are particular in that they are characteristics of the one space and the one time. Transcendental schemata can thus, as Gram suggests, only be construed as pure intuitions, while pure intuitions can be regarded as representations of the necessary and universal characteristics of space and time and thus of all objects qua appearances, in space and time.

Moreover, Kant himself strongly suggests such an interpretation when after initially describing transcendental schemata as "transcendental" (i.e., necessary and universal) "determinations of time," and claiming that "in addition to the function of understanding expressed in the category" (the logical function), pure a priori concepts "must contain a priori certain formal conditions of sensibility, namely, those of inner sense," he proceeds to directly link the notion of a transcendental schema to those conditions:

These conditions of sensibility constitute the universal condition under which alone the category can be applied to any object. This formal and pure condition of sensibility to which the employment of the concept of understanding is restricted, we shall entitle the *schema* of the concept. The procedure of understanding in these schemata we shall entitle the *schematism* of pure understanding.[69]

There are, of course, many difficulties involved in reconciling this or, indeed, any interpretation of Kant's doctrine of the schematism with all

[68] *Ibid.*, A142/B181.
[69] *Ibid.*, A140/B179.

of the diverse things that Kant says about it, both in the relevant chapter in the *Critique* and elsewhere. Moreover, since our present concern is largely with the relevance of this doctrine to the argument of *On a Discovery*, we cannot here engage in any detailed analysis of those difficulties. It may, however, be fruitful to point out that this view is not, as Gram supposes, incompatible with the initial description of the transcendental schema as a "mediating representation" or third thing. Gram rejects this notion on the grounds that it posits an incoherent, hybrid entity that is both sensible and intellectual, both a concept and an intuition.[70] This objection is based on the assumption that a pure intuition must be purely sensuous, and thus stand in no relation to the synthetic activity of the understanding. This, however, is a mistake, and it involves a confusion between pure intuition qua disposition or form of sensibility, and qua content or object of consciousness. The former alone is purely sensuous, as it is a pure receptivity or capacity to be affected. As the *Transcendental Analytic* makes quite clear, however, any determinate content of consciousness is the result of a synthetic activity, and the unity of space and time, wherein they can alone be "brought to the unity of consciousness" is itself the result of a transcendental synthesis.[71] A pure intuition qua content of consciousness is the result of a synthesis according to a priori concepts; it involves the sensuous realization or schematization of such concepts. It is therefore pure in that it involves the admixture of nothing empirical, but not in the sense that it involves nothing intellectual.

This interpretation of pure intuitions as schemata sheds a good deal of light on a number of contested points in the polemic between Kant and Eberhard, and offers a response to many subsequent criticisms of the Kantian conception of mathematics, which are often basically more sophisticated restatements of the Leibnizian position adhered to by Eberhard. First and foremost of these contested points is the alleged need to exhibit a concept in intuition in order to establish its objective reality or real possibility. Closely connected with this is Kant's thesis concerning the necessity of construction in pure intuition for mathematical demonstration; and both of these lead to the assertion of the synthetic a priori nature of mathematical propositions. Operating under the assumption that intuitions can only be images, Eberhard is easily able to deny both of these theses, as well as the claim that mathematics is synthetic (with synthetic naturally being understood in the Kantian sense). Thus, to use Eberhard's example, one would hardly wish to deny the objective reality of the concept of a chiliagon on the grounds

[70] Gram, *Kant, Ontology*, p. 93.
[71] Cf. *Critique of Pure Reason*, esp. A99–102.

that we cannot form a distinct image of such a figure, nor would we base a demonstration of the properties of a triangle on the features which we happen to find in a particular triangle (image) constructed on paper.

This however, was obviously never Kant's position, and such an interpretation is simply the consequence of confusing the image with the schema. Thus, while it makes no sense to say that a concept must be capable of being brought to an image, it makes perfectly good sense to claim that it must be schematizable if it is to relate to a possible object or have objective reality. This is because, unlike the image, the schema is not something extraneous to the concept, but is really the concept itself qua realized in intuition (a fact which may help to account for some of the diverse ways in which Kant characterizes schemata).[72] Just as sensibility apart from conceptualization is a mere disposition, or capacity to be affected in a certain manner, so a concept apart from its realization in sense (schematization) is merely an empty form of thought, which as such is not related to a possible object. Kant illustrates this in the *Critique* by means of the concept of a figure which is enclosed within two straight lines. Such a concept is shown to be logically possible in the sense that it is not self-contradictory, but not really possible in that is contradicts the essential nature of space; from which it follows that there can be no such figure corresponding to this concept, and thus, that the concept is empty.[73]

Moreover, the role of construction in geometrical demonstration is seen in a new light when it is realized that it is the schema and not the image which is constructed by the mathematician. The schema, unlike the image, can function in demonstration because it determines the essential properties of any figure falling under the concept. Since these properties are derived from the schema and the condition of its construction rather than from the mere concept, the ensuing judgment is synthetic. Since these properties derived from the schema necessarily pertain to all objects falling under the concept, the judgment is a priori. This latter point is clearly illustrated in a passage from the schematism chapter which almost seems as if it were written for Eberhard:

Indeed, it is schemata, not images of objects, which underlie our pure sensible concepts. No image could ever be adequate to the concept of a triangle in general. It would never attain that universality of the concept which renders it valid of all triangles, whether right-angled, obtuse-angled, or acute-angled; it would always be limited to a part only of this sphere.[74]

[72] Cf. Daval, *La métaphysique de Kant*, p. 147.
[73] *Critique of Pure Reason*, A220/B267.
[74] *Ibid.*, A140–41/B180.

In *On a Discovery* Kant presents these points in connection with an analysis of Eberhard's misunderstanding of Apollonius and his commentator, Borelli. Allegedly following Borelli, Eberhard had cited Apollonius's demonstrations concerning the properties of conic sections as an example of how a mathematician can proceed without any appeal to intuition or construction (with the implication that the metaphysician can do likewise). Kant counters this by showing that, far from counting against his theory, Apollonius's demonstrations provide the classic example of the role of construction in geometrical proof. Just as we have earlier suggested that determinate concepts are viewed by Kant as products of synthetic judgments, so here we see that the concept of a parabola is seen to be itself the result of an intellectual operation or construction, i.e., the cutting of the cone in accordance with a certain rule. All of the mathematical properties of the parabola are determined by the rule in accordance with which it is constructed, and it is only through this construction that the possibility of the figure is established. Moreover, Kant also claims that through this construction the parabola is presented in a priori intuition, and thus, as we have seen, that the product of such a construction is the schema of the concept.

This is underscored in the crucial footnote (192), wherein Kant comments upon the nature of geometrical construction. What is especially relevant here is the equation of pure with schematic construction and its opposition to empirical or technical (in the text, 'mechanical') construction. The mathematician, Kant points out, is only concerned with the former, and Eberhard's confusion stems from the fact that, having misunderstood Borelli's analysis of Apollonius, he failed to distinguish between these two radically different kinds of construction. He thus, in effect, only acknowledged the latter kind of construction, and having seen that it is irrelevant to mathematical demonstration, he jumped to the conclusion that all construction is equally irrelevant.

But what is pure or schematic construction if not the construction of a schema? We recall the passage from the *Critique* cited above. It points out that "schemata not images underlie our pure sensible" (i.e., mathematical) concepts. This is because it is only the schema, not the image, which has the required universality. This schema is the exhibition of the concept in intuition, and since the concept is a priori, the intuition is pure. Such a construction, Kant suggests, can occur either in the mere imagination, or it can result in an actual image, e.g., the triangle constructed on paper or the circle drawn in the sand. The important point, however, is that it is not the image in its particularity which concerns the mathematician, but its generic, conditioning features, viz., the schema or plan which is executed more or less imperfectly in the particular image. This schema, as we have already seen, is universal, as it holds of all geometrical figures of a given nature, and it is also particular, as it is presented in intuition as a specific delimitation of the one, all embracing space. It is therefore only by means of schemata that a priori concepts can be exhibited in intuition, and thus given objective reality; and similarly, it is only by means of the construction of these schemata that geometry is possible as a synthetic a priori science. The possibility of such schemata, however, at least in regard to geometrical concepts, rests on the a priori status of space as a form or condition of human sensibility. It is only because space has this status that its essential structure, delineated by the mathematician, possesses the requisite universality and necessity. Thus, the difference between Kant and Eberhard and, indeed, between Kant and Leibniz, concerning the nature of geometrical demonstration and the role of intuition and construction therein, is part and parcel of the more fundamental disagreement concerning the nature of sensibility.

With regard to arithmetic and algebra, however, the situation is far less clear. Kant, for his part, ignores them completely throughout the controversy, and the only discussion of these two branches of mathematics is a very brief treatment by Schulze of Eberhard's objections. Furthermore, not only is this response Schulze's rather than Kant's, but it also fails to meet Eberhard's objections on a number of important points. First of all, it completely ignores the Leibnizian-style demonstration of arithmetic propositions offered by Eberhard; secondly, the argument for the connection between number and the intuition of time is purely *ad hominem*, proving at most that Eberhard himself must acknowledge this connection; finally, Schulze's claim that characteristic construction is to be construed as a mere empirical aid, analogous to the five fingers in arithmetic, not only does not seem to jibe with the *Critique*, but even if it were granted, it sheds absolutely no light on the actual construction or presentation in intuition which is allegedly involved in algebra.

Nevertheless, Schulze's discussion is not totally without significance for our purposes, as it does at least point specifically to the schematism as the section of the *Critique* which provides the key both to the syntheticity of arithmetic and its relation to time. The passage which Schulze had in mind was obviously the description of number as "the pure *schema* of magnitude (*quantitatis*), as a concept of the understanding, . . . a representation which comprises the successive addition of homogeneous units." This is followed immediately by a further, and not obviously consistent characterization of number as "the unity of the synthesis of the manifold of a homogeneous intuition in general, a unity due to my generating time itself in the apprehension of the intuition."[75] This is a difficult passage, even by Kantian standards, and

[75] *Ibid.*, A142-43/B183.

Schulze, of course, provides absolutely no help in interpreting it. We can, however, without going too far afield, at least note that it strongly suggests that Kant conceives of number both as a concept or rule (the unity of the synthesis) and as a result of synthesis or schema (the schema of the pure concept of magnitude). Number in the latter sense would be a specific quantity or sum, and as Kant says elsewhere, including in a letter to Schulze, dated November 25, 1788,[76] such quantities can only be grasped in so far as they are given successively, and thus the grasping or conceiving of a sum is subject to a time condition. On this view then, time necessarily intervenes whenever the mathematician, rather than merely thinking of a number, attempts to realize that number, that is, construct it through an arithmetic operation.[77] The Kantian response to Eberhard's objections would thus be that it is because arithmetic calculation requires operations or constructions that it is synthetic (in Kant's sense);[78] and that it is because this construction is subject to time conditions, just as geometrical construction is subject to spatial conditions, that it necessarily involves a reference to intuition.

3

The Limitation of Knowledge and the Relation to Leibniz

The Kantian conception of the limitation of knowledge to appearances is itself a consequence of Kant's conception of sensibility, together with the closely related theory of the schematism. Thus, although this conception is the focal point of Eberhard's attack, and the central theme of the first and longest part of *On a Discovery*, it is best considered last in a systematic analysis of the dispute. Moreover, since much of the background for an analysis of this conception has already been presented in the previous discussion, the treatment can be relatively brief.

The crucial point to grasp is the precise nature of the connection between Kant's limitation thesis and his theory of sensibility. We have emphasized throughout the positive role which Kant grants to sensibility in human experience. Its forms (space and time) are a priori conditions of such experience, and this implies both their transcendental ideality and the impossibility of having any experience of objects independently of them. From this Kant concludes that we can only

---

[76] AK, X: 554–57. See also the letter to Rehberg, September 1790, AK XI: 207–10, and the *Critique of Pure Reason*, A102.

[77] Daval, *La métaphysique de Kant*, p. 140.

[78] For an excellent discussion of the constructive character of mathematics in Kant see Gottfried Martin, *Kant's Metaphysics and Theory of Science*, trans. P. C. Lucas (Manchester University Press, 1955), pp. 21–27.

intuit objects in so far as they are subject to those subjective conditions, and thus as they appear and not as they are in themselves. In this latter point Kant is in fundamental agreement with the Leibnizians. Eberhard, arguing on the basis of the Leibnizian theory of sensibility, admits that we can only have intuitive, i.e., sensible knowledge of phenomena. Against Kant, however, he also claims that we can have an inferential, purely conceptual knowledge of the "objective grounds" of these phenomena, of "true things," or things in themselves.

This shifts the locus of the dispute to Kant's claim that apart from its relation to sensibility and its conditions, mere thought can yield no genuine knowledge of an object. ("Thoughts without content are empty . . .") The very conditions which realize thought or which enable it to relate to an object also limit it to objects of a peculiar sort (phenomena). This is the note on which Kant ends the schematism chapter, where in reference to the pure concepts of the understanding he writes: "This (objective meaning) they acquire from sensibility, which realizes the understanding in the very process of restricting it."[79] Thus, by themselves and independently of their relation to sensible intuition (schematization), the pure concepts are empty forms of thought, which can provide no knowledge of any object, and certainly not of the non-sensible, objective grounds of appearances posited by Eberhard.

This line of thought is developed in the *Critique* in the chapter entitled "The Grounds of the Distinction of all objects into Phenomena and Noumena," which forms a bridge between the *Analytic* and the *Dialectic*. There Kant acknowledges that the conceptions of sensibility and appearance presented in the *Aesthetic* and *Analytic* require the drawing of the distinction between phenomena and noumena, i.e., between objects as known through the senses and the same objects "considered in their own nature" or "other possible things" which underlie the phenomena and are conceived through pure thought.[80] In *On a Discovery* this same thought is expressed through the assertion that the *Critique* affirms that space and time have objective as well as subjective grounds, and that their ultimate objective grounds are things in themselves. In the *Critique*, however, Kant emphasizes that knowledge of such objects would require a non-sensible, intellectual mode of intuition, which is itself a merely problematic concept, while in *On a Discovery* the emphasis is placed on the fact that these objective grounds of space and time are not themselves in space and time and are therefore unknowable. Kant therefore affirms in each work both the exist-

[79] *Critique of Pure Reason*, A147/B187.
[80] *Ibid.*, B06.

ence and the unknowability of things in themselves, thereby giving rise to one of the most famous objections to the critical philosophy.

In order to properly appraise this highly controversial aspect of Kant's philosophy, we must see it in light of the specifically Kantian conception of the finitude of human knowledge. It is, as we have seen, this conception which underlies Kant's whole polemic with Leibnizian rationalism. The human mind is not for Kant, as it is for Leibniz, a finite God, capable of grasping, albeit obscurely, what the divine intellect apprehends clearly and distinctly. Against this view Kant affirms the *sui generis* nature of the specifically human forms of knowing, and shows that these forms define the structure of experience and objectivity as it must necessarily be encountered by the human mind. From this perspective, the concept of the thing in itself or the noumenon in the negative sense assumes a legitimate role as a limiting concept. Rather than being, as with Leibniz, an ideal in terms of which human knowledge, with its attachment to sense, is found wanting, this noumenon is merely an x, in contrast to which the essential nature and reality of human knowledge is defined. Kant expresses this thought by asserting that the function of this concept is to "curb the pretensions of sensibility."[81] Now at first sight it might seem odd that Kant, who in opposition to Leibniz, affirms the positive role of sensibility, would express himself in this manner. The point, however, is that while Leibnizian rationalism does give to sensibility a merely limiting or distorting role in human cognition, at the same time it finds in this cognition an obscure apprehension of precisely the same content which is grasped adequately by the divine mind. It is *this* pretension that the Kantian theory is designed to curb, and far from contradicting other critical principles, the thing in itself, so conceived, is a necessity complement to the Kantian notion of sensibility.

As Kant goes on to show, however, in the *Transcendental Dialectic* in the *Critique*, neither this positive, constitutive role of sensibility, nor the limitation of knowledge to possible experience which it entails, have been generally recognized by metaphysicians. This failure leads directly to "transcendental illusion," and this to the antinomies. Moreover, as we have seen at length, Leibnizian rationalism, with its intellectualistic assumptions, its confusion of the concept and the thing, and with its confusion of logical conditions of thought with formal conditions of intuition and material conditions of existence, provides the classic example of this peculiar species of illusion. Eberhard, however, takes direct issue with this and, arguing in the name of Leibniz, attacks the notion of transcendental illusion in general; he argues in particular

[81] *Ibid.*, A255/B311.

for the "transcendental validity" of two metaphysical principles of pure reason: (1) the principle of sufficient reason, which provides a formal principle of knowledge, and is in addition the principle of synthetic, i.e., non-identical judgments; (2) the doctrine that space and time are ultimately composed of or grounded in simple, non-sensible elements, which provides a material principle of knowledge. In defending his critical thesis against Eberhard's attack, Kant relentlessly exposes the confusion and ambiguity in the former's position. It is therefore to these analyses, which constitute much of the actual text of *On a Discovery*, that we now turn.

1. *The Principle of Sufficient Reason*

Much of Kant's critique of Eberhard's interpretation and use of the principle has already been touched upon in connection with the discussion of its alleged role in synthetic judgments a priori. First of all, Kant points out that Eberhard's entire argument rests on the frequently mentioned confusion of a formal principle of judgment with a material principle of things. The distinction at issue is between the claim that every proposition has a reason, or ground, and the claim that every thing must have a ground or cause (the ambiguous German word "*Grund*" doing duty in both of these contexts). The former is a logical, analytic principle of thought, based on the principle of contradiction. As such it abstracts completely from all considerations of the relation of thought to its object. The latter is a transcendental, material, synthetic principle (again all of these are here synonymous), which makes a claim concerning the objects of human knowledge, and which therefore cannot be derived solely from the principle of contradiction.

This confusion involves a complete misunderstanding of the *Critique*, which sharply distinguishes between general (formal) and transcendental logic. This misunderstanding, Kant points out, is reflected in Eberhard's question as to whether the principle of sufficient reason (construed in the first sense as a formal principle of thought) has "transcendental validity." This is a misunderstanding because qua formal, the principle abstracts from all relations of thought to its object, and thus by definition cannot have such validity. This is obfuscated, however, by Eberhard's use of the ambiguous expression "all," which refers indifferently to propositions and to things, rather than the clear expression "every thing." The latter expression would make manifest the material, i.e., transcendental nature of the principle, and thus the absurdity of attempting to derive it from the principle of contradiction.

Moreover, Kant reasons that this confusion and obfuscation is deliberate and writes in reference to Eberhard: "He wishes to validate this concept of reason (and with it, unnoticed, the concept of causality) for all things in general, i.e., prove its objective validity without limiting it merely to objects of the senses, and thereby avoid the condition stipulated by the *Critique*, namely, the necessity of an intuition by means of which this reality is first demonstrable" (194–95). This goal is apparently achieved by basing this principle on the principle of contradiction "which is valid for all that we can possibly think, whether or not it is a sensible object with a corresponding intuition" (195). As such it would apply to non-sensible as well as sensible objects, and thus, serve as a positive principle of metaphysical knowledge. This line of reasoning, however, is a clear illustration of what Kant meant by transcendental illusion. The universality of the principle of contradiction is, after all, only achieved as a result of its formal nature. It holds of thought in general, without regard for its object. But such a principle is therefore merely logical, i.e., it abstracts from all considerations of the relation between thought and its object; and this is just the point at issue in the question concerning objective or "transcendental validity." It thus leads to the mistaken belief that something is being determined concerning the nature of reality, when in fact all that has been established is an analytic principle concerning the relation of concepts in a judgment.

After these preliminary considerations, Kant turns to Eberhard's actual demonstration of the principle, the details of which need not concern us here. Suffice it to point out that Kant attacks it from several perspectives, pointing out: (1) the ambiguity of its formulation (the word "all," as we have already noted, being able to refer either to every judgment or every being); (2) its lack of unity (Eberhard's variation of the demonstration being simply tacked on to Baumgarten's then standard version, thereby further confusing the issue); (3) the invalidity of the syllogism in which Eberhard formulates his demonstration (as Kant expresses himself to Reinhold, "the syllogism walks on all fours"); (4) the proposition "everything has a reason" which, if taken in its unlimited universality and applied to entities rather than to judgments, is false (this is because it implies a denial of the existence of God).

On the basis of these considerations Kant concludes that the attempt to provide a dogmatic demonstration of the principle of sufficient reason, construed in its real rather than its merely logical sense, must be regarded as a failure. This and indeed any a priori principle can only be established critically, i.e., in relation to possible experience and its conditions. Eberhard, however, not only endeavors to demonstrate the "transcendental validity" of the principle of sufficient reason but also to present it as the principle of synthetic judgments a priori. Kant does not address himself to this point in his actual refutation of Eberhard's demonstration, but he does in the second part of *On a Discovery*, in connection with his discussion of the analytic-synthetic distinction, as well as in his letter to Reinhold. But since this point has already been touched upon and since it involves the same charge of confusing a logical with a transcendental principle or the logical relation of ground and consequent with a real relation, it is not necessary to pursue it any further.

2. The Concept of the Simple

In addition to arguing for the "transcendental validity" of the principle of sufficient reason, Eberhard also attempts to demonstrate the validity of the concept of the simple, that is, the objective reality of simple, non-sensible beings (Leibnizian monads). By so doing he hoped, as we have seen, to demonstrate the possibility of genuine knowledge of the non-sensible, and thus to repudiate the Kantian limitation of knowledge to appearances. This, as we have also seen, was allegedly accomplished by arguing that concrete space and time—the space and time of experience—must be composed of simple, non-sensible elements which constitute their "objective grounds."

Kant devotes a good deal of attention to this argument, it being the subject matter of sections B and C of part one. Much of what he says there has already been discussed in connection with the analysis of Kant's conception of sensibility; although, in sharp contrast to the systematic, succinct treatment of the principle of sufficient reason, his analysis is repetitious and not always directly to the point. This is no doubt largely due to his desire to pursue Eberhard relentlessly and to expose every distortion of the *Critique*. Nevertheless, the basic points of Kant's polemic and their implications for an understanding of the *Critique* can be presented in a succinct fashion.

Basically, Kant sees in Eberhard's turn to the concept of the simple an attempt to advance beyond the position allegedly reached in connection with the principle of sufficient reason. Whereas with this latter principle, here equated with the causal principle, Eberhard had taken a principle with a legitimate empirical use and tried unsuccessfully to show that its use was not limited to that sphere, in the present instance he is concerned to establish the validity of a concept which has no empirical application. In the language of the *Critique*, he is therefore moving from a concept of the understanding to an idea of reason, the object of which is here described as an "object of the understanding" (*Verstandeswesen*). The whole project, however, is vitiated by the fact that Eberhard seeks this object in the elements of the sensible.

Kant presents two fundamental objections to this view, (1) that it contradicts mathematics, and (2) that it contradicts itself. The first point has already been touched upon in connection with the analysis of

Kant's conception of sensibility. It is based on the claim that mathematics demonstrates the infinite divisibility of space and time, from which Kant infers that neither can be composed of simple parts. The great bulk of Kant's attention, however, is directed to the second point, viz., the claim that Eberhard's position is self-contradictory. Here Kant shows in great detail, and with considerable repetition, both the confusion and what he takes to be the deliberate obfuscation in Eberhard's conception of the relation between the sensible and the non-sensible. In certain respects this treatment parallels Kant's analysis of Eberhard's deduction and application of the principle of sufficient reason. Just as in the former instance Kant's goal was to show that Eberhard sometimes took the principle in a purely logical sense (when he endeavored to show that it can be derived from the principle of contradiction) and sometimes in a transcendental or material sense (when he endeavored to demonstrate its "transcendental validity" or objective reality), in the present instance he endeavors to prove that Eberhard's whole argument rests on an illicit and unannounced shift from a position where the opposition between the sensible and the non-sensible is merely a matter of degree (in order to justify the move from the one to the other) to a position wherein the opposition is absolute (in order to refute the Kantian claim that we can have no knowledge of the non-sensible).

Kant regards this whole ploy as an attempt by Eberhard to appear to meet the demand of the *Critique* and thus to demonstrate the objective reality of the concept of the simple. Hence, although this concept refers to beings as objects of pure reason, Eberhard, according to Kant, seeks the reference of this concept in the elements of sensible objects. By so doing he hopes to be able to ascend from the sensible to its non-sensible grounds. However, this project fails because, in order to even get started, it must view in purely quantitative terms the opposition between the sensible and the non-sensible and their respective modes of intuition through which they are presented. On this line of thought, which was no doubt inspired by Leibniz's doctrine of small perceptions in the *New Essays*, the non-sensible is construed as that which can no longer be perceived because it is too small or too obscure, or no longer imagined because it is too complex. It is in this sense that Eberhard was able to regard the elements of space and time as non-sensible.

This obviously contradicts the critical, positive conception of sensibility, but Kant proceeds further and shows that it also contradicts common sense. Kant's basic argument is simply an appeal to the absurdity of the view that "the totality of an empirical intuition lies within the sphere of sensibility, but the simple elements of the same intuition lie completely outside this sphere" (203). In response to this, Kant points out: "The fact that there is no *image* of a simple part although it is itself a part of an image, i.e., of a sensible intuition, can not serve to raise it to the level of the super-sensible" (205). To cite Kant's own illustration, Newton's lamellae do not cease being sensible because we have no image or perception of them, and in the classic example of Eberhard's confusion, a chiliagon is not non-sensible simply because we can form no image thereof.

The argument thus once again turns on Eberhard's identification of the sensible with the imageable. This identification is clear in the example of the chiliagon, which is on Eberhardian grounds non-sensible because we cannot form an image of it, and it underlies his whole attempt to move from the sensible to its non-sensible ground. Kant's arguments are, in effect, addressed to this identification from the standpoint of his own conception of sensibility. He does not, however, put the manner in quite this way. Instead, the emphasis is placed on Eberhard's deliberate obfuscation, on his tendency to play with words, a charge which on this occasion at least does not seem to be justified.

There is, however, a sense in which it could be, and indeed was claimed by Eberhard in his subsequent contributions to the debate, that Kant himself was guilty of misrepresenting his position.[82] This misrepresentation concerns Kant's view that by the simple elements of sensible intuitions Eberhard meant parts rather than grounds. Kant not only attacks this view as absurd, but also accuses Eberhard of completely misunderstanding Leibniz on this point. Nevertheless, this leaves untouched the main force of Kant's critique. For although Eberhard does distinguish between parts and grounds, and does regard the non-sensible simple elements as grounds rather than parts of sensible intuitions, he also contends that we can gain a knowledge of these grounds from the intuitions by means of the principle of sufficient reason. Against this, the critical response is that, to be sure, space and time have "objective grounds," and that "if reason thinks a composite of substances as thing in itself (without relating it to the particular nature of our senses), it must by all means conceive it as composed of simple substances."[83] The point to be emphasized, however, is that this simple is to be met with in idea only, and thus:

The representation of an object as simple is a merely negative concept which reason cannot avoid, because it alone contains the unconditioned for every composite (as a thing, not as mere form), the possibility of which is always conditioned. This concept does not, therefore, serve to extend our knowledge, but merely characterizes a something in so far as it should be distinguished from objects of the senses (which all contain a composite). (209)

[82] *Philosophisches Magazin* III: 167, 170 ff., 420 ff.

[83] In his *Vorarbeiten* to the attack on Eberhard, Kant writes: "The proposition that a composite of things in themselves consists of simple parts is an analytic proposition." AK XX: 365.

Finally, Kant points out that not only is the ascent to the super-sensible which Eberhard attempts a total failure, only giving the appearance of success because of his equivocation with the notion of the non-sensible, but also that the ascent which Eberhard actually makes under this guise is merely logical. By this is meant that it does not lead to any genuinely new content, but simply moves from particulars given in sense experience to abstract concepts based on these particulars. Especially important in this regard is Eberhard's claim which Kant quotes: "We cannot have any general concepts which we have not abstracted from the things which we perceive through the senses or from those of which we are conscious in our own soul." Thus, even the categories or the most general ontological concepts are, on this view, ultimately derived through abstraction from sensible experience. But if this be the case, as Kant had already shown in the Inaugural Dissertation in terms of the distinction between the real and the logical use of the intellect, then despite their abstractness, these concepts must still be regarded as of sensible origin. Kant's point is simply that, just as Newton's lamellae do not cease being sensible objects, belonging to a possible experience, because they are invisible, so too general concepts, derived from experience by abstraction, do not lose their sensible status and become possible vehicles for the knowledge of non-sensible objects or noumena. Moreover, not only cannot such concepts yield knowledge of non-sensible objects, but since they are of empirical origin, they cannot fulfill the constitutive role in experience which Kant grants to pure concepts.

The outcome of this analysis is that Leibnizian rationalism, as practiced by Eberhard, is no more capable than Lockean empiricism of either establishing metaphysical principles yielding knowledge of noumena or of explaining the possibility of an empirical science of nature. In Kantian terms, this is equivalent to the claim that neither can explain the possibility of synthetic judgments a priori. What is especially interesting and clearly implied although not explicitly developed by Kant, however, is the suggestion that they cannot do so for essentially the same reason, and in fact that the rationalism and empiricism which are juxtaposed in Leibniz's *New Essays* are essentially two sides of the same coin. This sounds somewhat paradoxical, as it would appear that the Leibnizian "intellectualization of appearances" is dramatically opposed to the Lockean "sensualization of the pure concepts of the understanding." In the last analysis, however, this process of intellectualization or clarification of what is first presented obscurely through the senses can never, precisely because it is merely a clarification, get beyond the original sensible content. It can thus itself be viewed as a form of sensualization, albeit one which regards the sensible content as an obscure version of what is clearly and distinctly grasped by the divine intellect. Moreover, from the Kantian standpoint, both species of sensualization can be seen as consequences of an erroneous conception of sensibility. Not acknowledging that sensibility has an a priori form, and thus not recognizing the possibility of pure or a priori intuitions through which pure concepts can alone receive any meaning, neither rationalism nor empiricism can account for the possibility of pure concepts. Denying the possibility of a transcendental aesthetic, they at the same time both deny the possibility of a transcendental logic. In reference to Eberhard, it can perhaps be said that his fundamental error lay in his mistaken attempt to establish and extend the latter without acknowledging the possibility of the former.

Finally, we must at least briefly consider Kant's response to Eberhard's charge of a lack of originality. This charge, which seems to have particularly irked Kant, was directed to the critical philosophy as a whole, which is only held to be true insofar as it agrees with the Leibnizian, and to the distinction between analytic and synthetic judgments in particular. In regard to the latter, Eberhard had claimed that the distinction had long been recognized, albeit under different names, by the whole Leibnizian tradition, as well as by philosophers such as Locke, Reusch, and Crusius. Kant responds to this by pointing out that none of the above-mentioned thinkers really construed the distinction in the critical sense (the emphasis once again being placed on the fact that the distinction is to be taken in a transcendental and not merely logical manner). This is further supported by the claim that, if the above-mentioned thinkers had in fact grasped the true nature of this distinction, they would have been inevitably led to that revolution in metaphysics which was first inaugurated by the *Critique of Pure Reason*. But since this obviously did not occur, it follows that they did not really anticipate the *Critique* in regard to this distinction.[84]

The bulk of Eberhard's efforts in this direction, however, was devoted to the establishment of the originality and genuinely critical nature of the Leibnizian philosophy. This, as we have seen, was accomplished by means of innumerable, point-by-point comparisons of the doctrine of the two thinkers, with the Leibnizian doctrine being in each case either identical to the Kantian doctrine (and therefore original) or superior to it. Kant responds to this with a few remarks on the philosophy of Leibniz which really serve as an appendix to the text of *On a Discovery*. This half tongue-in-cheek, half serious response is epitomized by the claim that "the *Critique of Pure Reason* can thus be seen as the genuine apology for Leibniz" (250).

---

[84] In his *Vorarbeiten*, Kant acknowledges that with his two principles (contradiction and sufficient reason), Leibniz "had probably hit upon the distinction between analytic and synthetic judgments", *ibid.*, 376.

This is argued by means of a brief consideration of three of the basic tenets of the Leibnizian philosophy: the principle of sufficient reason, the doctrine of monads, and the pre-established harmony. A fourth basic tenet (at least according to the "Amphiboly of Concepts of Reflection"), the doctrine of the identity of indiscernibles, is omitted presumably because it is not mentioned by Eberhard. The reader can view Kant's treatment for himself, and it is not necessary to discuss it here in any detail. Suffice it to point out that, in at least the first and third case (the principle of sufficient reason and the pre-established harmony), Kant interprets these doctrines in a manner which does obvious violence not only to the Leibnizian texts but also to his other presentations and analyses of Leibnizian doctrines. The analysis of the doctrine of monads, however, constitutes somewhat of an exception to this rule. Here Kant points out that Leibnizian monads are not to be construed as parts of sensible bodies (a view which he attributes to Eberhard), nor as having any role in the explanation of phenomena, but as ideas of reason, pertaining only to the intellectual world. In regard to the first point at least, such an interpretation is quite feasible, and in fact was generally adopted by those who endeavored to distinguish sharply between the Leibnizian and the Wolffian position.[85] Moreover, Kant himself contrues the monadology in precisely the same manner in the *Metaphysical Foundations of Natural Science* (1786).[86]

Perhaps the most interesting aspect of this whole discussion, however, is Kant's interpretation of the pre-established harmony. This is construed as a harmony between the faculties of sensibility and understanding rather than between two distinct and totally independent beings. Moreover, this doctrine, thus construed, is brought into connection with the conception of teleology which Kant articulated in the *Critique of Judgment*. In all this Kant is obviously not giving a historically accurate account of the Leibnizian doctrine, but it is also obvious that this is not his intent. Rather, his concern is to underline the originality and revolutionary significance of the critical philosophy, while at the same time paying his respects to Leibniz as a thinker who, to be sure, did not really anticipate this revolution, but who nevertheless can be reinterpreted in its light in a fruitful way. By so doing he is applying to Leibniz precisely the same principle which he applied in the *Critique* to Plato, viz., that in the case of a past philosopher, it is often possible "to find that we understand him better than he has understood himself."[87]

---

[85] Cf. Hans Vaihinger, *Commentar zur Kant's Kritik der reinen Vernunft* (Stuttgart, Berlin, Leipzig, 1892), I:150-51.

[86] AK IV: 248; English translation by E. B. Bax, *Kant's Prolegomena and Metaphysical Foundations of Natural Science* (London, 1883), pp. 177-78.

[87] *Critique of Pure Reason*, A314/B370.

Conclusion

In casting a final retrospective glance over the Kant-Eberhard controversy, we note several items of iterest. First of all, from the latter's side, including the contributions of Maaß, we find an early statement of what have become classical objections to Kant's doctrine. These include attacks on the fixedness of the analytic-synthetic distinction, the necessity of intuition and construction in mathematical demonstration, the unknowability of things in themselves, the claim that space and time refer only to appearances, and the very conception of an a priori intuition. These objections are found together with some equally classical misinterpretations. These concern Kant's conception of intuition in general and pure intuition in particular, the notion of transcendental as distinguished from empirical ideality, and his understanding of the nature and significance of the analytic-synthetic distinction. Kant accuses Eberhard of deliberate obfuscation and misinterpretation on all of these points. In regard to the latter, however, we have seen that Kant's accusations are really not justified, and that some, although not all, of the fault must be placed on Kant for his somewhat misleading initial formulations.

When we turn to the Kantian response in *On a Discovery*, we find that its main philosophical significance lies in its discussion of the analytic-synthetic distinction. The starting point of this discussion, as we have seen, was the emphasis placed on the transcendental rather than the merely logical nature of this distinction. The first fruit of this corrective, which is articulated although clearly not sufficiently emphasized in both the *Critique* and the *Prolegomena*, is the recognition of the close kinship between, and, indeed, ultimate identity of the "critical problem" of the possibility of synthetic judgments a priori, and the allegedly "pre-critical problem" of explaining the possibility of the objective reality of pure or non-empirical concepts. Synthetic judgments, on this view, affirm such reality, while analytic judgments only affirm what is "contained in" or implied by a given concept. But the objective reality of a concept can, according to Kant, only be established by relating that concept to an intuition, and with pure concepts to pure intuitions. Thus, since synthetic judgments assert the objective reality of concepts, we were led to endorse Gram's thesis that in synthetic judgments concepts are predicated of intuitions, and in synthetic judgments a priori pure concepts of pure intuitions (with in both cases intuitions assuming a semantic function as part of the content of the judgments). Finally, we also saw that, on this line of interpretation, determinate (intuition-related) concepts are the products rather than the starting points of synthetic judgments, and that such judgments can therefore be viewed as acts of concept formation. The Kantian notion of syntheticity was thus seen to be intimately related to his theory of empirical concept formation, and this in turn provided a clue for the interpretation of the "Metaphysical Deduction."

The second main theme was the Kantian conception of intuition and sensibility. The importance of this theme arose as a natural consequence of the role given to intuitions in synthetic judgments. This was developed largely by way of a comparison of the Kantian and Leibnizian views. We saw there that the distinctive feature of the critical position—and this applies likewise to its relation to British empiricism—is the positive, constitutive function which it grants to sensibility. This function was further seen to provide the key to the understanding of Kant's doctrine of pure intuition, with such intuitions being equated with schemata.

In arguing for the above interpretation of the Kantian doctrines, we have moved continuously from *On a Discovery* to the *Critique of Pure Reason*, as well as other texts, and back again. This approach presupposes that the former work makes no major departures from the teachings of the *Critique*, and this is precisely what one would expect in a polemical writing designed to clarify and defend the doctrines of a previous work. To say this, however, is not to minimize its importance; for this importance lies primarily in its usefulness as a tool for the clarification and evaluation of the most important and hotly contested doctrines of the critical philosophy, as well as of the Kantian response to many of the objections which are often raised against these doctrines. Not only does *On a Discovery* cast a good deal of light on many of these doctrines taken singly but, more importantly, it clarifies some of the intrinsic connections between them. Moreover, it is largely able to do this because it reveals to us a Kant who is endeavoring to define and defend his position vis-à-vis Leibnizian rationalism. This was, of course, always a main concern of Kant, but one which has unfortunately been greatly neglected by Anglo-American interpreters and critics, who generally tend to view the *Critique of Pure Reason* almost exclusively as an answer, more or less adequate as the case may be, to Hume's scepticism. To view it in this way, however, is to miss a good deal of its significance, and it is hoped that the present translation and analysis of this almost completely neglected essay will make this fact evident. If it succeeds in doing this, it will provide a much needed corrective to the extremely one-sided manner in which the *Critique* has generally been approached in Anglo-American philosophy, and will therefore enable contemporary philosophers to view some of its distinctive doctrines in a fresh and more fruitful light.

Part Two

KANT'S *ON A DISCOVERY*

As he claims in his *Philosophisches Magazin* (vol. I, p. 289), Mr. Eberhard made the discovery that "the Leibnizian philosophy contains just as much of a critique of reason as the new philosophy, while at the same time still introducing a dogmatism based on a precise analysis of the faculties of knowledge. It therefore contains all that is true in the new philosophy, and in addition a well grounded extension of the sphere of the understanding." He does not, to be sure, explain why these things were not long ago recognized in the philosophy of the great man and in its daughter, the Wolffian. Yet how many discoveries regarded as new are not now clearly seen in the ancients by clever interpreters, once they have been shown what they should look for!

We could accept the denial of originality, were it not for the fact that the older critique contains in its results the exact opposite of the new one. If this were not so, the *argumentum ad verecundiam* (as Locke named it),[1] which Mr. Eberhard, fearing that his own might not suffice, craftily uses (sometimes, as on p. 298, with distortion of words), would be a great obstacle to the acceptance of the new critique. Yet it is a dubious enterprise to refute propositions of pure reason by means of books, which themselves can be based on no other source than that to which we are just as near as their author. Thus, as perspicacious as Mr. Eberhard generally is, he has perhaps not seen clearly this time. Moreover, he sometimes speaks as if he will not vouch for Leibniz (e.g., pp.381–93). It therefore seems best to leave the great man out of the picture and to consider the propositions which Mr. Eberhard offers in his name and uses as weapons against the *Critique* as his own assertions. Otherwise we would find ourselves in the nasty situation wherein the blows which he administers to us in Leibniz's name strike us, but we, in justifiably returning them, hit a great man, thereby drawing upon ourselves the hate of those who admire him.

[1] John Locke, *An Essay Concerning Human Understanding*, bk. IV, chap. XVII, sec. 19.

188   According to the example of the jurists in the conduct of a trial, the first item which we have to consider in this quarrel is the form. Mr. Eberhard explains his position concerning this in the following way (p. 255): "According to the arrangement of the journal we can break off or continue our journies as we choose, *we can proceed forwards or backwards and turn in all directions.*"—Now, one can readily accept the fact that a magazine can contain entirely different things in its different sections and issues. (Thus, in this one, a treatise on *logical truth* is followed immediately by a contribution to the history of *beards*, and this by a *poem*.) But Mr. Eberhard can hardly justify the mixing together of such unequal matters in one and the same section, or the turning of everything upside down, by means of this characteristic of a magazine (which would then become a mere garbage bin), especially if, as is here the case, his concern is with the comparison of two philosophical systems. Moreover, this is, in fact, far from the way in which he judges the matter.

This allegedly artless combination of themes is actually very carefully contrived. Its purpose is to entice the reader into accepting in advance, before he has acquired a touchstone of truth, propositions which require a close examination. It then demonstrates the validity of the touchstone, which is only selected afterwards, not, as it should be, on the basis of its intrinsic nature, but by means of those very propositions which the touchstone should test. This is an ingenious *hysteron proteron*, designed to gracefully avoid the long and difficult search for the elements of our a priori knowledge and the ground of their validity in respect to objects prior to all experience, therefore the deduction of their objective reality. It thus endeavors, where possible, to refute the *Critique* with a stroke of the pen, while at the same time making room for an unlimited dogmatism of pure reason. For as is known, the criticism of the pure understanding begins with this quest, which has as its goal the solution of the general question: how are synthetic propositions possible a priori? Moreover, it is only after a laborious examination of all of the conditions requisite for this that it can arrive at the

189   crucial conclusion, viz., that the objective reality of a concept can only be secured if it can be presented in a corresponding intuition (which for us is always sensible), and thus, that there is no knowledge which transcends the limits of sensibility, and consequently, of possible experience, i.e., no concepts of which one can be sure that they are not empty.—The magazine begins with the refutation of this proposition through the demonstration of its opposite, namely, that there is in fact an extension of knowledge beyond objects of the senses, and ends with the investigation of how this is possible a priori through synthetic propositions.

Actually, Mr. Eberhard offers us in the first volume of his *Philosoph-isches Magazin* a play in two acts. In the first the objective reality of our conceptions of the non-sensible is to be established, in the second the problem of how synthetic propositions are possible a priori is to be solved. As for the principle of sufficient reason, which he first ex-pounds (pp. 163–66), his purpose there is to establish the reality of the concept of reason (*Grund*) in this synthetic principle. According to the express words of the author (p. 316), however, it also pertains to the section about synthetic and analytic judgments, where something is for the first time to be established concerning the possibility of synthetic principles. All of the remainder, which either precedes this section or now and then interrupts it, consists of allusions to future proofs, ap-peals to earlier proofs, citations from Leibniz and other assertions, as well as attacks on expressions, usually with distortion of their sense, and similar matters. In all this he follows the advice which Quintilian gave to the orator in order to deceive the public in regard to an argu-ment of his which only deserved to be taken into consideration as a supplement: *Si non possunt valere quia magna sunt, valebunt quia multa sunt—Singula levia sunt et communia, universa tamen nocent; etiamsi non ut fulmine, tamen ut grandine.* [2] It is bad enough to have to do with an author who knows no order, but it is even worse to deal with one who affects disorder in order to allow superficial or false propositions to slip through unnoticed.

SECTION ONE

*Concerning the objective reality of those concepts
to which no corresponding sensible intuition
can be given, according to Mr. Eberhard*

190

Mr. Eberhard devotes himself (pp. 157-58) to this undertaking with a solemnity appropriate to the importance of the subject. He tells us of his long, unprejudiced efforts for the sake of a science (metaphysics), which he regards as a realm from which, if it were necessary, a consider-able portion could be abandoned, and yet an even more considerable area would remain. He speaks of flowers and fruits promised by the *uncontested*, fertile fields of ontology,* and even in regard to the con-

*But these are precisely the fields whose concepts and principles, as claims to knowl-edge of things in general, have been challenged, and have been limited to the much narrower field of objects of possible experience. This endeavor to dismiss out of hand the question concerning the *titulum possessionis* reveals here a manoeuver intended to deceive the judge about the actual point of the dispute.

[2] *Quintilian, Institutio Oratoria*, bk. V, chap. XII, l. 522. "If these arguments have no individual force because of strength, they will acquire it in virtue of their number.... Taken singly these arguments are trivial and commonplace, but their cumulative force is damaging."

tested fields of cosmology, he exhorts us not to stop working. This, he says, is because "We can always continue to work for its expansion, we can always seek to enrich it with new truths, *without having to first concern ourselves with the transcendental validity of these truths*" (which is here equivalent to the objective reality of its [cosmology's] concepts), and he adds: "*In this way have the mathematicians them-selves completed the delineation of entire sciences without saying a single word about the reality of their object.*" Moreover, desiring that the reader should be fully attentive to this point, he says: "This may be illustrated by a notable example, by an *example* that is too pertinent and *instructive* not to be allowed to be cited here." Yes, quite perti-nent; for never has a more excellent example been given as a warning *191* that one should not prove one's case by referring to sciences which one does not understand, not even to the pronouncements of other famous men, who are simply giving a report; for it is to be expected that one will not understand them either. Mr. Eberhard could not have more forcefully refuted himself and his announced project than through the judgment attributed to Borelli concerning the conics of Apollonius.[3]

Apollonius first constructs the concept of a cone, i.e., he exhibits it a priori in intuition (this is the first operation by means of which the geometer presents in advance the objective reality of his concept). He cuts it according to a certain rule, e.g., parallel with a side of the triangle which cuts the base of the cone (*conus rectus*) at right angles by its summit, and establishes a priori in intuition the attributes of the curved line produced by this cut on the surface of the cone. Thus, he extracts a concept of the relation in which its ordinates stand to the parameter, which concept, in this case, the parabola, is thereby given a priori in intuition. Consequently, the objective reality of this concept, i.e., the possibility of the existence of a thing with these properties, can be proven in no other way *than by providing the corresponding intui-tion.* Mr. Eberhard wanted to prove that one could extend his knowl-edge, and enrich it with new truths, without first considering whether one is proceeding with an entirely empty concept, one which can have no object (an assertion which is in plain contradiction with common sense), and he turned to the mathematicians to confirm his opinion. He could not, however, have hit upon a more unfortunate source. The misfortune stems from the fact that he was not acquainted with Apol-lonius himself and did not understand Borelli, who reflected on the

---

They may not have the overwhelming force of a thunderbolt, but they will have all the destructive force of hail." Kant's rendering differs in minor ways from the Latin text, suggesting that he was perhaps quoting from memory.

[3]J. A. Borelli (1608–79), Italian physician, physicist, and mathematician; he edited books V-VII of the *Conica* of Apollonius.

procedure of the ancient geometers. The latter speaks of the mechanical construction of concepts of conic sections (with the exception of the circle), and notes that mathematicians teach the properties of the conic sections without mentioning the mechanical construction. Now this is certainly a true, albeit a very insignificant remark; for instructions for drawing a parabola according to the prescription of the theory are of
192 interest only to the artist, not to the geometer.* Mr. Eberhard could have learned this from the passage from the remarks of Borelli which he himself cites and even has underscored. It says there: *Subjectum enim definitum assumi potest, ut affectionis variae de eo demonstrentur, licet praemissa non sit ars subjectum ipsum efformandum delineandi.*[4] It would, however, be grossly absurd to construe this as claiming that the geometer only expects to first prove the possibility of such a line, and consequently, the objective reality of his concept, from this mechanical construction. One could rather address to the modern geometers a reproach of the following nature: not that they derive the properties of a curved line from its definition without first being assured of the possibility of its object (for they are fully conscious of this together with the pure, merely schematic construction, and they also bring in mechanical construction afterwards if it is necessary), but that they arbitrarily think for themselves such a line (e.g., the parabola through the formula $ax=y^2$), and do not, according to the example of the ancient geometers, first bring it forth as given in the conic section. This would be more in accordance with the elegance of geometry, an elegance in the name of which we are often advised not to completely forsake the synthetic method of the ancients for the analytic method which is so rich in inventions.

*The following may serve to secure against misuse the expression "construction of concepts" of which the *Critique of Pure Reason* speaks several times, and by means of which it for the first time has carefully distinguished between the procedure of reason in mathematics and philosophy. In the most general sense one can call construction all exhibition of a concept through the (spontaneous) production of a corresponding intuition. If it occurs through the mere imagination in accordance with an a priori concept, it is called pure construction. (These are the constructions which the mathematician must make use of in all his demonstrations.) Hence, he can demonstrate by means of a circle which he draws with his stick in the sand, no matter how irregular it may turn out to be, the attributes of a circle in general, as perfectly as if it had been etched on a copper plate by the greatest artist. If, however, it is practised on some kind of material it could be called empirical construction. The first can also be called *schematic*, the second *technical*. The latter, and really improperly named, construction (because it belongs not to science but to art and takes place by means of instruments) is either the *geometrical*, by means of compass and ruler, or the *mechanical*, for which other instruments are necessary as, for example, the drawing of the other conic sections besides the circle.

---

[4] From Borelli's *Admonitio* to his edition of Apollonius, sec. XXII (reference cited by Eberhard, *Philosophisches Magazin* I: 159): "For one may assume the subject as defined, so that the variety of its affections may be shown, even if the manner of describing the formation of the subject has not been pre-supposed."

Mr. Eberhard therefore sets to work, not according to the example of a mathematician, but rather in the manner of the ingenious man who is capable of weaving a cord out of grains of sand.

193 He had already in the first issue of his magazine distinguished the principles of the *form* of knowledge, i.e., contradiction and sufficient reason, from the principles of the *matter* of knowledge (according to him, representation and extension). These he locates in the simple elements of which this matter is composed. Now, since no one contests the transcendental validity of the principle of contradiction, he seeks first to establish that of the *principle of sufficient reason,* and therewith the objective reality of the latter concept, secondly, the reality of the concept of simple being, without, as the *Critique* demands, requiring them to be verified through a corresponding intuition. For of what is true, it is not first necessary to ask if it is possible. So far logic has the principle *ab esse ad posse valet consequentia*[5] in common with metaphysics, or rather lends it to it.—In accordance with this division we wish now to proceed to our examination.

A. Demonstration of the objective reality
of the concept of sufficient reason
according to Mr. Eberhard

It is first of all worthy of note that Mr. Eberhard wishes to have the principle of sufficient reason regarded as a merely formal principle of knowledge, yet he nevertheless views it (p. 160) as a question, suggested by the *Critique: "If it also has transcendental validity"* (is in general a transcendental principle). Now, either Mr. Eberhard must have no conception of the difference between a *logical* (formal) and a *transcendental* (material) principle of knowledge, or, as is more likely, this is one of his clever manoeuvers, designed to substitute for the question at issue another which no one asks.

That *every proposition must have a reason* is the logical (formal) principle of knowledge, which is subordinated to, and not set beside,
194 the principle of contradiction.* That *every thing must have its reason* is

---

*The *Critique* has noted the distinction between problematic and assertoric judgments. An assertoric judgment is a *proposition.* The logicians are wrong in defining a proposition as a judgment expressed in *words;* for we must also, in thought, use words in judgments which we do not regard as propositions. In the conditional proposition: *if a body is simple, then it is unalterable,* there are two judgments, neither of which is a proposition, but only the consequence of the latter (the *consequens*) from the former (*antecedens*) constitutes the proposition. The judgment: *some bodies are simple* may, indeed, be contradictory, it can still set forth in order to see what follows from it, if it is regarded as an assertion, i.e., a proposition. The assertoric judgment: *every body is*

---

[5] "The inference from what is actual to what is possible is valid."

the transcendental (material) principle, which no one has ever proven or will prove by means of the principle of contradiction (and in general from mere concepts without relation to sensible intuition). It is clear enough, and has been stated countless times in the *Critique*, that a transcendental principle must determine a priori something in regard to the object and its possibility. It therefore does not, like the logical principles which completely abstract from everything concerning the possibility of the object, merely concern itself with the formal conditions of judgment. Mr. Eberhard, however, wished (p. 163) to put through his principle under the formula: *all* has a reason, and since, as his own example shows, he desired to smuggle in the actually material principle of causality by means of the principle of contradiction, he uses the word "*all*," and is careful not to say "*every thing*." Otherwise it would become too obvious that it is not a formal and logical but a material and transcendental principle of knowledge, which none the less can have its place in logic (as can any principle [*Grundsatz*] which rests on the principle [*Satz*] of contradiction).

It is, however, not without careful consideration, and with a purpose which he would gladly conceal from the reader, that he insists upon demonstrating this transcendental principle on the basis of the principle of contradiction. He wishes to validate this concept of reason (and with it, unnoticed, the concept of causality) for all things in general, i.e., prove its objective reality without limiting it merely to objects of the senses, and thereby avoid the condition stipulated by the *Critique*, namely, the necessity of an intuition by means of which this reality is first demonstrable. Now it is clear that the principle of contradiction is a principle which is valid for all that we can possibly think, whether or not it is a sensible object with a corresponding intuition; for it is valid for thought in general, without regard to any object. Thus, whatever violates this principle is obviously nothing (not even a thought). If he therefore wanted to introduce the objective reality of the concept of reason (*Grunde*), without allowing himself to be bound by its limitation to objects of sensible intuition, he had to construe it as a principle which is valid for thought in general. He had, however, to so present it that although it is of merely logical significance, it nevertheless seems to include within itself the concept of a real ground and, consequently, causality. He has, however, accorded to the reader more naiveté than he has a right to presuppose, even in reference to the most mediocre judgment.

195

---

divisible, says more than the merely problematic (let it be thought that every body is divisible) and stands under the universal logical principle of propositions, namely, that each proposition must be *grounded* (not be a merely possible judgment). This follows from the principle of contradiction, because otherwise there would be no proposition.

But, as so frequently happens with strategems, Mr. Eberhard entangled himself in how own. Previously he had hung the whole of metaphysics on *two* hinges, viz., the principles of contradiction and sufficient reason. He persists in this assertion when he holds, following Leibniz (at least according to the way in which he interprets Leibniz), that for the purpose of metaphysics the first needs to be supplemented by the second. Now, however, he says (p. 163): "The universal truth of the principle of sufficient reason can only be *demonstrated* from this (the principle of contradiction)," which he then confidently sets to work doing. Now once again all of metaphysics hangs upon a *single* hinge, whereas previously there were supposed to have been two. For the mere consequence of a principle, taken in its entire universality and without the addition of at least a new condition of its application, is certainly not a new principle which removes the defects of the previous one.

Yet before Mr. Eberhard presents this demonstration of the principle of sufficient reason (with it actually the objective reality of the concept of cause, but without requiring anything more than the principle of contradiction), he raises the expectations of the reader by means of the pompous division of his work (pp. 161–62), and what is more, by a 196 further comparison, as unsuccessful as the first, of his method with that of the mathematicians. Euclid himself is supposed to "have amongst his axioms propositions which actually require a demonstration, but which nevertheless are presented without demonstration." Now, speaking of the mathematician, he adds: "As soon as one of his axioms is denied, all of the theorems which depend upon it fall also. This is, however, *such a rare occurrence*, that he does not believe it necessary to sacrifice the simple elegance of his *exposition* and the beautiful proportions of his system. Philosophy must be more obliging." There is therefore now a *licentia geometrica*, just as there has long been a *licentia poetica*. If only this philosophy, which is so obliging in providing demonstrations, would also be obliging enough to produce an example from Euclid where he presents a proposition which is mathematically demonstrable as an axiom; for what can be demonstrated merely philosophically (from concepts), e.g., the whole is greater than its parts, does not strictly speaking belong to mathematics.

Now follows the promised demonstration. It is well that it is not lengthy; for its cogency is all the more apparent. We therefore wish to state it in its entirety: "Either everything has a reason or not everything has a reason. In the latter case, something could be possible and conceivable, the reason for which is nothing.—If, however, one of two opposite things could be without a sufficient reason, so likewise could the other be without a sufficient reason. If, for example, a portion of air could move towards the east and thus the wind could blow towards the east, without the air in the east becoming warmer and more rarified, then this portion of air would be *just as able* to move to the west as to the east. The same air would therefore be able to move *at the same time* in two opposite directions, to the east and to the west, and consequently, to the east and not to the east, that is to say, it could *at the same time* be and not be, which is contradictory and impossible."

This demonstration, through which the philosopher should, in respect to thoroughness, be even more obliging than the mathematician, has all the attributes which a demonstration must have in order to serve in logic as an example of how a demonstration should not be conducted.—*First of all*, the proposition to be demonstrated is ambiguously 197 formulated. Since the word *all* can signify either *every judgment*, which we take as a proposition about something or other, or *every thing*, it can be construed as either a logical or a transcendental principle. If it is construed in the first sense (it must then read: *every proposition has its reason*), it is then not only universally true, but even follows immediately from the *principle of contradiction*. If, however, by *all* is understood *every thing*, then an entirely different mode of demonstration would be required.

Secondly, the demonstration lacks unity. It actually consists of two demonstrations. The first is the well known Baumgartian demonstration, to which no one any longer appeals. Except for the missing conclusion ("which is self-contradictory"), which each must add for himself, the demonstration is completed where I have drawn the line. This is followed immediately by another demonstration, which by means of the word *however* is made to appear as a mere continuation of the chain of reasoning leading to the conclusion of the first demonstration. It is only necessary, however, to omit the word *however* in order to obtain a self-sufficient demonstration. Now, something more is required to find a contradiction in the proposition that *there is something without a reason* than in the first demonstration which found it immediately in this proposition itself. Thus, in order to conjure up a contradiction, he must add to this the proposition that *the opposite of the thing would also be without a reason*. Consequently, the second demonstration is conducted entirely differently from the Baumgartian, of which it is still supposed to form a part.[6]

---

[6]Kant is referring to Baumgarten, *Metaphysica*, § 20. Eberhard later explicitly denies this (*Philosophisches Magazin* III: 188); claiming that although his demonstration begins in the same manner as Baumgarten's, he actually offers a unified and original proof. This is because according to Baumgarten's version, the denial of the principle of sufficient reason implies that nothing is representable, i.e. regarded as something, while his formulation turns on the fact that the denial of the principle entails that something could exist at the same time as its opposite.

Thirdly, the *new direction* which Mr. Eberhard sought to give to his demonstration is very unfortunate. The line of reasoning which he uses has four steps. It can be reduced to the following syllogism:

(1) A wind which moves without reason to the east could just as well (*instead of this*) move to the west.

(2) Now (as the opponent of the principle of sufficient reason asserts) the wind moves without reason to the east.

(3) Consequently, it can move *at the same time* to the east and west, which is self-contradictory.

It is clear that I am fully justified in inserting the phrase *instead of this* in the major premise; for without such a restriction no one could accept it. If someone wages a certain sum on a roll of the dice and wins, he who would dissuade him from playing could very well say that he could have just as well rolled a loser and thus lost a good deal; but only *instead* of a winner, not winner and loser in the same roll. Similarly, the artist who carves a god out of a piece of wood could (instead of this) just as well have made a bench out of it. From this, however, it does not follow that he could have made both *at the same time*.

Fourthly, the principle itself, taken in the unlimited universality in which it there stands, is, if applied to entities, obviously false; for according to this principle, there could be absolutely nothing unconditioned. To seek, however, to avoid this embarrassing consequence by saying of a supreme being that he has, indeed, a reason for his existence, but that it lies within himself, leads to a contradiction. The reason for the existence of a thing, construed as its real ground, must always be distinguished from the thing. The thing must, therefore, be necessarily regarded as dependent upon another. I can very well say of a proposition that it has the reason (the logical reason) of its truth in itself; for the concept of the subject is something other than that of the predicate, and hence can contain the reason thereof. But if I allow no other reason for the existence of a thing to be accepted except the thing itself, I really mean by this that it has no real reason.

Mr. Eberhard has thus completely failed to accomplish what he intended in regard to the concept of causality, namely, to establish the validity of this category, and supposedly with it that of the remaining categories, for things in general, without limiting their use and validity to the knowledge of things as objects of possible experience. Moreover, it is in vain that he makes use of the sovereign principle of contradiction for this purpose. The teaching of the *Critique* therefore stands firm. No categories can contain or bring forth the least knowledge if they cannot be given a corresponding intuition, which for us human beings is always sensible. Thus, their use (in regard to the theoretical knowledge of things) can never extend beyond the limits of possible experience.

B. Proof of the objective reality
of the concept of the simple
in regard to objects of experience
according to Mr. Eberhard

Mr. Eberhard had previously spoken of a concept of the understanding (causality) which, although it can be applied to objects of the
199 senses, is nevertheless not limited to such an application, but is valid of
things in general. He thus sought to prove the objective reality of at
least *one* category, namely, that of cause, independently of the conditions of intuition. Now (pp. 169–73) he goes a step further and wishes
to secure the objective reality of a concept of that which admittedly
cannot be an object of the senses, namely, that of a *simple being*. He
will thus open the way to his exalted fertile fields of rational psychology and theology, from which the Gorgon's head of the *Critique* endeavored to deter him. His proof (pp. 169–70) proceeds thusly:

"Concrete* time, or the time which we sense, (which is probably
200 supposed to mean: in which we sense something) is nothing other than
the succession of our representations; for even the succession in motion
may be explained in terms of the succession of representations. Concrete time is therefore something composite, its simple elements being
representations. Since all finite things are in a continual flux (how does
he know a priori that this applies to all finite things and not merely to
appearances?), these elements can never be sensed. Inner sense cannot
perceive them separately, but only together with something which pre-

---

*The expression *"abstract time"*, (p. 170) in contradistinction to *"concrete time"* is
entirely incorrect, and should never be accepted, especially when it is a question of the
greatest logical precision, even if this misuse is, in fact, authorized by the new logicians.
One does not abstract *a concept* as a common mark, rather one abstracts *in the use* of a
concept, from the diversity of that which is contained under it. Chemists alone are able
to abstract something in the proper sense, as when they remove a liquid from other
matter in order to isolate it. The philosopher abstracts from that which he, in a certain
use of the concept, does not wish to take into consideration. He who wishes to formulate rules for education can do so either in regard to the concept of a child *in abstracto*
or a child in civil society (*in concreto*), without distinguishing between abstract and
concrete children. The distinction between abstract and concrete refers only to the use
of concepts, not to the concepts themselves. The neglect of this scholastic distinction
often falsifies the judgment concerning an object. If I say: abstract time or space has this
or that property, it seems as if time and space were first given in the objects of the
senses, like the red of a rose or cinnabar, and are only logically derived therefrom by
abstraction. If I say, however, that in time and space considered *in abstracto*, i.e., apart
from all empirical conditions, this or that property is to be noted, I at least leave it open
whether this can be known independently of experience (*a priori*), which I am not free
to do if I regard time as a concept merely abstracted from experience. I can in the first
instance judge, or at least endeavor to judge, by means of a priori principles about pure,
in contradistinction to empirically determined time and space, by abstracting from
everything empirical. In the second case, however, I am prevented from doing this, if (as
is claimed) I have only abstracted the concept from experience (as in the above example
of the red color).—Thus, those who with their semblance of knowledge endeavor to
avoid a careful examination must make use of expressions which will hide their sub-
trefuge.

cedes and follows. Furthermore, since the flux of alterations of all finite things is a *continuous* (this word is underlined by him), unbroken flux, no sensible part of time is the smallest or a completely simple part. The simple elements of concrete time therefore lie *completely* outside the sphere of sensibility.—The understanding, however, raises itself beyond this sphere by discovering the *unimageable* (*unbildliche*) simple, without which the image of sensibility, even in respect to time, is not possible. It (the understanding) therefore recognizes first of all that something objective pertains to the image of time, viz., the indivisible elementary representations. Together with the subjective grounds, which lie in the limits of the finite mind, these give to sensibility the image of concrete time. It is because of these limits that representations cannot be simultaneous, and because of the very same limits that they cannot be distinguished in the image." On page 171, he turns to space. There he tells us: "The great similarity between the other form of intuition—space—and time saves us from the labor of repeating in its analysis all that it has in common with time.—The first elements of the composite with which space arises are, just as the elements of time, simple and beyond the field of sensibility. They are objects of reason (*Verstandeswesen*), unimageable under any sensible form. They are, nevertheless, true objects, all of which they have in common with the elements of time."

201 Mr. Eberhard has chosen his demonstrations, if not with great logical rigor, at least after due deliberation, and considering his purpose, with a certain adroitness. Thus, no matter how much he, for easily discernible reasons, endeavors to disguise his purpose, it is nevertheless not difficult, and for its proper evaluation not irrelevant, to bring this plan to light. He wishes to demonstrate the objective reality of the concept of simple beings as objects of pure reason (*reiner Verstandeswesen*), and he seeks this reality in the *elements* of a sensible object, a project which is ill considered and contrary to his purposes. He has, however, good reasons for this. If he had, as is commonly done, presented his demonstrations from mere concepts, arguing that the origin of the complex must necessarily be sought in the simple, one could readily accept this, but not without adding: this, indeed, holds of our ideas, if we think of things in themselves of which we cannot have the least knowledge; it in no way, however, applies to objects of the senses (appearances), which are for us the only knowable objects. Hence, the objective reality of the concept is by no means demonstrated. He is thus forced to seek these objects of reason in objects of the senses. How is this to be accomplished? He had to give, by means of a shift unnoticed by the reader, a new meaning to the concept of the non-sensible, a meaning which is not only different from the one found in the *Critique*, but also from ordi-

nary usage. Hence, he sometimes uses it to refer to that part of the sensible representation which is no longer consciously apprehended, but whose existence is still recognized by the understanding. Such would be the small particles of bodies, or even the determinations of our faculty of representation, which we cannot represent clearly in a state of separation. Sometimes (especially when it is important that these small parts be recognized precisely as simple) the non-sensible refers to the unimageable, of which no image is possible, and which cannot be represented in any sensible form (in an image) (p. 171).—If ever one could justifiably reproach an author for the deliberate falsification of a conception (not confusion, which is not always deliberate), it is in this case. The *Critique* always understands by the non-sensible only that which can not at all, not even in the least part, be contained in a sensible intuition. It is therefore a deliberate deception of the unsuspecting reader to deny that something is a sensible object because no 202 image (by which is understood an intuition containing a manifold in certain relations, therefore a form) can be given. Having deceived the reader in this not very subtle manner, he believes that he can show him (without his noticing the contradiction) that the genuinely simple, which the understanding conceives in things but which is never encountered save in the idea, is in the objects of the senses, and that in this manner the objective reality of the concept is exhibited in intuition.

Let us now examine this demonstration more closely. It is based on two assumptions. The first is that concrete time and space consist of simple elements. The second is that these elements are objects of reason, not of sense. These assumptions are both erroneous, the first because it contradicts mathematics, the second because it contradicts itself.

We can be quite brief in regard to the first of these errors. Although Mr. Eberhard (despite his frequent allusions to them) seems to have no special acquaintance with mathematicians, he could, nevertheless, easily comprehend the demonstration, given by Keil in his *introductio in veram physicam*, which proceeds by the simple division of a straight line by an infinity of others.[7] He could then see, on the basis of the geometrical principle that not more than one straight line can be drawn through two given points, that there can be no simple parts in such a line. This mode of proof can be varied in many ways, and can also yield the demonstration of the impossibility of simple parts of time, if one bases it on the movement of a point along a straight line.

Now one cannot attempt to escape this conclusion by claiming that concrete time and space are not subject to those conditions which

[7] J. Keill, *Introductio ad veram physicam, seu lectiones physicae*, 2nd ed. (London, 1705), sec. III.

mathematics establishes in regard to abstract space (and time) as an imaginary entity. Not only would it follow from this that physics must in many cases (e.g., in the laws of the fall of bodies) be concerned about falling into error when it is following exactly the apodictic doctrines of geometry, but it also can be apodictically demonstrated that each thing in space or each alteration in time can, as soon as it occupies a portion of space or time, be divided into as many things or alterations as the space or time which it occupies. In order to avoid this paradox, which is felt to arise here because reason, which requires the simple as 203 the foundation of all composites, contradicts what mathematics establishes in regard to sensible intuition, one can and must admit that space and time are merely conceptual entities (*Gedankendinge*) and beings of the imagination. This is not to say that they are invented by the latter, but rather that they underlie all of its combinations and inventions. This is because they are the essential forms of our sensibility and the receptivity of our intuitions, through which all objects are given to us. Moreover, since these universal conditions of sensibility are likewise a priori conditions of the possibility of all objects of the senses as appearances, these appearances must therefore accord with them. The simple, either in temporal succession or in space, is therefore absolutely impossible. Hence, if Leibniz at times expressed himself in such a manner that his doctrine of simple being can be interpreted as implying that matter is a composite thereof, it is none the less fairer to him, as long as it is reconcilable with his express teachings, to understand him to mean by the simple not a part of matter but the non-sensible, and to us fully unknown ground of the appearance which we name matter (which may be a simple being even if the matter which constitutes the appearance is composite). If we cannot interpret Leibniz in this manner, we must reject his claims. For he is not the first, nor will he be the last great man who must allow for the freedom of others in research.

The second error involves such an obvious contradiction that Mr. Eberhard must have noticed it. He did the best he could, however, to gloss over it and cover up so as to render it imperceptible. It is, in effect, the claim that the totality of an empirical intuition lies within the sphere of sensibility, but the simple elements of the same intuition lie completely outside this sphere. He thus does not wish to have the simple construed as the ground of the intuitions in space and time (in which case he would be too close to the *Critique*), but rather that it be found in the elementary representations of sensible intuition themselves (albeit without clear consciousness). Furthermore, he demands that the composite of these elements be regarded as a sensible being, but its parts as objects of reason and not objects of the senses. "The elements of concrete time (as well as of concrete space) do not lack this intuitive aspect," he says (p. 170), although he adds (p. 171): "They cannot be intuited under any sensible form."

204   What led Mr. Eberhard to such a strange and manifestly absurd confusion in the first place? He realized that, unless a concept can be given a corresponding intuition, its objective reality must remain completely undetermined. But he wished to secure the objective reality of certain rational concepts, here the concept of a simple being, and to do so in such a way that this does not become (as the *Critique* claims) a completely unknowable object. If it were, the intuition, whose possibility the non-sensible object was designed to explain, would have to be regarded as a mere appearance, and he will likewise not grant this to the *Critique*. He thus had to compose the sensible intuition out of non-sensible parts, which is an obvious contradiction.*

How does Mr. Eberhard extricate himself from this difficulty? He does so by means of a mere play with words which, because of its ambiguity, is supposed to delay us for a moment. A *non-sensible (nicht-empfindbarer)* part is completely outside the realm of sensibility. Non-sensible, however, is that which can never be sensed *separately*. This applies to the simple in things as well as our representations. The second word, which is intended to make an object of reason out of the parts of a sensible representation or its object is the *"unimageable"* simple. This expression seems to please him most, for he uses it frequently in the sequel. To be non-sensible and still to constitute a part of the sensible seems even to him to be too striking a contradiction to serve as a means for bringing the concept of the non-sensible (*Nicht-sinnlichen*) into sensible intuition.

A *non-sensible* part here means a part of an empirical intuition, i.e.,
205 a part of which one is not *conscious*. Mr. Eberhard, however, does not want to admit this; for if he had done so he would also have had to admit that for him sensibility means nothing more than a state of confused representations in a manifold of intuition. This in turn would have exposed him to a censure by the *Critique* which he wishes to avoid. If, on the other hand, the word *sensible (empfindbar)* is used in its proper sense, it is obvious that if no simple part of a sensible object is sensible, then neither can the whole of it be so, and conversely, if

---

*It must here be carefully noted that he now does not wish to have sensibility consist in the mere obscurity of our representations, but also in the fact that an object is given to the senses (p. 299), precisely as if he had thereby affected something to his advantage. He attributed (p. 170) the representation of time to sensibility, because due to the limitations of the finite mind, its simple parts cannot be distinguished. (The representation is therefore confused.) Later (p. 299) he wishes to make this concept somewhat narrower, so as to avoid the solid objections to this view. He therefore adds to it precisely that condition which is the most disadvantageous to him. This is because he desires to establish that simple being as an object of reason, and in this way he brings a contradiction into his own assertion.

something is an object of the senses (*Sinne*) and sensation (*Empfindung*), all of its simple parts must be so, even though they may lack clarity of representation. Thus, the obscurity of the partial representations of a whole, as a result of which only the understanding can determine their presence in this whole and in its intuition, does not raise them above the sphere of sensibility and convert them into objects of reason. Newton's *lamellae*,[8] of which the colored particles of bodies consist, have not yet been seen through a microscope. Nevertheless, the understanding not only recognizes (or supposes) their existence, but also that they really are represented in our empirical intuition, albeit without being consciously apprehended. Yet this is no basis for regarding them as non-sensible, and hence as objects of reason, and they have never been understood in this way by his followers. There is, however, no difference between such small parts and completely simple parts, save in degree of dimunition. If the whole is an object of the senses, all of its parts must necessarily be so likewise.

The fact that there is no *image* of a simple part, although it is itself a part of an image, i.e., of a sensible intuition, can not serve to raise it to the level of the super-sensible. Simple beings must certainly (as the *Critique* shows) be conceived as raised beyond the limits of sensibility, and no image, i.e., no intuition, can be given which corresponds to their concept. Then, however, they cannot be considered as parts of the sensible. If they are, nevertheless (against all the evidence of mathematics), still regarded in this manner, it does not follow from the fact that no image corresponds to them that their representation is something super-sensible. Such a part would then be a simple sensation, therefore an element of sensibility; and the understanding would no more raise itself beyond sensibility by conceiving it than if it had conceived it as composite. For the latter concept, of which the former is merely the negation, is just as much a concept of the understanding. He could only have transcended the realm of sensibility if he had completely removed the simple from the sensible intuition and its objects, and with the infinite divisibility of matter (as expressed by mathematics) opened up the vista of a microcosm. He could then infer a simple which lies completely beyond the field of sensible intuition, precisely on the basis of the inadequacy of any internal principle of explanation of the sensible composite (which lacks complete division because of the total lack of a simple). Such a simple would therefore not be a part of this composite, but its wholly unknown ground which we only encounter in the idea. In that case, however, Mr. Eberhard would be forced to confess what he has tried so hard to deny, viz., that we cannot have the least knowledge of this super-sensible simple.

[8] I. Newton, *Optics*, bk II, pt III.

Actually, in order to avoid acknowledging this, he introduces into his alleged demonstration a curious equivocation. The place where it says "The flux of the changes *of all finite things* is a continuous, unbroken flux—no sensible part is the smallest or completely simple" sounds as if it had been dictated by the mathematicians. At the same time, however, there are simple parts in the same changes which, since they are not sensible, can only be recognized by the understanding. But if they are in it, then the *lex continua* of the flux of changes is false; for they occur discontinuously, and the fact that they are not, as Mr. Eberhard falsely expresses himself, sensed, i.e., consciously perceived, does not change their specific nature as parts of a merely empirical, sensible intuition. Does, indeed, all this suggest that Mr. Eberhard has a determinate concept of continuity?

In a word: the *Critique* has asserted that the objective reality of a concept can never be established, unless a corresponding intuition can be given to it. Mr. Eberhard wished to prove the opposite, and he based his demonstration on something which is notoriously false, namely, that the understanding knows the simple in things as objects in space and time, a view which we will nevertheless concede to him. We do so because in that case he has, in his own way, fulfilled rather than refuted the demand of the *Critique*. This required nothing more than that 207 objective reality be demonstrated in intuition, but this means that a concept must be given a corresponding intuition, which is precisely what it (the *Critique*) claimed and he wished to refute.

I would not dwell so long on so clear an issue if it did not furnish incontestable proof of how completely Mr. Eberhard ignored the *Critique* in regard to the distinction between sensible and non-sensible objects, or, if he prefers, how he misconstrued it.

C. The method of ascending from the sensible to the non-sensible according to Mr. Eberhard

Mr. Eberhard draws the following conclusion from the above demonstrations, especially the latter (p. 262): "Thus, the truth that space and time have both subjective and objective grounds has been proven completely apodictically. It was established that their *ultimate objective grounds* are things in themselves." Now every reader of the *Critique* will admit that these are exactly my assertions. Mr. Eberhard has therefore, with his apodictic demonstrations (to what extent they really are such can be seen from the previous analysis), asserted nothing against the *Critique*. It was further my opinion that these objective grounds, namely, the things in themselves, are not to be sought in space and time, but in what the *Critique* calls their extra or super-sensible substrate (noumenon). Mr. Eberhard wished to demonstrate the opposite of this, but he never, not even here in the statement of his conclusion, succeeds in clearly explicating his position.

Thus, he writes (p. 258, no. 3 and 4): "Besides the subjective grounds, space and time also have *objective* grounds, and these objective grounds are not appearances, but true, knowable things"; (p. 259) their *ultimate* grounds are things in themselves, all of which the *Critique* likewise literally and repeatedly affirms.[9] How is it then that Mr. Eberhard, who is usually keen enough to see what is to his advantage, this time did not see what is to his disadvantage? We have to do with a clever man who does not see something because he does not wish it to be seen. He actually did not want the reader to see that his objective grounds, which are not appearances but things in themselves, are merely *parts* (simple) of appearances; for the ineptness of such a manner of explanation would be noticed immediately. He therefore makes use of the word *grounds* (*Gründe*), because parts are also grounds of the possibility of a composite. Thus, he can speak with the *Critique* of ultimate grounds which are not appearances. Had he, however, straightforwardly spoken of parts of appearances, which are nevertheless not themselves appearances, of something sensible, whose parts are non-sensible, the absurdity of his position (even if one accepts the presupposition of simple parts) would have been readily apparent. But the word *ground* masks all of this. Thus, the unwary reader believes himself to understand thereby something which is entirely different from these intuitions, as does the *Critique*. He is therefore persuaded that Mr. Eberhard has demonstrated a capacity for knowledge of the super-sensible by the understanding, even in objects of the senses.

The most important thing, especially in the evaluation of this deception, is that the reader keep in mind what we have said about the Eberhardian deduction of space and time, as well as of sensible knowledge in general. According to him, we have sensible knowledge and its object, appearance, only as long as the representation of the object contains parts which are not, as he expresses himself, *sensible*, i.e., cannot be perceived in intuition with consciousness. It immediately ceases being sensible, and its object is no longer recognized as appearance, but as thing in itself, in a word it is henceforth noumenon, as soon as the understanding comprehends and discovers the first *grounds* of the appearance, which according to him should be its own parts. There is therefore no other difference between a thing as phenomenon

[9] Eberhard responds to this (*Philosophisches Magazin* III: 214 f.) by pointing out that if the *Critique* really affirmed this, then it is in complete agreement with the Leibnizian philosophy, but that this obviously contradicts what is said in the *Critique*. The emphasis here obviously falls on the notion that these objective grounds are knowable, which contradicts the basic Kantian doctrine of the unkowability of things in themselves. Kant's position in the essay as a whole, however, makes it clear that this must be regarded as a slip of the pen.

and the representation of the noumenon which underlies it than between a group of men which I see at a great distance and the same men when I am so close that I can count the individuals. It is only, he asserts, that we *could never come so close to it*. This, however, makes no difference in the thing, but only in the degree of our power of perception, which thereby always remains the same in regard to its mode. If this were really the distinction—which the *Critique* drew with so much effort in its *Aesthetic*—between the knowledge of things as appearances and the conception of them according to what they are as things in themselves, then this distinction would have been merely
209 childish nonsense, and even an extensive refutation of it would deserve no better name. But the *Critique* shows (to cite only a single example from among many) that in the world of bodies, as the totality of all objects of outer sense, there are certainly composite things, but the simple is not to be found in it at all. At the same time, however, the *Critique* demonstrates that, if reason thinks a composite of substances as thing in itself (without relating it to the particular nature of our senses), it must by all means conceive it as composed of simple substances. Because of what is necessarily included in the intuition of objects in space, reason can and should not conceive any simple element *in these objects*. From this it follows that, even if our senses were infinitely sharpened, it would still remain completely impossible even to come nearer to the simple, much less to finally arrive at it, because it is not to be found in such objects. Therefore, no choice remains but to admit that bodies are not things in themselves at all, and that their sensible representation, which we call corporeal things, is nothing but the appearance of something, which as thing in itself can alone contain the simple,* but which for us remains entirely unknowable. This is because the intuition, under which it can alone be given to us, does not provide us with the properties which pertain to it as it is in itself, but

---

*The representation of an object as simple is a merely negative concept which reason cannot avoid, because it alone contains the unconditioned for every composite (as a thing, not as mere form), the possibility of which is always conditioned. This concept does not, therefore, serve to extend our knowledge, but merely characterizes a something in so far as it should be distinguished from objects of the senses (which all contain a composite). If I now say: that which underlies the possibility of the composite, which therefore can alone be conceived as not composite, is the noumenon (which is not to be found in the sensible), I am not saying thereby: an aggregate of *so many simple beings*, as pure objects of reason, underlies body as appearance. Rather, I am saying that we cannot have the least knowledge of whether the super-sensible which grounds each appearance as substrate is, as thing in itself, either composite or simple. Further, it is a complete misunderstanding of the theory of sensible objects as mere appearances, to which something non-sensible must be attached, if one imagines or seeks others to imagine that what is meant thereby is that the super-sensible substrate of matter will be divided according to its monads, just as I divide matter itself. For then the *monas* (which is only the *idea* of a not further conditioned condition of the composite) would be placed in space, where it ceases to be a noumenon, and becomes again itself composite.

210 only the subjective conditions of our sensibility under which we can alone receive an intuitive representation of it.—Thus, according to the *Critique*, everything in an appearance is itself still appearance, however far the understanding may continue to divide it into its parts and demonstrate the existence of parts which the senses are no longer capable of clearly perceiving. According to Mr. Eberhard, however, they then immediately cease being appearances and become the things themselves (*die Sache selbst*).

Now it may perhaps seem unbelievable to the reader that Mr. Eberhard willfully perpetrated such an obvious misrepresentation of the conception of the sensible given by the *Critique* which he endeavored to refute, or even that he should have installed such an insipid and metaphysically useless distinction between objects of sense and objects of reason as one concerning the mere logical form of the mode of representation. Therefore, we wish to let him speak for himself.

After expending much unnecessary labor proving what no one ever doubted, and being, in passing, quite naturally astonished that critical idealism could have overlooked it, viz., that the objective reality of a concept, which in regard to particulars can only be demonstrated of objects of experience, is nevertheless certainly also demonstrable universally, i.e., of things in general, and that such a concept is not without any objective reality (although the conclusion is false that this reality can thereby also be demonstrated for concepts of things which cannot be objects of experience), he continues (pp. 271–72): "I must here make use of an example, the appropriateness of which will only become apparent later. The senses and imagination of man *in his present condition* are not capable of forming an exact image of a thousand-sided polygon, i.e., an image whereby it could, for example, be distinguished from one with nine hundred and ninety-nine sides. Nevertheless, as soon as I know that a figure has a thousand sides, my understanding can ascribe different predicates to it, etc. How then can it be proven that the understanding can neither affirm nor deny anything at all concern-
211 ing a *thing in itself* on the grounds that the imagination can form no image of it, or because we do not know all of the determinations which pertain to its individuality?" Subsequently (pp. 291–92), he explains himself thusly, concerning the distinction which the *Critique* makes between the logical and transcendental significance of sensibility: "The objects of understanding are *unimageable*, those of sensibility, on the other hand, are *imageable*," and he now cites from Leibniz* the exam-

---

*The reader will do well not to immediately ascribe to Leibniz all that Mr. Eberhard infers from his teachings. Leibniz wanted to refute the empiricism of Locke. For this purpose examples taken from mathematics were quite well suited to prove that such cognitions reach much further than our empirically acquired concepts could, and there-

ple of eternity, of which we can form no image, but of which we still have an intellectual conception (*Verstandesidee*). At the same time, however, he again refers to the example of the chiliagon, of which he says: "The senses and the imagination of man *in his present condition* can form no exact image whereby it can be distinguished from a polygon with nine hundred and ninety-nine sides."

One could not ask for a clearer proof than Mr. Eberhard here gives of a—I will not say deliberate—misrepresentation of the *Critique*, for it is far from being sufficiently plausible to succeed in that regard, but of a complete ignorance of the question at issue. A pentagon is, according to him, still an object of sense, but a chiliagon is already merely an object of reason, something non-sensible (or, as he terms it, *unimageable*). I suppose that a nonagon would already be more than half way from the sensible to the super-sensible; for if one does not count the sides with one's fingers, one can hardly determine the number by a mere glance. The question was whether we can hope to acquire a knowledge of that to which no corresponding intuition can be given. This was denied by the *Critique* in regard to whatever cannot be an object of the senses; because for the objective reality of a concept, we always stand in need 212 of an intuition, which for us, however, is always sensible, even that which is given in mathematics. Mr. Eberhard, on the other hand, *answers the question in the affirmative*, and cites, unfortunately, the mathematician, who always demonstrates everything in intuition, as if he could perfectly well attribute various predicates to the object of his concept through the understanding, without giving to his concept an exactly corresponding intuition in the imagination, and therefore gain knowledge of the object independently of that condition. Now, if Archimedes circumscribed a *polygon of ninety-six sides* around a circle, and inscribed another such figure in the circle, in order to determine how much smaller the circle is than the first and greater than the second, did he or did he not submit his concept of the above-mentioned regular polygon to an intuition? He necessarily did so, not that he actually drew it (which would be an unnecessary and absurd demand), but rather that he knew the rule for the construction of his concept, and therefore his ability to determine the magnitude of that figure as closely to that of the object itself as he wished, and consequently, to demonstrate the reality of the rule itself, and with it of this concept for the use of the imagination. If someone had asked him to find out how a

by to defend the a priori origin of the mathematical cognitions against Locke's attack. But it could not occur to him at all to affirm that the objects thereby cease being merely objects of sensible intuition, and presuppose another species of being as their underlying ground.

totality could be composed of monads, he would have confessed that, since they cannot be found in space, nothing can be said about them, because they are super-sensible beings, which are encountered only in thought, but never, as such, in intuition.—Mr. Eberhard, however, wants the latter (the monads) to be known as *non-sensible* objects (either in so far as they are too small for the degree of sharpness of our sense, or the number of them in intuition is too large for the present capacity of our imagination), about which we should be able to know a great deal through the understanding. We will not argue with him on this point; for such a conception of the non-sensible has nothing in common with that of the *Critique*. Moreover, since his very conception contains a contradiction, he will hardly have many followers.

213 It can be clearly seen from the above that Mr. Eberhard seeks the matter of all knowledge in the senses, and here he does not proceed incorrectly. He also wishes, however, to move from this matter to a knowledge of the supersensible. For this purpose he uses the principle or sufficient reason as a bridge. He not only accepts this principle in its unlimited universality, which requires an entirely different manner of distinguishing the sensible and the intellectual than he is willing to allow, but he also, according to his formula, prudently distinguishes it from the principle of causality, because otherwise it would conflict with his own purposes.* This bridge, however, is not sufficient; for on the far shore one cannot build with any of the materials of sensible representation. He uses these, to be sure, because he (like all other men) lacks any other materials. But he washes and purifies this simple (which he previously believed himself to have found as a part of sensible representations) of this stain. He does so by boasting that he *only introduced it into matter by way of demonstration*, since it could never be found in sensible representation through mere sense perception. Even if as alleged, however, the partial representation is actually in the matter as an object of the senses, there always remains, untouched by his demonstration, one small difficulty, viz., how can one secure the objective reality of a concept which has only been demonstrated of objects of the

---

*The proposition, *all things have their ground*, or in other words, everything exists only as a consequence, i.e., is dependent for its determination upon something else, holds without exception of things as appearances in space and time, but in no way of things in themselves, for the sake of which Mr. Eberhard actually attributed such generality to the proposition. It would, however, have been even less suitable to his purpose to express it in universal form as the principle of causality: everything which exists has a cause, i.e., exists only as effect; because he had just proposed to demonstrate the reality of the concept of a first being, which as such could not depend upon any cause. Thus, one finds it necessary to hide behind expressions which can be twisted at will. As an example, (p. 259) the word *ground* is used in such a way that one is led to believe that he has in mind something distinguished from the sensations. Actually, however, he understands it to refer merely to the partial sensations, which one can, in a logical perspective, equally well call the grounds of the possibility of a whole.

senses, if it should signify a being which cannot be an object of the senses at all (not even a homogeneous part of such an object)? For it remains uncertain whether, when one removes from the simple all of the properties whereby it can be a part of matter, anything at all remains which could be called a possible thing. Consequently, even had he established, through the demonstration, the objective reality of the simple as a part of matter, hence as an object which belongs merely to sensible intuition and a *possible* experience, he none the less would not have succeeded in doing so for every object, including the super-sensible, apart from a possible experience, which was precisely the question at issue.

214

In all that follows (pp. 263–306)—and is intended to serve as a confirmation of the above—nothing is to be found, as one can easily foresee, except the distortion of the propositions of the *Critique*. This is especially true of the misrepresentation and confusion of logical propositions, which concern merely the form of thought (without even taking an object into consideration) with transcendental propositions, which concern the way in which the understanding applies the form of thought, completely purely and without needing another source than itself, to the a priori knowledge of things. To the first belongs, among many other things, the translation of the conclusions of the *Critique* into a syllogistic form. Thus, he says (p. 270) that I conclude: "All representations which are not appearances are empty of the forms of sensible intuition (an unsuitable expression, which is nowhere found in the *Critique*, but which can remain standing).—All representations of things in themselves are representations which are not appearances (this expression is also contrary to the use of the *Critique*, where it says that they are representations *of things* which are not appearances).—Therefore, they are absolutely empty." Here are four principal concepts, and I would, he says, have to conclude: "Therefore, these representations are empty of the forms of sensible intuition."

Now only the latter conclusion can actually be drawn from the *Critique*, and Mr. Eberhard only read the first one into it. According to the *Critique*, however, there follows from this the following episyllogism, through which the former conclusion can finally be produced: representations which are empty of the forms of sensible intuition are empty of all intuition (for all our intuition is sensible).—Now, the representations of things in themselves are empty of such.—Therefore, they are empty of all intuition. And finally: representations which are empty of all intuition (to which, as concepts, no corresponding intuition can be given), are absolutely empty (without knowledge of their object).— Now, representations of things which are not appearances are empty of all intuition.—Therefore, they are (in knowledge) absolutely empty.

What is to be doubted here, the intelligence or the good faith of Mr. Eberhard?

215   Only a few examples can here be given of his complete misunderstanding of the *Critique* and of the groundlessness of what he purports to be able to put in its place in behalf of a better system; for even the most resolute comrade of Mr. Eberhard would grow weary of the labor of bringing his objections and counter-assertions into a coherent unity.

Having raised the question (p. 275) "What gives sensibility its matter, i.e., sensations?" he believes himself to have spoken against the *Critique* in that he says (p. 276): "We may choose what we will—we nevertheless arrive at *things in themselves*." Now this is precisely what the *Critique* constantly asserts. The only difference is that it places this ground of the matter of sensible representations not itself again in things as objects of the senses, but in something super-sensible, which *grounds* the sensible representations, and of which we can have no knowledge. It says: the objects as things in themselves *give* the matter to empirical intuition (they contain the ground of the determination of the faculty of representation in accordance with its sensibility), but they *are not* the matter of these intuitions.

After this, it is asked how the understanding works upon this matter (whatever its source may be). The *Critique* proves in the *Transcendental Logic* that this occurs through the subsumption of sensible (pure or empirical) intuitions under the categories which, as concepts of things in general, must be grounded completely a priori in the pure understanding. Mr. Eberhard, on the other hand, (pp. 276–79) bases his system on the claim: "We cannot have any general concepts which we have not *abstracted* from the things which we perceive through the senses or from those of which we are conscious in our own soul." He then carefully describes this abstraction from the particulars in the same paragraph. This is the first act of the understanding. The second consists (p. 279) in its again composing concepts out of this sublimated matter. The understanding therefore proceeds by means of *abstraction* (from sensible representations) to the categories, and now it advances from these and the essential characteristics of things to their properties. Thus he says (p. 278): "The understanding thus, with the help of reason, receives new composite concepts, just as it itself ascends by means of abstraction to ever more general and simple concepts, up to the

216   concepts of the *possible* and the grounded" etc.

This ascent (if that can be called an ascent which is only an abstraction from the empirical in the use of the understanding in experience, since then the intellectual, which we ourselves have previously put into experience in accordance with the nature of our understanding, i.e., the category, remains), is only logical, that is, to more general rules. But since these rules are abstracted from the use of the understanding in possible experience, wherein the categories are given a corresponding intuition, their use is likewise limited to this sphere.—For a truly *genuine* ascent, namely, to another species of being than can in general be given to the senses, even the most perfect, another mode of intuition, which we have named intellectual (because anything which belongs to knowledge, and is not sensible, can have no other name and significance) would be demanded. With such an understanding not only would the categories no longer be required, but they would have absolutely no use. But who can provide us with such an intuitive understanding, or, if it lies concealed within us, who can acquaint us with it?

Mr. Eberhard, however, has a remedy for this difficulty. According to him (pp. 280-81), "There are also *intuitions which are not sensible* (but also not intuitions of the understanding)—another intuition than the sensible in space and time."—"The first elements of concrete time and the first elements of concrete space are no longer appearances (objects of sensible intuition)." They are therefore true things, *things in themselves.* He distinguishes (p. 299) this non-sensible intuition from the sensible on the grounds that it is that in which something "is represented through the *senses unclearly* or confusedly," and he wishes (p. 295) to have the understanding defined as the "faculty of clear knowledge."—The difference between sensible and non-sensible intuition then consists in the fact that the simple parts in concrete space and time are represented obscurely in sensible and clearly in non-sensible intuition. Naturally, in this way the demand of the *Critique* is fulfilled in regard to the objective reality of the concept of simple beings, as a corresponding intuition (albeit non-sensible) is given to it.

217   *We ascend,* however, *only to fall much deeper.* For if these simple parts were subtly introduced into the intuition itself, then their representations would be established as parts contained in the empirical intuition, and the intuition would remain with them what it was with respect to the whole, namely, sensible. The consciousness of a representation makes no difference in its specific nature; for it can be combined with all representations. The consciousness of an empirical intuition is called perception. The fact, therefore, that these alleged simple parts are not *perceived* does not make the least difference to their nature as sensible intuitions. Hence, even if our senses were sharpened and our imagination strengthened so as to grasp the manifold of its intuition 218 with consciousness, we would not therefore, on account of the clarity* of this representation, perceive something non-sensible.

---

*For there is also a *clarity* in intuition, therefore in the representation of particulars, not merely of things in general (p. 295). This can be named *aesthetic*, and it is com-

It may occur to the reader to ask why, if Mr. Eberhard is by this evaluation beyond the sphere of sensibility (p. 169), he still always uses the expression *non-sensible*, and not rather *super-sensible*. Yet this happens with good reason. For with the latter it would be too apparent that he cannot derive it from sensible intuition, just because it is sensible. *Non-sensible*, however, characterizes a mere deficiency (e.g., in the consciousness of something in the representation of an object of the senses), and the reader will not immediately discern that the representation of a real object of another kind is being smuggled in. It is the same with the expression *universal things* (instead of *universal predicates of things*) of which we shall speak shortly, by which the reader believes that he must understand a special species of being, or the expression *non-identical* (instead of *synthetic*) judgments. It requires much skill in the choice of vague expressions to sell trivialities to the reader as significant things.

If, therefore, Mr. Eberhard has correctly interpreted the Leibniz-Wolff conception of the sensibility of intuition, viz., that it consists merely in the confusedness of the manifold of the representations in the intuition but that it nevertheless still represents the things in themselves, the clear knowledge of which, however, must come from the understanding (which recognizes the simple parts in that intuition), then the *Critique* has not falsely attributed anything to that philosophy, and it only remains to determine if it also has the right to say that the standpoint which it assumes in order to characterize sensibility (as a

---

pletely distinct from logical clarity through concepts (e.g., if a *New Guinea* savage first came to see a house, and was near enough to distinguish all of its parts, without having the least concept of it), but which, of course, is not contained in any logical textbook. It is therefore not permissible for this purpose to accept, as he demands, the definition of the understanding as the faculty of clear knowledge, instead of that of the *Critique* as the *faculty of knowledge through concepts*.[10] Most important, however, the *Critique's* definition is alone satisfactory, because the understanding is thereby also characterized as a transcendental faculty of concepts (categories) which originally spring only from it. His definition, on the other hand, refers merely to the logical capacity to produce clarity and universality, even in sensible representations, merely by the clear representation and abstraction of their marks. It is, however, of great concern to Mr. Eberhard to avoid these most important critical investigations by giving to his definitions equivocal marks. To this also pertains the expression (p. 295 and elsewhere), "a knowledge of *universal things*." This is an entirely objectionable scholastic expression, which can reawaken the conflict between nominalists and realists and which—although it can be found, to be sure, in many metaphysical compendia—still belongs merely to logic and not to transcendental philosophy. This is because it does not designate any difference in the nature of things, but only in the use of concepts, whether they are applied universally or particularly. Nevertheless, this expression, as well as the *unimageable*, serves to make the reader expect for a moment that a special kind of object, e.g., the simple elements, was thought.

---

[10] *Critique of Pure Reason*, A681/B93.

special faculty of receptivity) is incorrect.* He confirms the correctness
219 of the significance of the concept of sensibility, which the *Critique*
attributed to the Leibnizian philosophy (p. 303), by placing the subjective ground of appearances, as confused representations, in the *incapacity* to distinguish all the marks (partial representations of sensible intuition). Moreover, while rebuking the *Critique* for not acknowledging it,
he says (p. 377) that this ground consists in the limits of the subject.
The *Critique* itself asserts that besides these subjective grounds of the
logical form of intuition, the appearances also have *objective* grounds,
and in this it does not contradict Leibniz. It is, however, an obvious
contradiction to assert that—if these objective grounds (the simple
elements) lie as parts in the appearances themselves, and merely because
of their confusedness cannot be perceived as such, but can only be
known to be there by demonstration—they should thus be called sensible, and yet not merely sensible, but also, because of this latter reason,
intellectual intuitions. Leibniz's conception of sensibility and appearances can not be interpreted in this manner, and either Mr. Eberhard
has given an entirely erroneous interpretation of this opinion, or it must
be rejected without hesitation. One of the two: either the intuition of
the object is entirely intellectual, i.e., we intuit the things as they are in
themselves, and then sensibility consists merely in the confusedness
which is inseparable from such an all-inclusive intuition, or it is not
intellectual, and we understand by it only the mode in which we are
affected by an object which in itself is entirely unknown to us. Then,
however, sensibility so little consists in the confusedness, that sensible
intuition may contain even the highest degree of clarity, such that, if
simple parts were contained therein, they could be clearly distinguished, this intuition would still not contain anything more than mere
appearance. Both together cannot be thought in one and the same
concept of sensibility. Consequently, sensibility, as Mr. Eberhard attributes the concept of Leibniz, is distinguished from intellectual knowl-

---

*Mr. Eberhard ranted and raved in an amusing manner (p. 298) over the audacity of
such a rebuke (in addition to substituting an improper expression for it). If it ever
occurred to anyone to rebuke Cicero because he did not write good Latin, he would find
someone like Scipio,[11] (a grammarian reputed for his zeal), who would put him rudely,
but correctly in his place. For what constitutes good Latin is something which we can
only learn from Cicero (and his contemporaries). If, however, anyone believes himself to
have found an error in Plato's or Leibniz's philosophy, indignation over the claim that
there is something to criticize even in Leibniz would be ridiculous. For what is philosophically correct neither must nor can be learned from Leibniz, but rather from the
touchstone which lies equally near to all of us, common human reason. There are no
classical authors of philosophy.

---

[11] Kant is here referring to the philologist, Kasper Schoppe (1576–1649).

edge (*Verstandeserkenntnis*) either merely through the logical form (confusedness), whence it contains intellectual representations of things in themselves, or it is also distinguishable from it transcendentally, i.e., in regard to origin and content, in which case it contains nothing of the nature of the object in itself, but merely the mode in which the subject is affected, it may be as clear as one wishes. In the latter case we return to the affirmation of the *Critique*, to which we cannot oppose the first opinion without placing sensibility merely in the confusedness of the representation contained in the given intuition.

220

One cannot exhibit more clearly than Mr. Eberhard does against his will the infinite difference between the theory of sensibility as a special mode of intuition, which has its a priori form determinable according to universal principles, and the theory which views this intuition as a merely empirical apprehension of things in themselves, which (as sensible intuition) is only distinguished from an intellectual intuition by the clarity of the representation. From the *incapacity*, the *weakness*, and the *limits* of the faculty of representation (the exact expressions which Mr. Eberhard uses) one can derive no extension of knowledge, no positive determination of the object. The given principle must itself be something positive, which constitutes the substrate for such propositions, although only subjectively, and which only has objective validity in respect to appearances. If we grant to Mr. Eberhard his simple parts of the objects of sensible intuition, and allow him to explain, in the best manner that he can, their combination in accordance with his principle of sufficient reason, how and through what conclusions will he draw from his concept of monads and their connection through forces, the representation of space? How, for instance, will he be able to explain that space has three dimensions, and that of its three kinds of limit, two are themselves space, while the third, namely, the point, is the limit of all limits? Or, in respect to the objects of inner sense, how will he determine their underlying condition, time, as a magnitude, albeit only of one dimension, and (like space) as a continuous magnitude, from his simple parts, which in his opinion are perceived by the senses, although not separately, but which are conceived to be there by the understanding? Finally, how will he derive such a positive knowledge, which contains the conditions of the most extensive a priori sciences (geometry and universal physics) from these limits, from un-

221

clarity, and therefore from mere deficiencies? He must regard all these properties as false and merely invented (for they contradict the simple parts which he accepts), or he must seek their objective reality not in things in themselves, but in things as appearances. This would be to seek the form of their representation (as objects of sensible intuition) in the subject and in its receptivity, its quality of being susceptible of an immediate representation of given objects, which form now makes conceivable a priori (even before the objects are given) the possibility of a manifold knowledge of the conditions under which alone objects can appear to the senses. Now compare this with what Mr. Eberhard says (p. 377): "Mr. K. has not determined what is the subjective ground of appearances.—It is the limits of the subject" (that is now his determination). One can read and judge.

Mr. Eberhard is (p. 391) uncertain if I "understand by the form of sensible intuition the limits of the power of knowledge, by which the manifold is connected into the *images* of time and space, or these images in general themselves".—"He who conceives the images themselves as originally innate, rather than in their grounds, conceives a *qualitatem occultatem.* If, however, he accepts one of the two above explanations, then his theory is either completely or partially contained in the Leibnizian theory." He demands (p. 378) an elucidation concerning the *form* of *appearance*; "it may", he says, "be mild or harsh." He has opted in this paragraph for the latter tone. I wish to remain with the first, which is more appropriate for the position with superior reasons on its side.

The *Critique* admits absolutely no divinely implanted (*anerschaffene*) or innate (*angeborne*) *representations*. It regards them all, whether they belong to intuition or to concepts of the understanding, as *acquired*. There is, however, an original acquisition (as the teachers of natural right formulate it), consequently also of that which previously did not exist, and therefore did not pertain to anything before the act. Such is, as the *Critique* shows, *first of all*, the form of things in space and time, *secondly*, the synthetic unity of the manifold in concepts; for neither of these is derived by our faculty of knowledge from the objects given to it as they are in themselves, but rather it brings them out of itself a priori. There must, however, be a ground in the subject which makes it 222 possible for these representations to originate in this and no other manner, and which enables them to be related to objects which are not yet given. This ground at least is innate. (Since Mr. Eberhard himself notes that in order to justify the use of the expression "divinely implanted" the demonstration of the existence of God must already be presupposed, why does he use it rather than the old expression "innate" in a critique which deals with the first foundations of all knowledge?) Mr. Eberhard speaks of (p. 390): "the grounds of the general, still undetermined images of space and time, and the soul is created (*erschaffen*) with them." On the following page, however, he is again doubtful whether I understand by the form of intuition (or better: by the ground of all forms of intuition) the *limits* of the power of knowledge or these images themselves. It is inconceivable how he could enter-

tain the first supposition, even in a doubtful manner, since he must be aware that he wished to establish this conception of sensibility in opposition to the *Critique's*. The second one, however—namely, that he is doubtful if I mean the undetermined images of space and time—may be explained but not justified. For where have I ever regarded the intuitions of space and time, in which images are first of all possible, as themselves images (which always presuppose a concept of which they are the presentation, e.g., the undetermined image of the concept of a triangle, for which neither the relation of the sides nor of the angles are given)? He has committed himself so completely to the deceptive ploy of using the expression *image* instead of *sensible* that he cannot get away from it. The ground of the possibility of sensible intuition is neither of the two, neither *limit* of the faculty of knowledge nor *image*. It is the merely particular *receptivity* of the mind, whereby it receives representations in accordance with its subjective constitution, when affected by something (in sensation). Only this first formal ground, e.g., the possibility of a representation of space, is *innate*, not the spatial representation itself. For impressions are always required in order to first enable the faculty of knowledge to represent an object (which is always its own act). Thus, the formal *intuition*, which is called space, emerges as an originally acquired representation (the form of outer objects in general), the ground of which (as mere receptivity) is nevertheless innate and the acquisition of which long precedes determinate *concepts* of things that are in accordance with this form. The acquisi-
223 tion of these concepts is an *acquisitio derivativa*, as it already presupposes universal transcendental concepts of the understanding. These likewise are acquired and not innate, but their *acquisitio*, like that of space, is *originaria* and presupposes nothing innate* except the subjective conditions of the spontaneity of thought (in accordance with the unity of apperception). No one can be in doubt concerning the meaning of the ground of the possibility of a pure sensible intuition, except he who roams through the *Critique* with the help of a dictionary, but does not think it through.

The following example will show how little Mr. Eberhard understands the *Critique* in its clearest assertions, or perhaps, how he deliberately misunderstands it.

*After this one can judge in which sense Leibniz takes the word innate when he applies it to certain elements of knowledge. A treatise by Hißmann in the *Teutsche Merkur* (October, 1777) can facilitate this comprehension.[12]

---

[12] M. H. Hißmann, "Bemerkungen für die Geschichtschreiber der philos. Systeme; über Duten's Untersuchungen; und über die angeborenen Begriffe des Plato, Descartes und Leibniz," *Teutsch Merkur* (October, 1777), pp. 22–52.

It was said in the *Critique* that the mere category of substance (just as any other) contains absolutely nothing more than the logical function in respect of which an object is thought as determined, and therefore, that through it alone absolutely no knowledge of an object is produced, not even through the least (synthetic) predicate, *unless we provide it with a sensible intuition.* It was then inferred from this that, since we cannot judge of things at all without categories, absolutely no knowledge of the *super-sensible* (always taken in the theoretical sense) is possible. Mr. Eberhard pretends (pp. 384–85) to be able to provide this knowledge of the pure category of substance even without the help of sensible intuitions: "It is the *force* which effects the accidents." Force, however, is itself nothing other than a category (or the predicable thereof), namely, *causality*, of which I have likewise declared that without an underlying intuition its objective validity can be demonstrated just as little as that of the concept of a substance. Now in reality he bases (p. 385) this demonstration on the presentation of the accidents, hence also of force as its ground, in sensible (inner) intuition. For he really relates the concept of cause to a series of states of the mind (*Gemüt*) in time, of successive representations or grades thereof, whose ground is contained "in the thing which is fully determined throughout all its past, present and future alterations." "For this reason," he says, "the thing is a force; for this reason, it is a substance." The *Critique* itself, however, demands no more than the *presentation* in inner intuition of the concept of force (which is, as we noted in passing, entirely different than the concept for which he wished to secure objective reality, namely, substance*), and the objective reality of substance as a sensible being is thereby secured. The question, however, was whether the concept of force could be demonstrated as a pure category, i.e., even apart from its application to objects of sensible intuition, therefore, as valid of super-sensible objects, i.e., objects of mere thought. This question arises because in that case all consciousness which rests on temporal conditions, and consequently, every sequence

224

---

*The proposition, *the thing (the substance) is a force*, instead of the entirely natural proposition, *substance has a force*, is one which contradicts all ontological concepts, and is very disadvantageous to metaphysics. For the concept of substance, i.e., of the inherence in a subject, is thereby in reality completely lost, and instead of it, the concept of dependence on a cause is posited. This is just as Spinoza would have it, since he affirmed the universal dependence of all things in the world on an original being as their common cause, and by making the universal, effective force itself into a substance, he converted this dependence into inherence. A substance certainly has, in addition to its relationship of *subject* to accidents (and their inherence), also the relationship to them of *cause* to effect. But the former relationship is not identical with the latter. Force is not that which contains the ground of the existence of the accidents (for this is contained in the substance). Rather it is the concept of the mere relationship of the substance to the accidents in so far as it contains their ground, and this relationship is completely different from that of inherence.

of past, present, and future, together with the law of the continuity of changes of states of the mind (*Gemütszustandes*) must be removed (*wegfallen*), and thus nothing would remain by which the accidents could be given and which could serve as a support of the concept of force. If then, in accordance with Mr. Eberhard's demand, one removes (*wegnehmen*) the concept of man (in which the concept of a body is already contained), as well as that of representations whose existence is determinable in time, hence everything which contains conditions of outer as well as inner intuition (for this must be done if the reality of the concepts of substance and cause as pure categories, i.e., as concepts
225 which can serve for knowledge of the super-sensible, is to be secured), then there remains for him nothing of the concept of substance except a something, the existence of which can be thought only as a subject, and not as a mere predicate of another. Moreover, by the same token, nothing remains of the concept of cause except the concept of a relationship of something to something else in existence, according to which, if I posit the first, the other is also necessarily determined and posited. He can bring forth absolutely no knowledge of the things so constituted from these concepts, not even if such a constitution is even possible, i.e., if something could ever be given in which it was found. We are here not considering the question whether, in *regard to practical principles* a priori, the categories of substance and cause might receive objective reality in respect of the pure practical determination of reason when the concept of a thing (as noumenon) underlies them as a ground. For the possibility of a thing which can exist merely as subject and not again as predicate of another thing, or the property which, in respect to the existence of another, can have the relationship of ground and never the reverse, that of consequent of that other, must for the purpose of theoretical knowledge certainly be demonstrated by a corresponding intuition. For the former can possess no objective reality without the latter, and thus no knowledge of such an object could be acquired. Nevertheless, if these concepts should yield not constitutive but merely regulative principles for the use of reason (as is always the case with the idea of a noumenon), they could, as mere logical functions of the concepts of things, the possibility of which is not demonstrable, be indispensable for reason in its practical use. This is because they then hold, not as objective grounds of the possibility of noumena, but as subjective principles (of the theoretical or practical use of reason) in respect to phenomena.—Still, as has been said, the talk is here merely of the constitutive principles of knowledge of things, and if it is possible to acquire knowledge of any object at all by merely speaking of it through categories without establishing them through intuition (which for us is always sensible). Mr. Eberhard believes so, but for all his emphasis on

the fecundity of the arid ontological wilderness, he is not able to achieve it.

SECTION TWO

The solution of the problem,
How are synthetic judgments possible a priori?
according to Mr. Eberhard

226

This problem, considered in its generality, is the inevitable stone of offense on which all metaphysical dogmatists must unavoidably founder. They thus circumvent it as much as possible, and I have yet to find a single opponent of the *Critique* who has a solution to this problem which is valid for all cases. Mr. Eberhard addresses himself to this task, relying on his principles of contradiction and of sufficient reason (which he nevertheless only presents as an analytic principle); with what success, we shall soon see.

It seems that Mr. Eberhard has no clear conception of what the *Critique* means by *dogmatism*. Thus, he speaks (p. 262) of apodictic demonstrations which he claims to have furnished, and adds thereto: "If he is a dogmatist who accepts things in themselves with certainty, then we must, no matter what the cost, submit ourselves to the indignity of being called dogmatists," and then he says (p. 289) "that the Leibnizian philosophy contains just as much of a criticism of reason as the Kantian; for it grounds its dogmatism on a careful analysis of the faculties of knowledge, what is possible for each one." Now—if it really does this, then it does not contain a dogmatism in the sense in which our *Critique* always uses this term.

By *dogmatism* in metaphysics the *Critique* understands this: the general trust in its principles, without a previous critique of the faculty of reason itself, merely with a view to their success; by *scepticism*, the general mistrust in pure reason, without a previous critique, merely with a view to the failure of its assertions.* The *criticism* of the proce-

227

*The success in the use of a priori principles is their universal confirmation in their application to experience; for then one almost concedes to the dogmatist his a priori demonstration. The failure in the use of such principles, which gives rise to scepticism, is found solely in cases where only a priori demonstrations can be required, because experience can neither affirm nor deny anything in regard to them. This failure consists in the fact that a priori demonstrations of equal strength, which establish precisely the opposite principles, are contained in the universal human reason. The first (the successful principles) are only principles of the possibility of experience, and are contained in the *Analytic*. If, however, the *Critique* has not previously established them as such, these principles can easily be taken to be valid for more than merely objects of experience, thereby originating a dogmatism in respect to the super-sensible. The second (the unsuccessful ones) refer to objects, not as the first through concepts of understanding, but through ideas which can never be given in experience. Now, since the demonstrations through which the principles were thought merely for objects of a possible experience must, in such cases, necessarily contradict themselves, it follows that if one ignores the

dure of reason in regard to all that pertains to metaphysics (the doubt of the suspension of judgment) is, on the contrary, the maxim of a general mistrust of all of its synthetic propositions before the general ground of their possibility in the essential conditions of our faculty of knowledge has been determined.

One does not, therefore, free himself from the justified reproach of dogmatism by invoking, as Mr. Eberhard does (p. 262), allegedly apodictic demonstrations of his metaphysical assertions; for the failure of these demonstrations is so common, even if no visible error is to be found therein (which is there not the case), and the demonstration of its opposite so often opposes them with equal obviousness, that the sceptic, even if he can bring nothing specific against the argument, is still completely justified in placing his *non liquet* upon it. Only if the demonstration is produced in such a way that a mature criticism has previously established the possibility and general conditions of a priori knowledge can the metaphysician justify himself in the face of the charge of dogmatism, which for all its demonstrations is, without such a critique, completely blind. The canon of the *Critique* for this kind of judgment is contained in the general solution of the problem: *how is a synthetic knowledge possible a priori*? If this problem has not previously been resolved, then all metaphysicians until this point of time are not free of the charge of blind dogmatism or scepticism, no matter what their other services through which they justifiably possess so great a name.

228

Mr. Eberhard is not of this opinion. He proceeds as if such a warning, which in the *Transcendental Deduction* is justified through so many examples, were not addressed to the dogmatist. Thus he accepts as established, before the criticism of our capacity to judge synthetically a priori, a previously much-disputed synthetic proposition—namely, that time and space and the things in them consist of simple elements—without offering the least preceding critical investigations of the possibility of such a determination of the sensible through ideas of the super-sensible. This investigation, however, ought to be imposed itself upon him because of the contradiction of this proposition with mathematics. His own procedure gives us the best example of what the *Critique* calls dogmatism, which must ever remain excluded from all transcendental philosophy, and the significance of which he will now, I hope, more clearly grasp in his own example.

Critique, which can alone determine the boundaries, not only is a scepticism bound to arise in respect to all that is thought through mere ideas of reason, but ultimately a suspicion against all a priori knowledge, which leads in the end to a theory of universal doubt concerning metaphysics.

But before one proceeds to the solution of this principal problem, it is absolutely necessary to have a clear and determinate conception, *first*, of what the *Critique* in general understands by synthetic as distinguished from analytic judgments, *second*, of what it means by the characterization of such judgments as a priori as distinguished from empirical judgments.—The first point has been presented by the *Critique* as clearly and as repeatedly as one could wish. They are judgments through the predicate of which I attribute more to the subject of the judgment than I think in the concept to which I attach the predicate. This predicate, therefore, extends my knowledge beyond what is contained in that concept. This does not occur through analytic judgments, which serve merely to more clearly represent and assert what is already thought and contained in the given concept.—The *second point*, namely, what is an a priori as distinguished from an empirical judgment, here causes no difficulty; for it is a distinction long known and named in logic, and not as the first one (at least according to Mr. Eberhard) put forward under a new name. Still, considering Mr. Eberhard's intention, it is not superfluous to note that a predicate which is attributed a priori to a subject in a proposition is thereby affirmed to belong necessarily to it (be inseparable from the concept thereof). Such predicates can be said to belong to the essence (inner possibility of the concept, [*ad essentiam*] * *pertinentia*). Hence, all propositions which are valid a priori must contain such predicates. The others, that is to say, those which are separable from the concept of the subject (without prejudice to it) are called extra-essential marks (*extraessentialia*). The first predicates belong to the essence, either as constitutive parts thereof (*ut constitutiva*), or as consequences which have their sufficient reason therein (*ut rationata*). These are called essential parts (*essentialia*), which therefore contain no predicate which can be derived from other predicates contained in the same concept. Their totality constitutes the logical essence (*essentia*). The second are called properties (*attributa*). The extra-essential marks are either inner (*modi*) or relational (*relationes*) marks, and cannot serve as predicates in a priori propositions, because they are separable from the concept of the subject, and are therefore not necessarily connected with it.

229

Now, it is clear that, if one has not already given a criterion for a synthetic a priori proposition, the statement that its predicate is an attribute in no way illumines its distinction from an analytic proposition. For by naming it an attribute nothing more is said than that it can be derived as a necessary consequence from the essence. Whether it is

---

*In order to avoid even the least appearance of a circular explanation with these words, one can use instead of the expression *ad essentiam* the equivalent expression *ad internam possibilitatem pertinentia*.

derived analytically according to the principle of contradiction, or synthetically according to some other principle, remains thereby completely undetermined. Thus, in the proposition *every body is divisible*, the predicate is an attribute because it can be derived as a necessary consequence from an essential part of the concept of the subject, namely, extension. It is, however, an attribute which is represented as belonging to the concept of body according to the principle of contradiction. Thus, the proposition itself, despite the fact that it asserts an attribute of a subject, is nevertheless analytic. Permanence, on the other hand, is also an attribute of substance; for it is an absolutely necessary predicate thereof. It is, however, not contained in the concept of substance itself, and can not be derived from it by any analysis (according to the principle of contradiction). Thus the proposition *every substance is permanent* is a synthetic proposition. If it is therefore said of a proposition: it has as its predicate an attribute of the subject, it is not yet known if it is analytic or synthetic. One must therefore add, *it contains a synthetic attribute*, i.e., a necessary (albeit derived)—therefore, a priori knowable—predicate in a synthetic judgment. Thus, according to Mr. Eberhard, the explanation of synthetic judgments a priori is that they are judgments which assert synthetic attributes of things. Mr. Eberhard hurls himself into this tautology in order to, where possible, not only say something better and more determinate about the character of synthetic judgments a priori, but also with this definition to at the same time articulate their general principle, whereby their possibility can be judged; a task which the *Critique* was only able to accomplish after much difficult labor. According to him (p. 315): "Analytic judgments are those in which the predicate asserts the essence or some of the essential parts of the subject; synthetic judgments, however, (p. 316) if they are necessary truths, have attributes as their predicates." Through the word *attribute* he characterizes synthetic judgments as a priori (on account of the necessity of their predicate), but at the same time as judgments which assert the *rationata* of the essence, not the essence itself or some of its parts. He therefore gives an intimation of the principle of sufficient reason, by means of which the attribute can alone be predicated of the subject. He thus relies on the fact that it will not be noticed that the ground can here only be a logical ground, namely, one which indicates that the predicate can be derived from the concept of the subject, to be sure, only mediately, but still by virtue of (*zufolge*) the principle of contradiction. Then, however, although it asserts an attribute, such a proposition can still be analytic, and thus does not possess the defining characteristics of a synthetic proposition. Despite the fact that it must have occurred to him that this limitation is necessary, he is very careful not to frankly

230

admit that it must be a synthetic attribute in order for the proposition, for which it serves as a predicate, to be regarded as synthetic. Otherwise the tautology would be much too apparent. Thus he presents something which to the inexperienced seems to be new and substantive, but which in reality is merely an easily discerned smoke screen.

231 One can now also see what is signified by his principle of sufficient reason. He presents it in such a way that one is led to believe (especially judging in accordance with the example he sets forth), that he understands by it a real ground, since ground and consequent are in reality distinct from one another, and the proposition which combines them is for this reason a synthetic proposition. By no means! Rather, he had already well considered the future instances of the use of this principle, and formulated it in so indeterminate a manner that he could give it whatever meaning the occasion required. He therefore could also use it as a principle of analytic judgment without the reader noticing it. Is then the proposition *every body is divisible* any less analytic because its predicate is first derived by analysis from that which pertains immediately to the concept (to the essential part), namely, extension? If, from a predicate which is immediately recognized in a concept according to the principle of contradiction, another is inferred, which is likewise derived from this predicate according to the principle of contradiction, is the latter predicate derived from the concept any less according to the principle of contradiction than the former?

It is therefore apparent, first of all, that the hope of explaining synthetic propositions a priori through propositions which have attributes of their subject as predicate is destroyed, *unless one adds to this that they are synthetic*, and thus perpetrates an obvious tautology. It is also apparent that limits are set to the principle of sufficient reason, if it is to be presented as a separate principle, such that it can only be admitted as such into transcendental philosophy in so far as it justifies a synthetic connection of concepts. We may now compare this with the joyous proclamation of our author (p. 317): "So we would have thus already derived the distinction of judgments into analytic and synthetic, and indeed, *with the most precise determination of their line of demarcation* (that the first pertains merely to essences, the second to attributes), from the most fruitful and clearest principle of division (an allusion to his previously mentioned fertile fields of ontology), and *with the fullest certainty* that the division completely *exhausts* its principle of division."

However, despite his triumphant cry, Mr. Eberhard does not seem to be so completely certain of victory. For (p. 318) after he had taken it as fully established that Wolff and Baumgarten had long known and expressly characterized, albeit in different terms, that which the *Cri-*

tique brings to the fore under a different name, he becomes at once
232 uncertain which predicates in a synthetic judgment I might mean. But
now such a dust cloud of distinctions and classifications of predicates is
raised that the point at issue is lost sight of; all in order to demonstrate
that I *should have defined* the synthetic judgment, especially the a
priori variety, in distinction from the analytic judgment, *other* than I
have done. The talk is here not at all about my solution to the question
of how such judgments are possible, but only what I understand thereby, and that, if I accept one kind of predicate in them (p. 319), my
concept is too wide, but if I understand another kind (p. 320), it is too
narrow. It is, however, clear that if a concept first proceeds from a
definition, it is impossible for it to be too narrow or too wide; for it
then signifies nothing more or less than what the definition asserts of it.
The only thing that could be objected to in it would be that it contains
something inherently incomprehensible, which is of no value to the
explanation. The greatest master, however, in the obfuscation of that
which is clear can bring nothing against the definition which the *Critique* gives of *synthetic* propositions. They are propositions in which
the predicate contains more in it than is really thought in the concept
of the subject; in other words, through the predicate of which something is added to the thought of the subject, which is not contained
therein. Analytic propositions are those in which the predicate only
contains what was thought in the concept of the subject of this judgment. Now the predicate of the first kind of propostion may, if they
are a priori propositions, be an attribute (of the subject of the judgment) or who knows what else; yet this determination neither can nor
ought to enter into the definition. Even if the attribute were demonstrated to pertain to the subject in as incisive a manner as Mr. Eberhard
has effected it, this still belongs to the deduction of the possibility of
the knowledge of things through such a mode of judgment, which must
first appear *after* the definition. Now, however, he finds the definition
incomprehensible, too wide or too narrow, because it does not accord
with his own allegedly more precise determination of the predicates of
such judgments.

Mr. Eberhard uses all means in order to bring as much confusion as
possible into a completely clear and simple thing. The effect, however,
is entirely contrary to his purpose.

"The whole of metaphysics," he claims (p. 308), "according to Mr.
Kant, *contains solely analytic judgments*," and he cites in support of
233 this a passage from the *Prolegomena* (p. 33).[13] He presents this as if I

[13] Eberhard was referring to *Prolegomena*, p. 271 (Beck translation, p. 20), wherein Kant
claims: "We can be shown indeed many propositions, demonstrably certain and never ques-
tioned; but these are all analytical, and rather concern the materials and the scaffolding for
metaphysics than the extension of knowledge. . .".

had there spoken of metaphysics in general, whereas actually the concern in this place is only with previous metaphysics *in so far as its propositions are grounded in valid demonstrations.* Of metaphysics itself the *Prolegomena* asserts (p. 36): "Metaphysical judgments properly so called are all synthetic." But even in regard to previous metaphysics, the *Prolegomena* states, immediately after the above passage, "that it also presents synthetic propositions, *which are readily granted to it,* but which it has never demonstrated a priori."[14] It is therefore not that previous metaphysics contains no synthetic propositions, (for it has more than enough of them) and among them some that are perfectly valid (i.e., those which are principles of a possible experience), but only that it has not demonstrated them from a priori grounds, which is affirmed in the passage in question. Thus, in order for Mr. Eberhard to refute me, he has only to introduce one such apodictically demonstrated proposition; for the principle of sufficient reason, with its demonstration (pp. 163-64), certainly does not refute my assertion.

It is equally falsely claimed (p. 314) "that I assert that mathematics is the only science which contains synthetic judgments a priori." He has not cited the place where I have allegedly said this, and if he had not been so desirous of seeing precisely the contrary of this, the second part of the main transcendental question, how pure natural science is possible (*Prolegomena*, pp. 71-124), would have made it perfectly obvious to him that I expressly assert the opposite. He ascribes to me the assertion (p. 318): "Apart from the judgments of mathematics, only the judgments of experience are synthetic"; this despite the fact that the *Critique* (First Edition, pp. 158-235) presents the idea (*Vorstellung*) of a complete system of metaphysical, and, indeed, synthetic principles, and establishes them through a priori demonstrations. My assertion was that these principles are, however, only principles of the possibility of experience. He construes this to mean "that they are only empirical judgments." He therefore makes what I consider a ground of experience into a consequent thereof. Thus is everything which comes into his head from the *Critique* changed and distorted in order to allow it to appear for a moment in a false light.

As still another trick in order to avoid being entirely pinned down in his counter assertions, he presents them in a completely general manner, and as abstractly as possible. Moreover, he avoids giving an example whereby one could know with assurance what he is saying. Thus, he divides (p. 318) the attributes into those which we can know either a priori or a posteriori, and says that *it seems to him* that I understand by my synthetic judgments "merely the not absolutely necessary truths, and of the absolutely necessary truths pertaining to the latter species of

234

[14]*Prolegomena*, p. 273 (Beck translation, p. 18).

judgment, those in which the necessary predicates can only be known a posteriori by the human understanding." It seems to me, however, that something else must have been meant by these words than is actually said; for as they stand they contain an obvious contradiction. Predicates which are known only *a posteriori*, but still are *necessary*, and attributes of such a nature that they (p. 321) "cannot be derived from the essence of the subject" are, according to the explanation which Mr. Eberhard himself gave of the latter, completely inconceivable things. If, however, something is really meant thereby, and if the objection which Mr. Eberhard raises by this, to say the least, incomprehensible distinction, against the usefulness of the definition which the *Critique* gave of synthetic judgments is to be answered, then he must still at least give an example of that strange species of attribute; for I cannot refute an objection to which I cannot attach any meaning. He avoids as much as possible introducing examples from metaphysics, but restricts himself, as long as he can, to those taken from mathematics, whereby he proceeds entirely in accordance with his best interests. He thus wants to escape from the hard reproach that metaphysics has *up until now* been absolutely unable to demonstrate its synthetic a priori propositions (because it regards them as valid of things in themselves, and wants to demonstrate them from concepts). Thus, he always chooses examples taken from mathematics, where the propositions can be grounded in a rigorous demonstration because they are based upon a priori intuition. He cannot, however, acknowledge this to be an essential condition of the possibility of *all* synthetic propositions a priori, without at the same time giving up all hope of extending his knowledge to the supersensible, to which no intuition possible for us correponds, and thus leaving uncultivated his promised fruitful fields of psychology and theology. If therefore we can applaud neither his insight nor his willingness to shed light on a controversial subject, we can at least render homage to his prudence in not missing the smallest visible advantage.

235   Yet whenever Mr. Eberhard by chance comes up against an example taken from metaphysics, he invariably meets with the misfortune of establishing precisely the opposite of what he endeavors to prove. He tried in the first place to establish that there must be another principle of the possibility of things beside the principle of contradiction. He also says, however, that this principle must be deduced from the principle of contradiction, and he thus endeavors to derive it. Now he says (p. 319): "The principle *everything which is necessary is eternal, all necessary truths are eternal truths* is *obviously* a *synthetic* proposition, and yet it can be known a priori." It is, however, obviously analytic, and one can sufficiently see from this example what a distorted conception Mr. Eberhard continues to have of this distinction of propositions, with

which he claims to be perfectly familiar. For he cannot wish to regard truth as a particular thing existing in time, whose existence is either eternal or only lasts for a certain time. That all bodies are extended is necessarily and eternally true, they may now exist or not, exist for a long or short time, or throughout all time, i.e., eternally. The proposition says only that these truths do not depend upon experience (which must take place at a determinate moment in time), and that they are therefore not limited by any temporal conditions, i.e., they are knowable as truths a priori, which is completely identical with the proposition that they are knowable as necessary truths.

The same can be said of the following example, which also serves as an example of his accuracy in referring to the *Critique*. He says (p. 325): "I do not see how one can wish to deny to metaphysics all synthetic judgments." Now far from doing this, the *Critique* has rather (as has already been pointed out) presented an entire and complete system of such judgments as true principles; only it has at the same time shown that these principles, without exception, merely express the synthetic unity of the manifold of intuition (as condition of the possibility of experience), and are therefore solely applicable to objects in so far as they can be given in experience. The metaphysical examples which he now offers of synthetic propositions a priori (albeit with the prudent qualification *if metaphysics demonstrates such propositions*), *all finite things are alterable, and the infinite thing is unalterable*, are both analytic. For in reality, that is, in so far as existence is concerned, the alterable is that which has determinations which can follow one another in time. Therefore, only that is alterable which cannot exist other than in time. This condition, however, is not necessarily connected with the concept of a finite thing in general (which does not have all reality), but only with a thing qua object of sensible intuition. But since Mr. Eberhard wishes to affirm his a priori propositions independently of this latter condition, his proposition that all finite beings are as such alterable (i.e., in accordance with their mere concept, and thus, also as noumenon) is false. Thus, the proposition *everything which is finite is, as such, alterable* is to be understood only from the determination of its concept, therefore logically, since then, under the alterable, is meant that which is not thoroughly determined in its concept, and which can thus be determined in many opposing ways. Then, however, the proposition that finite things, i.e., all things except for the *ens realissimum* (*allerrealesten*) are logically alterable (in regard to the concept which one can form of them) would be an analytic proposition. For it is completely identical to say: I consider a thing as finite on the grounds that it does not possess all reality, and to say: it is not determined through the concept of it what, or how much reality I should attribute to it; i.e., I can attribute now this, now that to it, and change its determinations in many ways without affecting the concept of its finitude. It is in precisely the same manner, namely, logically, that the infinite being is unalterable. For if by such a being is understood one which, on account of its concept, can have nothing but reality as predicate and, consequently, which is thoroughly determined by this concept (to be understood in regard to predicates of which we are certain whether or not they are truly real), then no single predicate can be changed without prejudice to the concept. This, however, at the same time shows it to be a merely analytic proposition, namely, one which attributes no other predicate to its subject than those which can 237 be developed from it through the principle of contradiction.* If one plays with mere concepts without considering their objective reality, then one can very easily bring forth thousands of illusory extensions of knowledge without needing intuition. Things are quite otherwise, however, when one endeavors to extend one's knowledge of an object. To such a merely apparent extension belongs also the proposition *the infinite being (taken in the metaphysical sense) is itself not really alterable*, i.e., its determinations do not follow in it in time (for the reason that its existence as mere noumenon cannot without contradiction be thought in time). This is likewise a merely analytic proposition, if one presupposes the synthetic principles of space and time as formal intuitions of things as phenomena. In that case it is identical with the proposition of the *Critique* that the concept of the *ens realissimum* is not a concept of a phenomenon,[15] and far from extending the knowledge of the infinite being with a synthetic proposition, it excludes all extension of its concept by denying it intuition.—Still, it is to be noted

*To the propositions which belong merely to logic, but which through the ambiguity of their expression find their way into metaphysics, and thus, although really analytic, are regarded as synthetic, belongs also the proposition *the essences of things are unalterable*, i.e., one cannot modify anything in that which pertains essentially to their concept, without at the same time giving up the concept itself. This proposition, which is found in Baumgarten's *Metaphysics* § 132, and, indeed, in the main section on the alterable and unalterable, where (as is quite correct) alteration is explained through the existence of the successive determinations of a thing, therefore through their succession in time, nevertheless sounds as if it were presenting a law of nature which extends our concepts of the objects of the senses (especially since the talk is of existence in time). Thus, philosophical novices believe themselves to have learned something considerable thereby, and affirming that the essences of things are unalterable, they reject, for example, the opinion of some mineralogists that silicon can be gradually transformed into aluminum. Only this metaphysical motto is a poor identical proposition which has nothing at all to do with the existence of things and their possible or impossible alterations. Rather it belongs entirely to logic, and inculcates something which no one could dream of denying anyway, viz., that if I wish to maintain the concept of one and the same object, I can change nothing in it, i.e., I must not predicate of it the opposite of what I think in this concept.

[15] *Critique of Pure Reason*, A576/B604.

that having enunciated the above-mentioned proposition, Mr. Eberhard prudently adds, "if metaphysics can demonstrate it." I have together with this proposition indicated the line of argument (*Beweisgrund*) through which metaphysics is accustomed to create the illusion that it is dealing with a synthetic proposition. This line of argument is also the only possible way to employ determinations (such as the unalterable), which have a certain significance in relation to the logical essence (of the concept), afterwards in a completely different sense in relation to the real essence (the nature of the object). The reader is not asked to be put off with dilatory answers (which will in the end still be referred to dear Baumgarten, who also took the concept for the thing), but can judge for himself on the spot.

One can see from the entire discussion in this section that either Mr. Eberhard has no conception of what is meant by synthetic judgments a priori, or, more probably, that he deliberately seeks to confuse the issue, so that the reader will come to doubt what is immediately apparent. The only two metaphysical examples which he wishes to let pass as synthetic, although closely considered both are analytic, are *all necessary truths are eternal* (he could have here just as well have used the word unalterable), and *the necessary being is unalterable*. The paucity of examples, while the *Critique* offers an abundance of examples of genuine synthetic judgments, is easy to explain. It was necessary for him to have those predicates for his judgment which he could demonstrate to be attributes of the subject from the mere concept of this subject. Since this cannot occur if the predicate is synthetic, he had to seek one of those which has long been played with in metaphysics, namely, the concept of the alterable and unalterable. This is at one time considered in its merely logical relation to the concept of the subject and, at another time, in its real relation to the object; while it is yet believed that a single meaning is to be found therein. Now, if one presupposes the existence of its subject in time, this predicate (the concept of the alterable and the unalterable) certainly yields an attribute of this subject and a synthetic judgment. Then, however, sensible intuition and the thing itself, although only as phenomenon, are also presupposed, which Mr. Eberhard was not willing to accept as a condition of synthetic judgments. Instead of only applying the concept of the unalterable to things (in their existence), he applies it to the concept of things; for then unalterability surely becomes an attribute of all predicates in so far as they necessarily pertain to a certain subject, although the concept itself may have an object corresponding to it or may be simply an empty concept.—Previously he had played the same game with the principle of sufficient reason. One is led to believe that he is presenting a metaphysical proposition, which determines something of things a priori, and it is a merely logical assertion, which says nothing more than that, in order for a judgment to be a proposition, it must be represented not merely as possible (problematic), but at the same time as grounded (it is indifferent whether it be analytic or synthetic). The metaphysical principle of causality lay near at hand, but he was careful about touching it (for the example which he gives of it does not accord with the universality of that alleged supreme principle of all synthetic judgments). The reason for this is that he wanted to let pass a logical rule, which is entirely analytic, and which abstracts from all conditions of objects, as a natural principle with which metaphysics has alone to deal.

Mr. Eberhard must have feared that the reader would finally be able to see through this deception. Thus, in order to turn the reader's attention away from this issue once and for all, he says at the conclusion of this section (p. 361) that "the dispute as to whether a proposition is analytic or synthetic is, in regard to its logical truth, trivial." This is, however, in vain. Mere common sense must acknowledge this question as soon as it is clearly posed. The daily increase of my knowledge through an ever richer experience teaches me that I can extend my knowledge beyond a given concept. But if it is said that I can extend it beyond the given concept even without experience, i.e., can judge synthetically a priori, and one adds thereto that for this something more is necessarily demanded than to have this concept, that a ground is also required whereby I can truthfully add to my concept more than what I already think in it, then I would laugh at him if he were to tell me that the proposition *I must, beside my concept, still have another ground in order to say more than lies in it*, is that principle itself, which already suffices for every extension, since I need only represent to myself as an attribute this more which I think a priori as pertaining to the concept of a thing, but which is still not contained in it. For I wish to know what is the ground through which, beside what is essentially proper to my concept and which I already know, I can become acquainted with additional features and, indeed, with those which necessarily pertain to a thing as attributes, although they are not contained in the concept of the thing. Now I found that the extension of my knowledge through experience rests upon empirical (sense) intuition, in which I encountered much that corresponded to my concept, but could learn of still more as connected with this concept that was not thought in it. Now I can easily conceive, if only it is pointed out to me, that if an extension of knowledge beyond my concept is to take place a priori, then, just as in the former instance, an empirical intuition was necessary, so here a pure intuition a priori is required. I am only puzzled as to where this is to be found and how its possibility is to be explained. But now I am instructed by the *Critique* to remove all that is empirical or actually sensible in space and time, therefore to negate all things qua empirically represented, and I then find that space and time remain, each as an individual being, the intuition of which precedes all concepts of them and of the things in them. Given the nature of these original modes of representation, I can only regard them as merely subjective (but positive) forms of my sensibility (not merely as the deficiency of the clarity of the representations obtained through this sensibility), not as forms of *things in themselves*, therefore only as forms of objects of sensible intuition, and hence of mere appearances. It thereby becomes clear to me not only how synthetic knowledge a priori is possible in mathematics as well as natural science, since these a priori intuitions make this extension possible, and the synthetic unity which the understanding must in each case give to the manifold in order to think an object thereof makes it actual, but I must also come to see that since the understanding for its part cannot intuit, these synthetic propositions a priori cannot be extended beyond the limits of possible experience, because all concepts going beyond this field are empty and must be without a corresponding object. In order to arrive at such knowledge I must either omit something from the conditions which I require for knowledge of objects of the senses, which in such knowledge can never be omitted, or I must combine the remainder in a way in which it can never be combined in sensible knowledge, and so dare to form concepts about which, although they do not contain a contradiction, I can never know whether or not an object ever corresponds to them, and which therefore remain completely empty for me.

241 The reader may now compare what is said here with what Mr. Eberhard proclaimed (p. 316) in his exposition of synthetic judgments, and judge for himself which one of us has presented the problem with empty verbiage rather than grounded knowledge.

The defining characteristic of synthetic judgments is still (p. 316) that "in *eternal truths*, they have attributes of the subject; in *temporal truths*, contingent properties or relations as predicates." Mr. Eberhard now compares this "most fruitful and illuminating" (p. 317) principle of division with that which the *Critique* gives of it, namely, that synthetic judgments are those in which the principle is not the principle of contradiction! "But what is it then?," Mr. Eberhard asks indignantly, and thereupon announces his discovery (allegedly drawn from Leibniz's writings), namely, the principle of sufficient reason, which next to the principle of contradiction, on which analytic judgments turn, constitutes the second hinge on which the human understanding moves, namely, in its synthetic judgments.

One can now see from what I have just presented as the succinct result of the analytic portion of the critique of the understanding, that this expounds with all necessary detail the principle of synthetic judgments in general, which follows necessarily from their definition, viz., *that they are only possible under the condition that an intuition under-lies the concept of their subject*, which, if the judgments are empirical, is empirical, and if they are synthetic judgments a priori, is a pure intuition a priori. Every reader can easily see for himself the conse-quences of this proposition, not only for the determination of the limits of the use of human reason, but even for an insight into the true nature of our sensibility (for this proposition can be demonstrated independently of the derivation of the representations of space and time, and thus serve as basis for the demonstration of their ideality, even before we have deduced it from their inner nature).

Compare this with the alleged principle which the Eberhardian deter-mination of the nature of synthetic propositions a priori entails, "They are those which assert of the concept of a subject its attributes," i.e., those attributes which pertain to it necessarily but only as conse-quences, and because considered as such, they must be related to some ground, their possibility is conceivable through the principle of reason (*Prinzip des Grundes*). Now, however, one justifiably asks if this ground 242 of their predicate is to be sought in the subject according to the princi-ple of contradiction (in which case the judgment, in spite of the princi-ple of reason, would always be only analytic), or if it cannot be derived from the concept of the subject according to the principle of contradic-tion, in which case the attribute is alone synthetic. Therefore neither the name "attribute" nor the principle of sufficient reason (*Satz des zureichenden Grundes*) distinguishes analytic from synthetic judgments. Rather, if by synthetic judgments are meant judgments a priori, then according to this label nothing more can be said than that their predi-cate is in some way *grounded* in the essence of the concept of the subject, and is therefore an attribute, not, however, merely as a conse-quence of the principle of contradiction. But how, as synthetic attrib-ute, it can come into connection with the concept of the subject, since it cannot be derived from an analysis of this concept, is not to be learned from the concept of an attribute and the proposition that it has some ground. Mr. Eberhard's formulation is therefore completely empty. The *Critique*, however, clearly demonstrates the ground of this possibility, namely, that there must be a pure intuition underlying the concept of the subject, which makes possible, yes, which can alone make possible, the a priori connection of a synthetic predicate with a concept.

What is here decisive is that logic can give absolutely no information concerning the question: how synthetic propositions are possible a priori. If it wishes to tell us: derive from that which constitutes the essence of your concept the suffieicntly determined synthetic predicates thereof (which are then called attributes), we are no further along then before. How should I proceed in order to go with my concept beyond this concept itself, and to assert more of it than is thought in it? This problem will never be solved if one, as logic does, takes into consideration the conditions of knowledge merely from the side of the understanding. Sensibility must also be considered, even as a faculty of intuition a priori, and he who imagines himself to find consolation in the classifications which logic makes of concepts (since it, as it must, abstract from all objects of these concepts) is wasting his work and his efforts. Mr. Eberhard, however, does judge logic from this point of view, and following the information which he derives from the concept of attribute (and from the principle of synthetic judgments a priori which pertains exclusively to it, the principle of sufficient reason), he

243 judges it as *so fecund and promising for the solution of the dark questions in transcendental philosophy*, that he even (p. 322) outlines a new table of the division of judgments for logic (in which, however, the author of the *Critique* declines to occupy the place assigned to him), which was suggested to him (p. 320) by an allegedly new division of these judgments by Jacob Bernoulli.[16] One could well say of such new discoveries in logic what was once said in a learned journal: "*Alas!* someone has once again invented a new thermometer." For so long as one must be satisfied with the two fixed points of division, the freezing and the boiling points of water, without being able to determine the relation of the heat at either point to absolute heat, it is immaterial whether the interval is divided into eighty or one hundred degrees, etc. So long, therefore, as we are not in general taught how the attributes (here understood as synthetic) which, although they cannot be developed from the concept of the subject, yet come to be necessary predicates of this subject (p. 322), or even become able to be received as such with it, any systematic division which is intended to explain the possibility of judgments, which it can only do in a very few cases, is a completely unnecessary burden on our memory, and would have difficulty finding a place in a new system of logic. This is because not even the mere idea of synthetic judgments a priori (which Mr. Eberhard very absurdly calls *non-essential* judgments) belongs to logic.

Finally, something concerning the claim brought forth by Mr. Eberhard and others that the distinction between analytic and synthetic judgments is not new but has long been known (and allegedly because of its unimportance only casually treated). It can matter little to one who is concerned with truth, especially if he uses a distinction in a

[16] According to the editors of the Academy edition, vol. 8, p. 497, the reference is probably to Jacob Bernoulli the elder (1654–1705), Professor of mathematics at Basel. Eberhard does not cite the source of this reference.

hitherto at least untried manner, if it has already been made by others. Moreover, it is the common destiny of everything new in science that, if one cannot oppose anything to it, it is at least discovered to have been known for ages. But, if from an observation presented as new important consequences strike one immediately in the eye, consequences which it would have been impossible to have overlooked had it been made previously, then a suspicion must arise in regard to the correctness or 244 importance of that division itself, a suspicion which could stand in the way of its use. If, however, this division is put beyond doubt, and at the same time the necessity with which it brings forth from itself these consequences becomes apparent, then one can assume with the highest degree of probability that it had yet not been made.

Now the question of how knowledge is possible a priori has long been raised and treated, especially since the time of Locke. What would then be more natural than that as soon as the distinction between the analytic and synthetic in such knowledge had been clearly noted, that this general question would have been delimited to the particular one: how are *synthetic* judgments possible a priori? For as soon as this question was raised, it would have become apparent immediately that the success or failure of metaphysics depends entirely upon the way in which this problem is resolved. Moreover, all dogmatic procedures of metaphysics would certainly have been suspended until sufficient information was received concerning this single problem, and the idea of a "critique of pure reason" would have become the rallying cry before which even the strongest trumpeter of dogmatic assertions would be powerless. But since this has not happened, one can only judge that this manner of distinguishing judgments has never been properly conceived. This was inevitable if it is viewed in the manner of Mr. Eberhard, who amongst predicates merely distinguishes attributes from the essence and essential parts of the subject, and therefore assigns it to logic. Since logic has nothing to do with the possibility of knowledge in regard to its content, but merely with its form in so far as it is a *discursive* knowledge, the investigation of the origin of a priori knowledge of objects must be left exclusively to transcendental philosophy. Nor could this insight and positive usefulness have been achieved by the mentioned division if it exchanged for the expression *analytic–synthetic* one as badly chosen as *identical–non-identical.* The latter does not provide the least clue as to the possible mode of connection of such representations a priori. However, the notion of a synthetic judgment (in opposition to analytic) immediately brings with it a reference to an *a priori synthesis* in general and must naturally suggest the investigation which is no longer logical but already transcendental: whether there are 245 not concepts (categories) which express nothing but the pure synthetic unity of the manifold (of any intuition) with regard to the concept of an object in general, and which underlie a priori all knowledge thereof. Moreover, since this concerns merely the thought of an object in general, the question also arises as to whether the manner in which the object must be given (namely, the form of its intuition) must not likewise be presupposed a priori for such synthetic knowledge. Then the attention directed to this point would have inevitably transformed that logical distinction, which otherwise can be of no use, into a transcental problem.

It was therefore not merely a verbal quibble, but a step in the advance of knowledge, when the *Critique* first made known the distinction between judgments which rest entirely on the principle of identity or contradiction, from those which require another principle through the label "analytic" in contradistinction to "synthetic" judgments. For the notion of synthesis clearly indicates that something outside of the given concept must be added as a substrate which makes it possible to go beyond the concept with my predicate. Thus, the investigation is directed to the possibility of a synthesis of representations with regard to knowledge in general, which must soon lead to the recognition of intuition as an indispensable condition for knowledge, and pure intuition for a priori knowledge. Such a result, however, could not be expected through the explanation of synthetic judgments as non-identical, and it never was the outcome of such an explanation. In order to assure oneself on this point it is only necessary to consider the examples which have hitherto been produced to prove that the distinction in question has been well known in philosophy, although under other names. The first one (which I myself cited, although only as something analogous) is by *Locke*[17] who in distinguishing between what he called knowledge of co-existence and of relation, places the first in empirical and the second in moral judgments. He does not, however, name the synthetic aspect of judgments in general, nor has he derived the least rule for pure knowledge a priori in general from the distinction of such propositions from identical propositions. The example from *Reusch*[18] belongs entirely to logic, and only shows the two different ways to bring clarity to given concepts, without being concerned with the ex-

[17] Locke, *Essay Concerning the Human Understanding*, Bk IV, Ch. 3. In the *Prolegomena*, p. 270 (Beck, pp. 19–20); Kant refers to this section in the Essay and writes: In Locke's *Essay*, however, I find an indication of my division. For in the fourth book (Chapter III, §9, seq.), having discussed the various connections of representations in judgments, and their sources, one of which he makes "Identity or contradiction" (analytical judgments) and another the co-existence of ideas in a subject (synthetical judgments), he confesses (510) that our (a priori) knowledge of the latter is very narrow and almost nothing."

[18] Johann Peter Reusch (1691–1758), a Wolffian and author of *Systema logicum*, first edition 1734 and *Systema metaphysicum*, first edition, 1734.

tension of knowledge, especially a priori, in regard to objects. The third, from *Crusius*[19] only refers to metaphysical propositions which cannot be demonstrated through the principle of contradiction. No one therefore has conceived this distinction in its universality with regard to a critique of reason in general. If someone had, mathematics, with its great riches in synthetic knowledge a priori, would have had to have been cited as an example of the first order, the comparison of which with pure philosophy and the latter's poverty in respect to such propositions (although it is rich enough in the analytic variety), would have inevitably given rise to an investigation into the possibility of the former. In the meanwhile, it is left to each to judge for himself whether or not he is conscious of having already recognized this distinction in general and found it in other authors; so long as, for this reason alone, he does not regard this investigation as superfluous, and its goal as already having been long achieved.

* * *

May we be finished for now and for ever with this debate over a pretended critique of pure reason which only reiterates an earlier one which justified the great claims of metaphysics. It has emerged with sufficient clarity that, if there were such a critique, Mr. Eberhard was not capable of seeing, understanding, or remedying at any point—even second hand—this need of philosophy.—The other courageous men, who through their objections have labored to keep alive the critical enterprise, will not so interpret this single exception to my intent (not to become involved in any formal controversies), as if I have granted any less importance to their arguments and philosophical status. It occurred only this one time, in order to make conspicuous a certain behaviour which is worthy of attention and, it seems to me, which is particularly characteristic of Mr. Eberhard. As for the rest, may the *Critique of Pure Reason* continue to maintain itself, if it can, through its intrinsic solidity. Once put in circulation, it will not disappear without at least calling forth a more solid system of pure philosophy than has hitherto been at hand. If, however, one tries to envisage such an event, the present state of affairs provides ample material to recognize that the apparent harmony which now reigns amongst opponents of the *Critique* is really a disguised disharmony in that they are miles apart in the principles which they propose to set in its place. It would therefore provide us with an exhibition as amusing as it is instructive if they would for a time set aside their conflict with their common enemy in

[19] Crucius, *Weg zu Gewißheit und Zuverläßigkeit der menschlichen Erkenntniß*, (Leipzig, 1746), § 260.

order to try to reach an accord on the principles which they wish to accept. They would then, however, proceed no further than he who tried to construct a bridge the length of the stream rather than across it.

Given the anarchy which unaviodably rules in the philosophical world because it only recognizes an invisible thing, reason, as its legitimate sovereign, it has always been necessary to rally this restless group around some single great man as a unifying point. But for those who did not bring their own understanding, or had no desire to use it, or, if not deficient in either, still acted as if theirs could only be supported by that of another, to understand such a great man was a difficulty which has hitherto prevented the formation of a durable constitution and which will remain an obstacle for some time to come.

Leibniz's metaphysics contains basically three defining characteristics: 1) The principle of sufficient reason, and this, to be sure, in so far as it should merely show the insufficiency of the principle of contradiction for the knowledge of necessary truths. 2) The monadology. 3) The doctrine of the pre-established harmony. On account of these three principles, he has been attacked by many opponents who did not understand him. He has also, however, (as a great knower and worthy panegyrist remarked on a certain occasion) been mistreated by his alleged followers and interpreters.[20] In this, his fate has been similar to the fate of other past philosophers who could well have said: "God protect us only from our friends; as for our enemies, we can take care of them ourselves."

I. Is it realy credible that Leibniz wished to have his principle of sufficient reason construed *objectively* (as a natural law) when he attributed a great importance to it as an addition to previous philosophy? It is actually so universally known and (under proper limitations) so manifestly clear that not even the weakest mind could believe itself to have made therein a new discovery. He has, therefore, been much scorned by his uncomprehending opponents. In fact, however, this was only understood by Leibniz as a *subjective principle*, namely, merely one which pointed toward a critique of reason. For what does it mean to claim that another principle is necessary in addition to the principle of contradiction? It is to say, in effect, that only that which already lies in the concept of the object can be known according to the principle of contradiction. Should one now wish to assert something more of this object, then something must be added beyond the concept, and in order to be able to do this, another principle, distinct from the principle of contradiction, must be sought, i.e., it must have its special

248

[20]M. Hißmann, *Versuch uber das Leben des Freih. von. Leibnitz* (Münster, 1783), pp. 58–60, 69 ff.

ground. Now, since the latter kind of proposition is (now at least) called synthetic, Leibniz wanted to say nothing more than that it is necessary to add to the principle of contradiction (as the principle of analytic judgments) still another principle, namely, that of synthetic judgments. This was certainly a new and noteworthy indication of metaphysical investigations which were not yet carried out (and which have only recently taken place). If, however, his disciple takes this indication of a special principle, which at that time was not yet found, for the (already found) principle (of synthetic knowledge) itself, discovered by Leibniz—does he not expose Leibniz to ridicule just when he thinks that he is providing him with an apology?

II. Is it really believable that Leibniz, the great mathematician, held that bodies are composed of monads (and hence space composed of simple parts)? He did not mean the physical world, but its substrate, the intelligible world, which is unknown to us. This lies merely in the Idea of reason, and in it we must certainly represent to ourselves everything which we think as a composite substance as composed of simple substances. He also seems, with Plato, to attribute to the human mind an original, although now only obscure, intellectual intuition of these super-sensible beings. He infers nothing from this, however, concerning sensible beings. He wishes these latter to be considered as relative to a special mode of intuition, of which we are only capable in regard to knowledge which is possible for us, thus, as mere appearances in the strictest sense, dependent upon (specific, particular) forms of intuition. We cannot, therefore, be disturbed by his explanation of sensibility as a confused mode of representation, but rather must set in its place another one which is more in accordance with his purpose. Otherwise his system will contradict itself. The acceptance of this error as a deliberate and wise precaution (in the manner of imitators who, in order to become perfectly similar to their models, even copy their mistaken gestures and pronunciations) can hardly be regarded as a contribution to the glory of the master. The innateness of certain concepts, as an expression for a *fundamental faculty* in respect to a priori principles of our knowledge—which he used merely against Locke, who only recognizes an empirical origin—is likewise incorrectly understood if it is taken literally.

III. Is it possible to believe that, by his pre-established harmony between soul and body, Leibniz should have understood an adaptation of two beings which are by their nature completely independent of one another and incapable of entering into relationship through their own power? This would be to proclaim idealism; for why should one accept bodies in general, if it is possible that everything which occurs in the soul can be viewed as an effect of its own power, which would occur in this way if it were in complete isolation? The soul and the substrate of the appearances which we call bodies, a substrate which is completely unknown to us, are, to be sure, two completely different beings. These *appearances* themselves, however, which are conditioned by the form of their intuition belonging to the constitution of the subject (soul), are mere representations. Thus, one can well conceive of the connection, according to certain a priori laws, between understanding and sensibility in the same subject, and at the same time the necessary and natural dependence of the latter upon external things, without surrendering these things to idealism. As for the harmony between understanding and sensibility in so far as it makes possible an a priori knowledge of universal laws, the *Critique* has essentially shown that without it no experience is possible. This is because, without such a harmony, objects (which partly, in regard to their intuition, accord with the formal conditions of our sensibility, and partly, in regard to the connection of the manifold, accord with the principles of its arrangement in one consciousness as a condition of the possibility of a knowledge thereof) could not be taken up by us into the unity of consciousness and enter into experience, and would therefore be nothing for us. We could, however, still provide no reason why we have precisely such a mode of sensibility and an understanding of such a nature, through the combinations of which experience becomes possible. Nor could we explain why they, as two otherwise completely heterogeneous sources of knowledge, always agree so well as to permit empirical knowledge in general and especially (as the *Critique of Judgment* points out) as to permit an experience of nature under its manifold *particular* and merely empirical laws, of which the understanding teaches us nothing a priori, as if nature were deliberately organized in view of our power of comprehension. This we could not (nor can any one else) further explain. In naming the ground of this relation a *pre-established* harmony, Leibniz especially had regard for the knowledge of bodies, and under this first of all of our own, as the middle ground of this relation. In so doing he obviously did not explain, nor did he wish to explain, this agreement, but only to indicate that we must conceive a certain purposiveness in the arrangement by the highest cause of ourselves as well as of all things outside of us. This may, to be sure, be understood as already placed in creation (pre-determined), not, however, as the pre-determination of externally existent things, but only of the powers of the mind in us, sensibility and understanding, each related to the other in accordance with its particular nature. This is just what the *Critique* teaches when it holds that they must stand in a reciprocal relationship in the mind in order to permit a knowledge a things a priori. That this was his true, although not clearly expressed, opinion may be surmised from the fact that he extended that pre-established harmony much further than to the agreement of soul and body, namely, to the agreement between the realm of *nature* and the realm of *grace* (the realm of purposes in relation to the final purpose, i.e., mankind under moral laws). This harmony between the consequences of our concepts of nature and those of our concept of freedom must be conceived of as a harmony between two completely different faculties in us, standing under completely heterogeneous principles, and not as a harmony between two sorts of things *externally* existent to one another. Moreover, this harmony, which is required by morality, absolutely cannot, as the *Critique* shows, be conceived from the nature of the beings in the universe. Rather, as an agreement which for us at least is accidental, it can only be conceived through an intelligent first cause.

251   The *Critique of Pure Reason* can thus be seen as the genuine apology for Leibniz, even against his partisans whose eulogies scarcely do him any honor; just as it can be for many different past philosophers, to whom many historians of philosophy, with all their intended praise, only attribute mere nonsense. Such historians cannot comprehend the purpose of these philosophers because they neglect the key to the interpretation of all products of pure reason from mere concepts, the critique of reason itself (as the common source of all these concepts). They are thus incapable of recognizing beyond what the philosophers actually said, what they really meant to say.

Appendix A
KANT'S LETTERS TO REINHOLD

1. *Kant to Reinhold*, May 12, 1789 (AK XI: 33-40)

The sincerest thanks, my most treasured and dearest friend, for the communication of your kind opinion of me, which arrived together with your beautiful gift on the day after my birthday! The portrait of me, done without my consent, by Mr. Loewe, a Jewish painter, is, according to my friends, supposed to resemble me somewhat. But a man who knows painting said at first glance: a Jew always paints people to look like Jews; the proof of which is to be found in the nose. But enough of this.

I could not send you my judgment of Eberhard's new attack earlier, as our shop did not even have all three of the first issues of his magazine, and I could find them only in the public library. Thus the delay in my answer.—*That Mr. Eberhard, along with several others*, has not *understood me*, is the least one can say (for that could be partly my fault). But as I shall in part show you in the following remarks, he actually sets out not to understand me, and even to make me incomprehensible.

In the first issue of the magazine he tries to appear as a man who is conscious of his own importance in the eyes of the philosophical public. He speaks of "sensations" aroused by the *Critique*, of "sanguine hopes" which were "surpassed," of the many people who were stupified, and of the many who are not yet able to recover (as if he were writing for the theater or the boudoir about a rival), and like a man who is fed up with watching the show, he is determined to put an end to it.—I wish that he might be reproached a bit for this wanton charlatanry.—The first three issues of the magazine more or less constitute a unit, of which the third, from p. 307 on, attacks the chief point of my Introduction in the *Critique*, and concludes (p. 317) triumphantly: "We should therefore now. . . ." I cannot here omit making a few remarks about this, in order that those readers who make the effort to check up on it will not overlook the deceitfulness with which this man, who is dishonest in every line he writes, in those matters wherein he is weak, as well as in those wherein his opponent is strong, puts everything in an ambiguous light. I will only indicate the pages and the beginning of the places I discuss with a few words, and I beg you to look up the rest for yourself. The refutation of the fourth part of the third issue will serve to reveal the whole man, his insight as well as his character. My remarks will chiefly concern pp. 314-19.

On pp. 314-15 he says: "According to this distinction would be. . . if we make anything definite out of this."[1]

---

[1] The passage in Eberhard reads: "According to this the distinction between analytic and synthetic judgments would be this: analytic judgments are those in which the predicate states

His explanation of a synthetic judgment a priori is a pure deception, namely, a flat tautology. For it is already implicit in the expression: "a judgment a priori" that its predicate is necessary. It is likewise implicit in the expression "synthetic" that the predicate is not the essence nor an essential part of the concept which serves as subject; for otherwise it would be identical with the concept, and the judgment would thus not be synthetic. Now whatever is thought as necessarily connected with a concept, but not through identity, is thought as necessarily connected through something *distinct* from the essence of the concept, i.e., through a ground. For it is one and the same thing to say that the predicate is not thought in the essence of the concept but still as necessary through it, or to say that it is grounded in the essence, that is, it must be thought as an attribute of the subject. Thus, his allegedly great discovery is nothing more than a shallow tautology whereby, through the surreptitious substitution of other meanings for the technical terms of logic, he creates the illusion of having provided a real *basis for explanation*.

But the pretended discovery has yet a second inexcusable flaw, viz., that it, as an alleged definition, is not convertible. For I can say in any case: in all synthetic judgments, the predicates are attributes of the subject, but not the converse: every judgment that asserts an attribute of a subject is a synthetic judgment a priori. For there are also *analytic* attributes. Extension is an essential part of the concept of a body; as it is a *primitive* mark of this concept, which cannot be derived from any other inner mark. Divisibility, however, is also a necessary predicate of the concept of body, but only as one which can be inferred (as subaltern) from the former predicate (extension). It is therefore an attribute of body. Now divisibility can be derived from the concept of the extended (as composite) according to the principle of identity, and the judgment *every body is divisible* is a judgment a priori, which has an attribute of the thing for a predicate (the thing itself is the subject) and is therefore not a synthetic judgment. Consequently, the fact that the predicate in a judgment is an attribute does not at all serve to distinguish synthetic judgments a priori from analytic judgments.

All similar errors, which begin as confusions and end as deliberate deceptions. are based on the fact that the logical relation of ground and consequent is mistaken for the real relation. A ground is (in general) that whereby something else (distinct from it) is made determinate (*quo positio determinate* ponitur aliud*).[2] A consequent (*rationatum*) is *quod non ponitur nisi posito alio*.[3] The ground must therefore always be something distinct from the consequent, and he who can provide no

---

*This expression must never be left out of the definition of a ground. For the *consequent* is likewise something that, if I posit it, I must at the same time think something else is posited, that is, it always belongs to something or other as its ground. But when I think something as consequent, I merely posit *some ground or other*, which one is undetermined. (Thus, the hypothetical judgment is based on the rule: *a positione consequentis ad positionem antecedentis non valet consequentia*).[4] On the other hand, if the ground is posited, the consequent is determined.

---

the essence or some of the essential parts of the subject; those in which the predicate asserts no determination belonging to the essence or to the essential parts of the subject are synthetic. This is what Mr. Kant must want to say if he presents the distinction so that the first are merely explicative and the latter are ampliative, in so far as we can make anything definite out of his explanation."

[2] English: that which being posited determines something else.

[3] English: that which is not posited unless something else is posited.

[4] English: the movement from the consequent to the antecedent is not valid.

ground but the given consequent shows that he knows (or that the thing has) no ground! Now this distinction is either merely logical (in the manner of representation) or real, that is, in the object itself. The concept of the extended is logically distinct from the concept of the divisible; for the former, to be sure, contains the latter, but much more besides. In the thing (Sache) itself, however, the two are identical; for divisibility is really contained in the concept of extension. But it is real distinctness that is required for synthetic judgments. When logic proclaims that all (assertoric) judgments must have a ground, it does not concern itself with the real distinction at all. Logic abstracts from it because this distinction relates to the content of knowledge. If one says, however, that every thing has its ground, one always means thereby the real ground.

Now, when Eberhard names the principle of sufficient reason as the principle of synthetic judgments in general, he can mean by this nothing other than the logical axiom (Grundsatz). This axiom, however, also allows for analytic grounds, and, indeed, can be derived from the principle of contradiction. Then, however, it is a clumsy absurdity on his part to justify his so-called non-identical judgments on the basis of the principle of sufficient reason, a principle which on his own admission is merely a consequence of the principle of contradiction (a principle that is absolutely incapable of grounding any but identical judgments).

I remark only in passing (so that as a result people may more easily take note of Eberhard's procedure), that the real ground is again twofold: either the formal ground (of the intuition of the object), e.g., as the sides of the triangle contain the ground of the angle—or the material ground of the existence of the thing. The latter determines that whatever contains it will be called cause. For it is quite customary for the conjurors of metaphysics to make sleights of hand, and before one realizes it, to leap from the logical principle of sufficient reason to the transcendental principle of causality, assuming the latter to be already contained in the former. The proposition that nihil est sine ratione, which in effect says that everything exists only as a consequent, is in itself absurd, or else they give it some other meaning. Thus, the entire discussion of essence, attributes, etc. absolutely does not belong to metaphysics (wherein Baumgarten and several others have placed it) but merely to logic. For I can easily find the logical essence of a given concept, namely, its primitive constitutiva, as well as the attributes, as rationata logica of this essence, by means of the analysis of all that I think under my concept. The real essence (nature), however, that is, the primary, inner ground of all that necessarily pertains to a given thing, is impossible for man to discover in regard to any object. Thus, extension and impenetrability constitute the whole logical essence of the concept of matter, that is, all that is necessarily and primitively contained in my, and every man's, concept of matter. Knowledge of the real essence of matter, however, of the primary, inner, sufficient grounds of all that necessarily pertains to it, far surpasses all human capacities. Nor can we discover the real essence of water, earth, or any other empirical object, and even the real essence of space and time—and the basic reason why the former has three, the latter only one dimension—escapes us. The reason for this is precisely that, since the logical essence is known analytically and the real essence can only be known synthetically and a priori, there must be a ground of the synthesis of the latter; and there, for us at least, the matter must stand.

The reason that mathematical judgments only yield synthetic attributes is not because all synthetic judgments a priori have to do merely with attributes, but rather, that mathematical judgments cannot be other than synthetic and a priori. On p. 314, where Eberhard introduces such a judgment as an example, he says cautiously: "The question as to whether there are such judgments outside of mathematics may for the present be set aside." Why did he not offer for comparison at least one of the various examples which are found in metaphysics? It must have been difficult for him to find one that could withstand such a comparison. On p. 319, however, he considers the following, which he claims to be obviously synthetic, although it is obviously analytic and an unfortunate choice. The proposition is: *everything necessary is eternal: all necessary truths are eternal truths*. This latter judgment says only that necessary truth is not restricted by any accidental conditions (and therefore not restricted by any position in time), but this is identical with the concept of necessity, and is an analytic proposition. If, however, he wanted to assert that necessary truth actually *exists* at all times, then this is an absurdity to which we cannot be expected to assent. He could not, however, have possibly intended the first proposition to refer to the existence of a *thing* at all times; for then the second proposition would be totally unrelated to it. (Initially I thought that the expression *eternal truths* and its opposite *temporal truths* were merely affectations employing figurative terms, and rather inappropriate for a transcendental critique. Now, however, it seems as though he meant them literally.)

On pp. 318–19 it reads: "Mr. Kant seems to mean merely the not necessary truths . . . only the experiential judgments are necessary."[5] This is such a crude misunderstanding or rather deliberate misrepresentation of my position that one can predict in advance how *genuine* the consequences will be.

He says several times of his opponents that their distinction between synthetic and analytic judgments has long been known. Perhaps so! Nevertheless, the importance of the distinction was not seen because all judgments a priori were placed in the latter category, and only experiential judgments in the former. Thus, the whole point of the distinction was lost.

And now to conclude. Mr. Eberhard says (p. 316): "One seeks in vain for Kant's principle of synthetic judgment." But this principle is completely unambiguously presented in the whole *Critique*, from the chapter on the schematism on, though not in a specific formula. It is: *All synthetic judgments of theoretical knowledge are only possible through the relation of a given concept to an intuition*. If the synthetic judgment is experiential, the underlying intuition must be empirical; if it is a judgment a priori, the intuition must be pure. Since (for us men) pure intuition is only possible (since no object is given) in so far as it consists merely of the form of the subject and of his receptivity to representations, that is, his capacity to be affected by objects, the actuality of synthetic propositions a priori is already sufficient to prove that these propositions concern only sensible objects and cannot transcend appearances. This is therefore shown even without our having to know that space and time are these forms of sensibility, and that the concepts to which we relate our intuitions, in order to have synthetic propositions a priori, are categories. However, once we recognize these categories and their origin as mere forms of thinking, we become convinced that they cannot yield, by themselves, any knowledge and, together with those intuitions, any theoretical knowledge of the super-sensible, although they can be used as Ideas for a practical purpose without

[5] Kant refers to the first part of this passage in *On a Discovery* (pp. 233–34) where it reads in full that Kant understands by synthetic judgments "merely the not absolutely necessary truths, and of the absolutely necessary truths pertaining to the latter species of judgment, those in which the necessary predicates can only be known a priori by the human understanding." The remaining part of the passage in Eberhard reads: "Apart from the judgments of mathematics, only experiential judgments are synthetic." Kant has here thus misquoted Eberhard.

transcending their sphere. This is because the limits of our capacity to give objective reality to our concepts determines neither the bounds of the possibility of things, nor of the use of the categories in respect to the super-sensible, as concepts of an object in general, which ground actually gives practical Ideas of reason. Thus, the principle of synthetic judgments a priori has an infinitely greater fruitfulness than the principle of sufficient reason, which determines nothing and which, considered in its universality, is merely logical.

*   *   *

These then, dear friend, are my remarks concerning the 3rd issue of Eberhard's magazine, which I put entirely at your disposal. The delicacy with which you set out upon your projected work and which is so in accord with your restrained character, may not only be undeserved by this man but actually disadvantageous, if you are driven too far. I shall have the honor of sending you the conclusion of my remarks on the second issue during the next week. This will serve to reveal to you his truly malicious nature, as well, of course, as his ignorance. Since he is inclined to regard all mildness as weakness, he can only be held in check by a clear presentation of his absurdities and misrepresentations. I wish that you would use these remarks as you see fit. They are only hints to help you recall what you have already learned through your own diligent study of these matters. Meanwhile, I even give you full permission to use my name whenever and wherever you see fit.

My sincerest thanks for your lovely book, but I have not yet had time to read it through. I am very interested in your theory of the faculty of representation which should appear next Michaelmas together with my *Critique of Judgment* (a part of which is the "Critique of Taste"). My warmest greetings to Messrs. Schütz, Hufeland, and your distinguished father-in-law.

With the greatest respect and true friendship,
I am, devotedly,
  I. Kant

(see enclosure)

2. *Kant to Reinhold*, May 19, 1789 (AK XI: 40–48)

I am adding to my remarks sent to you on the 12th some more concerning the first two issues of the *Philosophisches Magazin*. This is a most unpleasant task (as it involves setting aright pure equivocations). It is also one which you did not require of me, but which nevertheless still seems necessary in order to show the public in the very beginning the shallowness and duplicity of an author whose only inclination is to deceive.

P. 12: "Plato and Aristotle excluded. . . ."[6]
(Of the latter precisely the opposite is the case. The *nihil est in intellectu, quod non antea fuerit in sensu*[7] of the Aristotelian school—a principle which agrees with Locke's—is actually the criterion for distinguishing the Aristotelian from the Platonic school).

---

[6]The full passage in Eberhard reads: "Plato and Aristotle excluded certainty from any knowledge through the senses and limited it merely to the region of non-sensible ideas or ideas of the understanding. The newest philosophy banishes it from this region and limits it only to the world of the senses."

[7]English: nothing is in the intellect which was not first in the senses.

P. 23: "The metaphysics of this philosophy. . . ."[8]
(the materials for this purpose are completely, without any exception, to be found in the *Critique*).

Pp. 25-26: "If it means: the sensible concepts. . . ."[9]
(Here is a double absurdity. Pure concepts of reason (*Vernunftbegriffe*) which Eberhard equates with pure concepts of the understanding (*Verstandsbegriffen*) are presented by him as concepts which are derived from sensible concepts (like extension and color, which are initially situated in sensible representations). This is precisely the opposite of what I presented as the defining characteristic of pure concepts of the understanding. And then, the notion of "mediate intuition" is contradictory. I say only that a *corresponding* intuition can be given to a pure concept of the understanding. This intuition, however, contains nothing of that concept, but only the manifold to which the concept of the understanding applies the synthetic unity of apperception. It is therefore for itself a concept of an object in general, be the intuition what it may).

P. 156: "That means nothing other than. . . ."[10]
(Here he speaks of necessary laws etc., without noticing that in the *Critique* the task is precisely to show which laws are objectively necessary, and how one can be guaranteed that they hold of the nature of things, i.e., how they can possibly be synthetic and yet a priori. For otherwise one is in danger, like Crusius, whose language Eberhard uses here, of taking a merely subjective necessity, based either on habit or on an inability to grasp an object in any other way, for an objective necessity.)

Pp. 157-58: "I for one am. . . ."
(Here one might well ask, as did the foreign scholar when shown the Sorbonne lecture hall: "They have argued here for 300 years; what have they decided?")[11]

P. 158: "We can always continue to work for its (metaphysics') extension. . . ."—One must here bring him to a halt. For his declaration concerns an important point, namely, whether or not a critique of reason must precede metaphysics. From pp. 157-59 he reveals his confused notion of what the *Critique* is about, as well as displaying his ignorance just when he wishes to parade as learned.

---

[8]The full passage in Eberhard reads: "The metaphysics of this philosophy (Leibniz-Wolffian) is regarded by Kant as useless, and he refers to a future metaphysical system. There can, however, be no likelihood of its construction since the *Critique* has already precluded any access to the materials which are necessary for it."

[9]The full passage in Eberhard reads: "A second reason why Mr. Kant rejects the pure concepts of reason is that they do not given any object. What does it mean: objects are given? If it means: they are actual outside of the representations, then I do not see why objects of sensible ideas must be more actual than objects of the understanding simply because the former are imageable and the latter are not. If it means: the sensible concepts are intuitive, then this is certainly true, they are *immediately intuitive*. But concepts of the understanding are also intuitive, only they are *mediately intuitive*. For they are derived from sensible concepts, and can be intuited in the latter, and if they are constructed from abstract concepts, they still bring with them immediately intuitive marks of the abstract concepts out of which they have been constructed."

[10]The full passage in Eberhard reads: "How can we assure ourselves of its logical truth, if this logical truth consists in the agreement of our knowledge with its objects? This question has been answered: its logical truth follows necessarily from its metaphysical truth. The one is inseparably bound up with the other. That means nothing other than that as soon as the power of representation conceives something as possible and actual outside of itself, according to its necessary laws, then it must be possible and actual outside of it, and it can only be possible and actual insofar as the power of representation is necessitated, through the very same necessary laws, to conceive it."

[11]In the passage referred to, Eberhard argues for the possibility of progress in metaphysics.

This passage also serves by itself to reveal the deceitfulness which he will proceed to exhibit. On p. 157 he speaks of metaphysical truth (in the beginning of the section it was transcendental truth) and its demonstration, contrasting this with logical truth and its demonstration. But all judgmental truth (*Wahrheit eines Urteils*), insofar as it rests on objective grounds, is logical. The judgment itself may belong to physics or metaphysics. One tends to contrast logical with aesthetic truth (that of the poet), e.g., to represent heaven as a vault and the sunset dipping into the sea. In the latter case we demand only that the judgment have the appearance of truth to all men, that is, that it agree with subjective conditions of judgment. When, however, we speak of the objective determining grounds of a judgment, then we don't distinguish between geometrical, physical, metaphysical—and logical truth.

Now he says, (p. 158): "We can always continue to work for its extension, without having to first concern ourselves with the transcendental validity of these truths." (Previously (p. 157) he had claimed that the genuineness of logical truth was being called into doubt, and now (p. 158) he says that we don't have to concern ourselves with transcendental truth (by which he presumably means the very same thing which he had just said was being doubted.) At the place (p. 158) where he claims: "In this way have the mathematicians completed the delineation of entire sciences, *without saying a single word about the reality of their object,*" etc., he shows the grossest ignorance, not merely in his pseudo-mathematics, but also in his complete misunderstanding of what the *Critique* demands with respect to intuitions, through which alone the objective reality of concepts can be secured. We must therefore dwell a moment on his own examples.

Mr. Eberhard wishes to free himself for the demand, so irksome to all dogmatists but nevertheless unavoidable, that no concept be admitted to the rank of cognition if its objective reality is not shown through the possibility of the object being exhibited in a corresponding intuition. He thus calls on the mathematicians, who are not supposed to have said a word about the reality of the objects of their concepts and have still completed the delineation of entire sciences. He could not have hit upon a more unfortunate example to justify his procedure. For the situation is precisely the opposite. The mathematician can not make the least claim in regard to any object whatsoever without exhibiting it in intuition (or, if we are dealing merely with quantities without qualities, as in algebra, exhibiting the quantitative relationships thought under the chosen symbols). He has, as usual, instead of investigating the subject itself, merely skimmed through some books which he has not understood, and found a place in Borelli, the editor of Apollonius's *Conica*, which seems to suit his purpose: "*Subjectum enim . . . delineandi.* Had he even the least notion of what Borelli was talking about, he would find that the definition which Apollonius gives, e.g., of a parabola, is itself the exhibition of a concept in intuition, namely, the intersection of a cone under certain conditions, and in establishing the objective reality of the concept, that the definition here, as always in geometry, is at the same time the construction of the concept. If, however, in accordance with the property of the conic section derived from this definition, namely, that the semi-ordinate is the mean proportional between the parameter and the abscissa, the problem is posed as follows: given the parameter, how is the parabola to be drawn? (i.e., how are the ordinates to be applied upon the given diameter?); then the solution, as Borelli correctly says, belongs to art, which follows science as a practical corollary. For science has to do with the properties of objects, not with the way in which they can be produced under given conditions. If a circle is defined as a curved line on which all points are equidistant from a center, is not this concept given in intuition? Moreover, is not this the case even though the practical proposition that follows: *to describe a circle* (as a straight line is rotated uniformly about a point), is not even considered. Mathematics is the great model for all synthetic use of reason, just because it is never lacking in the intuition *with which* it confers objective reality upon its concepts. In philosophy, however, and indeed, in theoretical knowledge, we cannot always satisfactorily comply with this demand. Then, however, we must acknowledge that our concepts have no claim to be ranked as cognitions of objects, but only as Ideas, merely regulative principles in respect to objects which are given in intuition, but which can never be completely known in terms of their conditions.

P. 163: "Now this principle of sufficient reason can . . . ."[12] (He here makes a confession which will not appeal to many of his allies in attacking the *Critique*, namely, the empiricists. It is that *the principle of sufficient reason is only possible a priori*. At the same time, however, he explains that this principle could only be demonstrated by means of the principle of contradiction. He thereby makes it *ipso facto* into merely a principle of analytic judgments, and thus undermines at the outset his plan to explain the possibility of synthetic judgments a priori by means of it. The demonstration therefore turns out wretchedly. First he treats the principle of sufficient reason as a logical principle (which it must be if he wishes to derive it from the principle of contradiction). Thus construed, the principle says in effect: *every assertoric judgment must have a ground*. In the course of his demonstration, however, he proceeds to construe it as the metaphysical principle: *every event has its cause* [*Ursache*], which involves an entirely different conception of ground. In the latter case it refers to the real ground or principle of causality, the relation of which to the consequent cannot, as with the logical ground, be thought according to the principle of contradiction.)

The demonstration begins (p. 164) with the claim that *two propositions which contradict one another at the same time cannot both be true*. Now, if this principle be compared with the example (p. 163), where it is said that a portion of air moves to the east, the application of the logical principle of sufficient reason would read: the proposition *the air moves to the east* must have a ground. For without having a ground, i.e., without having another representation besides the concept of air and of a movement to the east, the subject is entirely undetermined in respect to the predicate. The above proposition, however, is experiential. Consequently, it is not merely thought problematically but assertorically, as *grounded*, and, to be sure, in experience, as a knowledge through connected perceptions. But this ground is identical to that stated in the proposition (I speak of what is present through perception, not what is merely possible through concepts). It is therefore an analytic ground of *judgment*, in accordance with the principle of contradiction, and thus has nothing in common with the real ground, which concerns the synthetic relationships between cause and effect in the objects themselves. Eberhard therefore begins with the analytic principle of sufficient reason (as a logical principle), and leaps to the metaphysical and thus always synthetic principle of causality, which is never mentioned in logic. He has thus failed completely to demonstrate what he set out to do, but rather something that is never disputed, and he therefore committed a crude *fallaciam ignorationis Elenchi*. But outside of this attempt to

---

[12] The full passage in Eberhard reads: "Now this principle (the principle of sufficient reason) can only be demonstrated a priori; for a demonstration through induction is impossible. The grounds of things are in many cases so hidden, that experience can not always discover them. Thus, those who deny its universality can cite just as many experiences against it, as its defenders for it. If, therefore, the principle of sufficient reason is to be demonstrated a priori, then we must derive it from a higher principle. Now there is no higher principle except the principle of contradiction. The universal truth of the principle of sufficient reason can therefore only be demonstrated from this higher principle."

lead the reader astray, the paralogism (p. 163). "If, for example," to (p. 164) "is impossible" is too awful for words. Put in syllogistic form it reads: if there were no sufficient reason why a portion of air moves toward the east, it could just as well (instead of this; for this is what Mr. Eberhard must really mean, otherwise the consequence of the hypothetical proposition would be false) move toward the west. Now there is no sufficient reason why, etc. Therefore, the wind could just as well move toward the east and toward the west at the same time, which is self-contradictory. This syllogism walks on all fours.

In so far as Mr. Eberhard has demonstrated it, the principle of sufficient reason is therefore still only a logical principle and analytic. Considered from this point of view, there are not two but three principles of knowledge: (1) the principle of contradiction, for categorical judgments; (2) the principle of (logical) ground, for hypothetical judgments; (3) the principle of division (excluded middle between two mutually contradictory propositions), for disjunctive judgments. On this basis, all judgments must conform, first, as *problematic* (as mere judgments), in so far as they express *possibility*, to the principle of contradiction; secondly, as *assertoric* (as propositions) in so far as they express logical *actuality*, i.e., truth, to the principle of sufficient reason; thirdly, as *apodictic* (as certain knowledge) to the principle of excluded middle. The reason for the latter is that apodictic truth can only be thought through the denial of its opposite, and therefore through the division of a predicate into two contradictories and the exclusion of one of them.

The attempt (p. 169) to demonstrate that the simple, as the intelligible, can nevertheless be made intuitive, turns out to be even more pathetic than the rest. For he speaks of *concrete* time as something composite, the simple elements of which are supposed to be representations, and he does not notice that the pure intuition of time, wherein the representations should succeed one another, must already be presupposed in order to represent the succession of this concrete time. Since there is nothing simple in this pure intuition, which the author terms unimageable (or non-sensible), it follows unquestionably that the understanding does not in any way raise itself above the sphere of sensibility in the representation of time. With his alleged first elements of the composite in space, namely, the simples, he crudely repudiates (p. 171) not only Leibniz's actual opinion, but the whole of mathematics. You can judge the worth of what he writes from pp. 244–56 and the *objective* validity of his principle of sufficient reason from my remarks concerning p. 163. He wishes (p. 156) to infer from the subjective necessity of the principle of sufficient reason (now construed as the principle of causality) and from the representations of which it consists and their combination, that the ground of this principle must not lie merely in the subject, but in the object; although I am doubtful if I understand him correctly in this confused discussion. But why does he need to make such circumlocutions, when he thinks that he can deduce it from the principle of contradiction?

I do not recall whether in my previous letter I made mention of this man's strange and extremely provocative misinterpretation or misrepresentation (pp. 272–74) of my account of Ideas of reason, that is, Ideas for which no corresponding intuition can be given, and of the super-sensible in general. He claims that the concept of the chiliagon is such an Idea, and that we can none the less have a great deal of mathematical knowledge concerning it. Now this is such an absurd misrepresentation of the concept of the super-sensible, that a child could notice it. For the question is just whether there can be an exhibition of the representation in an intuition that is possible according to our *kind* of sensibility; the degree thereof, i.e., the power of the imagination to grasp the manifold, may be as great or as small as he wishes. Thus, even if something were presented to us as a million-sided figure, and we could note the lack of a single side at first glance, this representation would not cease being sensible. Only the possibility of exhibiting the concept of a chiliagon in intuition can ground the possibility of the object itself for mathematics; for then the combination of the figure can be completely prescribed in accordance with all of its requirements, without having to worry about the size of the measuring stick that would be necessary in order to make the figure with all of its parts observable to the eye.—One can judge what manner of man he is from this misrepresentation.

He is also good at giving false citations, for example, pp. 19-20, and especially p. 36. On pp. 290 and 298, however, he outdoes himself; for he there becomes a veritable Falsarius. He cites p. 44 of the old edition of the *Critique of Pure Reason*[13] where I said: "The philosophy of Leibniz and Wolff, in thus treating the difference between the sensible and the intelligible as merely logical, has given a completely wrong direction to all investigations into the nature and origin of our knowledge," and presents it thusly: "Here Kant has accused the philosophy of Leibniz and Wolff of falsifying the concept of sensibility and appearance . . . ." Now just as certain people finally come to believe themselves the lies that they have often repeated, so Eberhard becomes so carried away in regard to the alleged use of this presumptuous expression against Leibniz, that he attributes the word "falsify," which exists only in his brain, three times on one page (298) to the author of the *Critique*.[14] What does one call someone who deliberately falsifies a document in a legal trial?

I content myself with these few remarks and I beg you to use them as you see fit, but where possible in a forceful manner. For restraint is not to be expected from this man, for whom bragging has become a maxim in order to surreptitiously gain respect. I would do battle with him myself, and in my own name, but for the time which it would take, which I would rather use to complete my project. Already I am aware of the infirmities of age, and so I must leave the struggle to my friends, if they think it worth pursuing. Basically, I cannot but be pleased with the general commotion which the *Critique* not only inspired, but still calls forth, despite all of the alliances which have been formed against it (although the opponents of the *Critique* have been disunited and will remain so); for it serves to focus attention on the work. In addition, the unending misunderstandings or misrepresentations provide a stimulus for the clarification of the expressions which can give rise to misunderstandings. Thus, in the end, I do not at all fear these attacks, so long as things are conducted calmly. Still, it is a good deed to the community to expose at once the endeavors of a man whose very nature is to deceive and who is acquainted with, and through long habit adept at, all of the tricks through which the casual reader can be seduced into giving his blind trust, e.g., the appeal to misinterpreted passages in the works of famous men. Feder[15] is for all his limitations at least honest, a property which is not to be found in Eberhard's way of thinking.

With warmth and friendship, and with the greatest respect for the integrity of your character, I am faithfully,

Your completely devoted friend and servant,

I. Kant

---

[13] Kant is here referring to the first edition, hence to A44.

[14] It should be noted that in the preceding paragraph of the *Critique* (A43/B61), Kant does claim that the concept of sensibility and of appearance would be falsified. . ." if we were to accept the Leibnizian view.

[15] J. G. H. Feder (1740-1821) an outspoken critic of the Kantian philosophy, and collaborator with Christian Garve in the famous Garve-Feder Review of the Critique which greatly irked Kant.

Appendix B

SCHULZE ON EBERHARD

Selections from Schulze's Review
of the Second Volume of the *Philosophisches Magazin*,
and Kant's notes to Kästner's Treatises
(AK: XX)

Defense of the doctrines (1) *that the general concept of space precedes all sensations* and (2) that *apodictic certainty of all geometrical principles rests upon the a priori necessity of this concept.* (Schulze, pp. 397–403)

Concerning the first point, to which Mr. Eberhard only addresses himself briefly, the subject is entirely incorrectly and the predicate very ambiguously expressed. The *Critique* says (2nd edition, p. 38): *Space is not an empirical concept which has been derived from outer experiences, but a necessary a priori representation, which underlies all outer intuitions.* To this Eberhard replies: "From the premise on which this claim is based, it follows only that the outer sensations cannot be without the concept of space. It is, however, still possible that the concept either precedes or is only coexistent with these representations." This is incorrect; for the premise also says that, in order that certain sensations be referred to something outside me, and similarly, in order that I may be able to represent them as *outside* and *alongside* one another, the representation of space *must already* be *presupposed.* Now, it follows from this not merely that outer sensations *cannot be without* the concept of space, but that they first become possible through it, and therefore that they already presuppose it as something independent of them, i.e., as representation a priori.

Mr. Eberhard dwells somewhat longer on the second proposition and opposes to it the following: "The *necessity of geometrical truths* can not at all be grounded in the *imageable marks of their concepts.*" Now, without even considering the here entirely inappropriate expression *the imageable*, this proposition is formulated in such a manner that the reader will entirely lose sight of the true question at issue, and Kant could completely accept it. For he in no way grounds the *necessity* of geometrical propositions on the *intuitability* of its concepts (for it only follows from this that they are *synthetic*), but on the fact that the intuition on which the construction of the concepts rests is an a priori intuition and therefore a *necessary* one. Nevertheless, let us here consider his two demonstrations. The *first* one is taken from the *contingency and alterability of the subjective grounds of these images or intuitions.* He says: (1) "the concepts of absolutely necessary and eternal truths must be absolutely necessary and eternal, the truths themselves only in their objects, the concepts, however, in the divine understanding. In the divine understanding, however, there is immediately no imageable representation of space. Thus, the necessity of the concept in eternal truths in no way lies in the imageable." This is a striking enterprise, seeking the certainty of geometrical propositions partly in things in themselves, partly in the divine understanding! The reviewer is not at all ashamed to acknowledge his complete ignorance concerning that which is to be found in things in themselves, as well as in the divine understanding, and I can say nothing more than that I understand nothing of this super-earthly argument. The errors in Mr. Eberhard's conception of eternal and necessary truths, however, have already been pointed out by Kant in his essay. (2) Mr. Eberhard concludes: "The *imageable* in space has only subjective grounds, namely, in the limits of the representing subject. This *subjective* element, however, is *alterable* and *contingent.* It is therefore impossible for it to be the sufficient ground of the *absolute necessity* of eternal truths. This ground can only be in the *objective* element (in things in themselves)." This argument rests merely on a misconception of the necessity of space. According to Kant, the ground of the representation of space is *merely subjective*, and it lies, as he has proven, not in the limits of the power of representation, but merely in the *innate, special constitution* of our capacity for intuition (*Anschauungsfähigkeit*). Now, to be sure, it certainly *cannot* be proven that *this* space is absolutely necessary, i.e., that every being capable of thought has it and must represent those things which we call "outer" as things in space. For us, however, the representation which we have of *space* is given with such unconditional necessity and unalterability through the original constitution of our capacity for intuition, that it is for us absolutely impossible to *think away* space, or to think it in any other manner. Thus, if we wished to change even a single predicate which is known by us to belong to it, the entire representation of space would be abolished and become a non-entity (*Unding*). The absolute necessity of the connection of the predicate with the subject, and therefore the apodictic certainty of all geometrical postulates and axioms, is grounded *immediately* in the absolute necessity to represent space exactly as it is *given* to us through the original constitution of our capacity of intuition and not otherwise. (Whoever would deny this must give up the whole of space itself as the object of geometry.) Moreover, this is also the *mediate* ground of the certainty of all of those problems and theorems which can be derived merely from these postulates and axioms. If, on the other hand, that particular, original constitution of our capacity for intuition were given up, then space in its entirety would be *nothing*, and in that case all geometrical concepts and propositions would likewise be *nothing*. From this it is therefore also clear what an erroneous conception Mr. Eberhard forms of the eternity and necessity of geometrical truths when he says (p. 83): "If the truth *between two points only one straight line is possible* is an eternal and absolutely necessary truth, then it must be true even if all of the *subjective* limits of the power of representation, and with them all *sensible* representation, are abolished." This amounts to saying that, if all geometrical points and straight lines were to be abolished and become nothing, it would still be true that between two nothings only one nothing is possible. If Mr. Eberhard, therefore, really wishes to refute the Kantian thesis, he must first *prove* that space is not, as Kant has shown, something *merely subjective*, but at the same time is something in the things in themselves. For until he produces this proof, his entire argument is in vain.

Mr. Eberhard bases his second demonstration on the *impossibility* of *a priori intuitions.* Space, he says, is *infinite.* The *imageable* concept or *intuition* of space, however, must always be *determinate* or *finite.* Thus, an imageable concept or a pure intuition of an infinite space is completely impossible, a *non-entity*, an *illusion*, a *chimera.* Consequently, the concept of such a space must be *unimageable*, a concept of the *understanding*, which only contains the general determinations of the ultimate grounds of the image of space. But this forceful argument unfortunately really rests on a misconception of the infinity of space. For to say that space is infinite means that it is nowhere terminated, that no *absolute* limit is possible beyond which there would be no more space. Now the pure intuition of space, which is immediately given to us through the original constitution of our capacity for intuition, is of such a nature that we may limit it where we will, we can nevertheless not conceive of any of these limits as absolute, i.e., as one through which space is wholly terminated. Thus, our pure intuition of space is most certainly an intuition of an infinite space. All efforts to obscure this immediately obvious matter are therefore in vain. The whole deception consists in imagining that we can completely survey (*überschauen*) infinite space in its entirety, i.e., that we must grasp that which never terminates in our representation as somewhere terminated. This is an obvious contradiction, but it is also, as we have already shown, one which is not necessary for the demonstration of the infinity of space. Moreover, were it in fact necessary, then it would also follow that no conceptual representation of infinite space would be possible, because the understanding is no more capable than sensibility of completely grasping the infinite. Thus, Mr. Eberhard must completely deny the infinity of space. But how could be then use it as the basis of his demonstration that a pure intuition of space is a chimera? As for the rest, if Mr. Eberhard regards it as an entirely false idea that particular spaces are parts of one and the same, single space, *because no infinite aggregate can be a totality*, this rests entirely on the completely erroneous notion that we can only arrive at the concept of the whole of a single, infinite space by first composing it as an aggregate out of infinitely many parts. He thus neglects the unique feature, which is found in no other composite besides space and time. This is the fact that space is given to us in pure intuition as a magnitude, in which the *possibility* of representing parts *already presupposes the representation of an infinite whole*; for we cannot conceive the least finite space, the shortest line, or the smallest triangle or prism, without representing it as *in a whole, infinite space*. It follows uncontestably from this that space is not a composite which can be thought through concepts of the *pure understanding*, because with these the representation of parts does not first require the representation of the whole, but rather just the reverse. It is therefore grounded merely in our *sensibility*, and if one abstracts from this, it is nothing at all. Consequently, a space which is an objective predicate of things in themselves, as well as a geometry whose truth rests on the general determinations of things in themselves, are shown to be non-entities. Mr. Eberhard, to be sure, does not claim that this argument is entirely irrefutable. Nevertheless, he in fact treats it as such, as he concludes the essay in the following solemn manner: "The knowledge of non-sensible objects would thus be saved.—Mr. Kant has performed the service of inducing this saying.—German philosophy, which perhaps like a surfeited victor has rested on its laurels, has him to thank that his attack necessitated it to muster anew its neglected treasures." This triumph of German philosophy over the allegedly un-German *Kantian* one has come, however, somewhat too early. For up until now, it has not recaptured a single foot of its lost fertile fields of ontology, cosmology, etc., and it will hardly be able to do so through the merely general, undetermined assertion of the possibility of synthetic propositions a priori from concepts, without establishing this possibility in a genuine manner, even in regard to a single proposition of this kind, of which the *Critique* had demonstrated it for several. The shortest way would rather be if Eberhard, as Mendelssohn has done, were to really show us his dogmatic treasures, if, for example, he would actually derive for us the images of space and time from objective grounds, and make conceivable, from the merely conceptual representations of the relation of a manifold, that we can only represent to ourselves the relations of outer things to one another in three dimensions, but the inner determinations and their relations in only a single dimension; further, if he could explain to us the absolute inner of matter, and clearly present his theory of the simple elements of body, or, assuming the existence of a necessary being, demonstrate for us its attributes from its mere concept—all this, however, without any rhetorical embellishments, in dry, precise demonstrations, as the pure metaphysician can and must do it. For in this way the act itself would show without any further detours on which side the victory falls.

* * *

On the Apodictic Certainty of Arithmetic and Analysis
(Schulze, pp. 407–8)

What Mr. Eberhard has to say concerning the apodictic certainty of *arithmetic* and *analysis* is based chiefly on the consideration that the pure intuition of time does not lie in the concept of number itself as its object, but only in the limits of our power of representation. But if that is the case, then Mr. Eberhard himself must admit that the concept which we have of a number is merely sensible, and thereby actually holds the intuition of time within itself. This is so because, according to his system, the limits of the power of representation are precisely the source of sensibility. He therefore unavoidably contradicts himself, because *counting* units without adding them *successively* to one another is an obvious contradiction. Indeed, Mr. Eberhard believes that only Kant's commentators have brought the intuition of time into arithmetic; for he says that he does not recall having seen this in any of Kant's writings. Nevertheless, the matter is presented clearly and in detail in the chapter on the *Schematism of the Pure Concepts of the Understanding*, in the first as well as the second edition of the *Critique*, first edition, pp. 142–46. Moreover, just these passages clearly show at the same time that by this example of fingers and points, which Mr. Eberhard seems to ridicule, as well as by the *characteristic* construction, Kant understands nothing more than empirical aids, whereby one only seeks to facilitate the presentation of numbers in the pure intuition of time.

* * *

The Analysis of Maaß's discussion of the Analytic-Synthetic Distinction
(Schulze, pp. 408–9)

The reviewer can only briefly consider the essay of Mr. Maaß. Its purpose is to convincingly confirm the previous essay of Mr. Eberhard through an analysis of the most essential teaching of the Kantian *Critique*; and in fact, Mr. Maaß does here address himself to the most important question of all, to the question *how are synthetic judgments possible a priori.* He first attacks the Kantian division of judgments into analytic and synthetic and the definition of both on the grounds that this division is not sufficiently determinate. Now, one would think that no logic in the world could find something to quarrel with in this division: "In each judgment the predicate either lies in the concept of the subject, or it does not, i.e., either the predicate may be derived from the concept of the subject by means of the mere principle of contradiction, or it may not. Thus, if one terms the first kind of judgment analytic and the second synthetic, all judgments are either analytic or synthetic" as this division is itself derived immediately from the principle of contradiction.

Nevertheless, Mr. Maaß finds divisions of this sort not sufficiently determinate, and thus also not satisfying. For according to this division, he believes, one could not definitively say of any given judgment whether it is analytic or synthetic. This is because one person could think this, another that, the one more and the other less, under the concept of the subject. This latter point is, to be sure, true. Only if one wishes to decide about a judgment, one must in each case know previously what should be thought under the subject as well as the predicate. Now, suppose that I find, in a judgment which two philosophers express in the same words, that one of them connects the subject with a rich concept in which the predicate is already contained, while the other, on the other hand, connects it with a concept in which the predicate in question is not contained. I would then be entirely correct in saying that the judgment of the first one is analytic, and of the second one synthetic. For although their judgments seem to be one and the same, since they are expressed with the same words, they are nevertheless in this case in fact not one but two different judgments. Let one place just so many marks (*Merkmale*) in the concept of the subject that the predicate, which he wishes to prove of the subject, can be derived from its concept through the mere principle of contradiction. This trick (*Kunststück*) does not help him at all. For the *Critique* grants to him without dispute this kind of analytic judgment. Then, however, it takes the concept of the subject itself into consideration, and it asks: how did it come about that you have placed so many different marks in this concept that it already contains synthetic propositions? First prove the objective reality of your concept, i.e., first prove that any one of its marks really belongs to a possible object, and then, when you have done that, prove that the other marks belong to the same thing that the first one belongs to without themselves belonging to the first mark. The entire dispute as to how much or how little should be contained in the concept of the subject has not the least effect on the merely metaphysical question: how are synthetic judgments possible a priori?, but belongs merely in the logical theory of definition, and this without doubt demands that one not introduce more marks into a definition than are necessary for the distinction of the defined thing from all others. It therefore excludes from the definition of a thing all those marks about which one can demand proof as to how and by what grounds they pertain to the requisite marks.

In this way not only everything Mr. Maaß brought forth against the division in question, but also the invalid attempt, already exposed in its nakedness by Kant, to dismiss the problem of the *Critique* on the grounds that he, together with Mr. Eberhard, regards the predicate of a synthetic judgment as an attribute, collapses by itself, and with it his entire first section (pp. 188–216). The *Critique* has already presented a series of propositions which it, taking the words in its sense, regards as synthetic a priori, e.g., there is something permanent in each appearance, everything that happens has a cause, the absolutely necessary being is wise and good, etc. Now Mr. Maaß may, if he wishes, call the predicate in these propositions an attribute. That has no bearing on the matter. The *Critique* only demands of him a proof that in these propositions the predicate necessarily belongs to the subject.

*   *   *

The Infinity of Space, a Comparison of the Metaphysical and
the Geometrical Treatments (Kant-Schulze, pp. 419–22)

Metaphysics must show how one *has* the representation of space, geometry, however, teaches how one *describes* a space, i.e., can present it a priori in a representation (not through a drawing). In the former, space is considered as it is *given*, before all determinations, in accordance with a certain concept of an object. In the latter it is considered as it is generated (*gemacht*). In the former it is *original* and only one (single) *space*. In the latter it is *derived* and there are (many) *spaces*. The geometrician, however, in agreement with the metaphysician, and as a consequence of the fundamental representation (*Grundvorstellung*) of space, must confess that these spaces can only be thought as parts of the one original space. Now one can only view as *infinite* a magnitude in comparison to which each specified homogeneous magnitude is equal to only a part. Thus, the geometrician, as well as the metaphysician, represents the orginial space as infinite and, indeed, given as such. For the representation of space (together with that of time) has a *peculiarity* found in no other concept, viz., that all spaces are only possible and thinkable as parts of one single space, so that the representation of parts already presupposes that of the whole. Now, if the geometer says that a straight line, no matter how far it has been extended, can still be extended further, this does not mean the same as what is said in arithmetic concerning numbers, viz., that they can be continuously and endlessly increased through the addition of other units or numbers. In that case the numbers to be added and the magnitudes generated through this addition are possible *for themselves*, without having to belong, together with the previous ones, as *parts of a magnitude*. To say, however, that a straight line can be continued infinitely means that *the space in which I describe the line is greater than any line which I might describe in it*. Thus, the geometrician expressly grounds the possibility of his task of infinitely increasing a space (of which there are many) on the original representation[1] of a single infinite space, as a singular representation, in which alone the possibility of all spaces, proceeding to infinity, is given. He therefore generates space merely by limiting, either fully or partially, the possible finite and infinite parts of the single infinite space which is given to him. The question, however, as to how this single infinite space is given, or how we have it, does not occur to the geometrician, but concerns merely the metaphysician. Moreover, it is just here that the *Critique* proves that space is not at all something objective, existing apart from us (*außer uns*), but rather consists merely in the *pure form of the mode of sensible representation of the subject as an a priori intuition*. This is also in perfect agreement with what, according to Mr. Kästner's citation (p. 418), Raphson[2] holds, namely, that mathematicians have to do only with an *infinito potentiali*, and that an *actu infinitum* (the metaphysical given) *non datur a parte rei, sed a parte cogitantis*.[3] This latter mode of representation, however, is not for this reason invented and false. On the contrary, it absolutely underlies the infinitely progressing construction of geometrical concepts, and leads metaphysics to the *subjective* ground of the possibility of space, i.e., to its *ideality*. . . .

The reviewer finds Mr. Kästner in complete agreement with the *Critique of Pure Reason*, even where he says (p. 419) at the end of his second essay on geometry:

---

[1] In Kant's handwritten version the parallel passage reads: ". . . of a single, infinite, subjectively given space. This agrees very well with the fact that the geometrical and objectively given space is always finite. For it is only given in so far as it is generated. To say, however, that the metaphysical, i.e., original, but merely subjectively given space, which (because there is not a plurality of them) cannot be brought under any concept capable of construction, but which still contains the ground of the possibility of all geometrical concepts, is infinite, means only that it consists in the pure form of the mode of sensible representation of the subject, as an a priori intuition, and therefore as a singular representation, in which the possibility of all space, proceeding to infinity, is given."

[2] The reference is to the British mathematician, Joseph Raphson, *Analysis Aequationem Universalis*, 2nd ed. (London, 1696), Ch. 3.

[3] English: not given on the side of the object, but on the side of the thinker.

"One never concludes from the image, but from that which the understanding thinks in connection with the image." For he undoubtably means by the first the empirical sketch, and by the second the pure intuition in accordance with a concept, i.e., a rule of the understanding, namely, the construction of the concept, which is not an empirical presentation of it. If, however, he cites the *Philosophisches Magazin* in the belief that he has thereby presented and affirmed Eberhard's conception of the *imageable* in contrast to the *intelligible*, then he is very much mistaken. For he (Eberhard) understands by the *imageable* not a form in space, as geometry might regard it, but space itself (although it is hard to conceive how one could form an image of something external without presupposing space), and his *intelligible* is not the concept of a possible object of the senses, but of something which the understanding must represent, not as in space, but as its underlying ground, from which space can be explained. This misunderstanding, however, will be readily excused by anyone who has felt the difficulty of connecting a consistent meaning with this expression *the imageable*, which Mr. Eberhard uses in so many different senses. . . .

Appendix C

EBERHARD'S SUMMARY COMPARISONS OF THE LEIBNIZIAN AND KANTIAN PHILOSOPHIES

I. Philosophisches Magazin I: 284–88

Kantian Critique of Pure Reason	*Leibnizian Critique of Pure Reason*
1. Something which is not appearance must correspond to appearance.	1. Appearances must have as an ultimate ground something which is not appearance.
2. Of this something I know nothing.	2. I do not distinguish, and have no clear idea of the proper determinations of the particularity of this something.
3. I have no concept at all of it.	3. I only have a concept of what pertains to its genus. I can present this concept in a definition which contains essential aspects and attributes of the thing.
4. This something, to which the appearances are to be related is, therefore, not to be called *noumenon*.	4. This something, which is not appearance or *phenomenon*, can therefore be called *noumenon*. For I can define it, and derive various truths from its definition. These are eternal truths. I can through definitions distinguish between the infinite being, a finite being such as the human soul, and the elements of body by means of their generic conceptions. The faculty of knowledge which does this is the understanding, and the objects of the understanding are *noumena*, as the objects of the senses are *phenomena*.
5. If this something were to be a noumenal object, another intuition besides the sensible one would be necessary.	5. The non-sensible intuition is representation; for this is the simplest object of inner sense, and the simplest matter of concrete time.
6. There must be an intuition for each object. We cannot, however, prove that there can be another intuition be-	6. Even if we had no intuitive idea of the simplest matter, we could still establish many of its general determina-

side the sensible; although we likwise cannot prove the opposite.

tions. Wolff has pioneered in this way in regard to the elements of body. Leibniz believed himself able to determine this matter, and it is in the simplest object of inner sense, the simplest element of concrete time, representation.

7. That something, which corresponds to the appearances, is only a transcendental object, a something = x, of which we know nothing, nor (according to the present condition of our understanding) can we ever know anything.

7. That something, which is the ultimate ground of appearance, contains general determinations = a, which are knowable to us, and to which the particularity = x, which is not clearly knowable by us, belongs. Therefore, the entire something is, in respect to its knowability, a + x.

II.

II. Philosophisches Magazin I: 393-404

Kantian Critique of Pure Reason

Leibnizian Critique of Pure Reason

1. Sensible intuitions are singular representations, which depend upon the organization (*Einrichtung*) of the representing subject.
2. They therefore relate not to things in themselves, but merely to appearances.

1. Representations of particulars have their ground in the object as much as in the representing subject.

2. They are appearances, and as such have no noticeable similarity with the object, because they cannot distinguish its particular reality. The universal determinations in the manifold of the object are distinguished through the understanding. The determinations proper to its particularity are not cognizable by the finite power of representation. But what does it mean to refer to appearances (*auf Erscheinungen gehen*)? Does it mean that they are appearances?—This we have presupposed—or does it mean that their objects are appearances?—That would mean that the objects of appearances are appearances, which is absurd.

3. That which enables the manifold of appearances to be intuited is the *form* of appearances.
4. The pure forms of intuition are space and time.

3. The limits of the finite subject are the subjective grounds of the *form* of appearance.
4. Space and time are appearances, for they have subjective grounds in the finite power of representation. The limits of the finite power of representation are therefore (1) the forms of the appearances of space and time. (2) But space and time can be thought

without the modifications and differences of things which are their ultimate objective ground. They can also be thought without a determinate quantity, without determinate limits and degrees, just as motion can be conceived without a determinate velocity. They are then abstract, general time and space, i.e., undetermined space, undetermined time, in respect to both their inner determinations and their outer limits. It is not fully clear to me in which sense critical idealism uses the expression "pure form of intuition," whether in sense one or two.

5. These forms of sensible intuition are a priori in the mind; for (1) they are the receptivity of the subject to be affected by objects, and thus must necessarily precede all intuitions of these objects.

5. If by the *form* of sensible intuition is meant the *receptivity* of the *subject*, it is then the subjective ground of appearances, and in the rational analysis (*verstandliche Erklärung*) of appearances, this must be thought before (in the logical not the temporal sense) the appearances themselves.

6. But (2) as forms of all appearances they must also be given before all actual perceptions.

6. If perceptions are sensations with consciousness, then they are representations of actual, and therefore of particular, completely determinate things. These lower things cannot be without the determinations of the higher things to which they belong. In the subordination of things the higher therefore precede the lower. The lower, on the other hand, cannot be thought without the determinations of the higher. They therefore follow them in the subordination of things. It does not follow from this, however, that the higher precede the lower, in time; for with the development of the concept to clarity the order is reversed. Thus, if one understands under the pure form of intuition general time and general space, then in the development of concepts the perception precedes the form.

7. Nothing that can be intuited in space is a thing in itself.

7. That can mean: (1) no extended or spatially actual thing is a thing in itself. This is, to be sure, true, and was first taught by Leibniz. (2) That extended or spatially actual things have

8. Space is not an empirical concept which has been derived from outer experience. For in order that certain sensations may be referred to something outside me (i.e., to something in a region of space other than that in which I find myself) and, similarly, in order that I may be able to represent them as outside and alongside one another—and accordingly, as not only different but as in different places,—the representation of space must be presupposed.

9. Space is the single a priori, representation of outer sense; for no one can have a representation of a color or a taste a priori.

no objective grounds which are things in themselves; and this is false; for the extended thing is, as every appearance, a *phenomenon bene fundatum*, i.e., it has subjective and objective grounds. What we know of these grounds through the understanding has already been shown.

8. The apperception, or the clear concept of space, is certainly an empirical concept, one which has been derived from outer experience. For all our sensible concepts become clear through sensation. Otherwise these clear concepts would be innate in us, which no one will admit. What is innate in us are the grounds of our concept of space, which is obscure, as has been proven in the present treatise, before all sensation through outer sense. It therefore must first become clear through sensation and abstraction. There is thus no contradiction between the proposition: (1) the pure intuitions or simplest characteristics of sensible knowledge precede all perceptions or sensations; and (2) they are abstracted from them. For as *obscure* concepts they precede perception, and as *clear* concepts they are abstracted from it.

9. The co-existence of simple substances in accordance with the law of continuity can be thought without their modifications and effects, and the soul thus has the ground of space in itself, and can have an obscure general concept of space without color and impenetrability. Moreover, if the actual extended thing is not visible or tangible, as is generally the case with air, then space is recognized through its visible and tangible limits. As soon as actual space is visible, it cannot be sensed without colors. Since these colors are sensed through their effects on the sense of sight, they cannot be sensed without an extended thing; for activities must inhere in substances and forces, and their continuous co-existence is the objective ground of

the appearance of extension. This is the reason why extension can be represented without color, but not color without extension.

10. Space and time are intuitions which are originally in the soul.

10. The grounds of the images of space and time have their origin in the soul. Since, however, they are appearances, they are not originally in the soul in the sense that they are not explicable in terms of something which is not space and time. Otherwise they would be *qualitates occultae.* They are *phaenomena bene fundata,* namely, grounded in the simple, with which the soul is created, and which it intuits in itself. The images of space and time are therefore explicable in terms of these simple grounds, and hence, their general concepts cannot be original.

INDEX

THE JOHNS HOPKINS UNIVERSITY PRESS

This book was composed in Baskerville text and Baskerville Bold
display type by Jones Composition Company, Inc. from a design by
Joyce Woods. It was printed on 60-lb. Sebago, regular finish, and
bound in Joanna Bancroft by The Maple Press Company.

Library of Congress Cataloging in Publication Data

Kant, Immanuel, 1724–1804.
  The Kant-Eberhard controversy.

  Includes bibliographical references.
  1. Eberhard, Johann August, 1739–1809. 2. Knowledge,
Theory of. I. Allison, Henry E., ed.
II. Title.
B2779.E3213   121   73-8113
ISBN 0-8018-1456-1